How to Do *Everything* with **JavaScript**

How to Do *Everything* with **JavaScript**

Scott Duffy

McGraw-Hill/Osborne

New York Chicago San Francisco Lisbon
London Madrid Mexico City Milan New Delhi
San Juan Seoul Singapore Sydney Toronto

McGraw-Hill/Osborne
2600 Tenth Street
Berkeley, California 94710
U.S.A.

To arrange bulk purchase discounts for sales promotions, premiums, or fund-raisers, please contact **McGraw-Hill**/Osborne at the above address. For information on translations or book distributors outside the U.S.A., please see the International Contact Information page immediately following the index of this book.

How to Do Everything with JavaScript

1234567890 FGR FGR 019876543

ISBN 0-07-222887-3

Publisher:	Brandon A. Nordin
Vice President	
& Associate Publisher:	Scott Rogers
Acquisitions Editor:	Megg Morin
Project Editors:	Leslie Tilley, Madhu Prasher
Acquisitions Coordinator:	Tana Allen
Technical Editor:	Warren Raquel
Copy Editor:	Leslie Tilley
Proofreader:	Paul Tyler
Indexer:	Valerie Robbins
Computer Designers:	Carie Abrew, Lucie Ericksen
Illustrators:	Melinda Lytle, Michael Mueller, Lyssa Wald
Series Design:	Mickey Galicia
Cover Series Design:	Dodie Shoemaker
Cover Illustration:	Eliot Bergman

This book was composed with Corel VENTURA™ Publisher.

This book is dedicated to:

My wife, Liez'l. Words cannot adequately express
how important you are to my life.

My mother, who taught me the true meaning of strength
and perseverance. God bless.

My father, who at this very moment is surely telling the angel
next to him, "That's my son." I miss you, Dad.

About the Author

Scott Duffy has been providing IT consulting services to medium- and large-sized businesses and government organizations for more than six years. Before embarking on a career as a consultant, Scott worked at two of the largest corporations in Canada as a software developer.

His 12 years of professional experience cover a wide range of platforms and technologies, including programming in mainframe, client-server, and web-based application environments. He is actively involved in every stage of the software development process, including team management.

When he's not designing software applications for clients, Scott keeps himself busy with his writing projects. He is currently working on his next book for McGraw-Hill/Osborne, a study guide for the Microsoft MCSD 70-300 exam.

To contact Scott to discuss your organization's business needs, or about any other matter, please e-mail him at scott.duffy@mydemos.com or visit his web site at http://www.mydemos.com.

Contents at a Glance

Contents

Acknowledgments

Programming today is a race between software engineers striving to build bigger and better idiot-proof programs, and the Universe trying to produce bigger and better idiots. So far, the Universe is winning.

—Rich Cook

I very much appreciate the efforts of everyone who was involved in getting this book published. I certainly don't want to imagine what would have been created had I been left to my own devices. I am extremely happy with how this book turned out, and I owe a great debt of gratitude to many people for that:

Megg Morin, my acquisitions editor at Osborne. Thank you for all your help in developing the concept and for giving the book the strong push in the right direction that it needed at the beginning.

Leslie Tilley, my copy editor and project editor. Thank you, thank you, thank you. I really appreciate your hard work and attention to detail. You're the primary reason this book turned out so well.

Tana Allen, my acquisitions coordinator. Thanks for keeping the project on track.

Madhu Prasher. Thanks for doing what you do so well. It's always good to meet someone who loves her job.

Warren Raquel, my technical editor. Thanks for your diligent efforts.

Jawahara Saidullah, my agent at Waterside Productions. Thanks for getting me this gig and hopefully many more to come.

And last but not least, my wife Liez'l. With you beside me, I can climb mountains and slay dragons.

Introduction

Netscape introduced JavaScript with great fanfare in December 1995 as an "open, cross-platform object scripting language." It was billed as the perfect complement to the much-anticipated Java programming language, since the two languages can communicate with each other inside a browser window.

Today, almost 10 years later, JavaScript is ubiquitous across the Internet landscape. It is estimated that 25 percent of web pages on the Internet today contain JavaScript code. Some of them use that code to perform some very basic scripting effects, such as controlling mouse rollovers and setting the browser status bar. Many of them contain complex dynamic menus and automated forms. No other scripting language comes close to JavaScript's domination of the web browser environment.

The key to JavaScript's success has been its ease of use. For instance, a single JavaScript statement can create an interesting browser effect, and a small handful of statements is all that's required for a completely interactive browser environment.

You don't even need any special tools to create these effects. A simple text editor, such as Windows Notepad, is all that is required. If you can create HTML web pages, you have all the tools you'll need to get started.

With the impending release of version 2.0, JavaScript will finally be usable side by side with programming languages such as C++ and Visual Basic. For instance, Microsoft has included a version of JavaScript 2.0, called JScript .NET, in its popular .NET programming environment. JScript .NET can access almost all the .NET Framework classes and can be used to create Windows Forms applications that run on your desktop. In fact, the next new word processor you use may be coded entirely in JavaScript.

Who Should Read This Book

This book is designed to help anyone interested in adding elements of interactivity to their personal web pages. Some experience with a PC is required, as we will not cover how to access the Internet or how to use a web browser. You don't have to be an HTML expert, although it will help if you have some experience with that language. When encountering new HTML for the first time, I will briefly explain what's going on, but always in the context of JavaScript.

How This Book Is Organized

How to Do Everything with JavaScript is organized into three main sections. Each section focuses on a different set of JavaScript skills:

Part I   Chapters 1–5 take you through the basics of JavaScript. This part covers the fundamental aspects of the programming languages, including statements, objects, and data types.

Part II   Chapters 6–12 show you how to integrate JavaScript into a web site. This part looks at using JavaScript with the Document Object Model, browser events, frames, and web forms.

Part III   Chapters 13–15 cover advanced JavaScript topics. This part deals with debugging a JavaScript program, errorproofing code, and communicating with other objects embedded in a web page.

Often, the best way to learn a programming language like JavaScript is to play around with it. Don't be afraid to try some of the JavaScript examples in the book yourself. Type them in and change them to something of your own design—you will gain a better understanding of how things work. Ask yourself, "What will happen if I do this instead?" Then go ahead and try it— nothing can go seriously wrong. The worst that can happen is that something you try doesn't work. And that's OK. Simply shrug your shoulders and try again.

Part I

Learn JavaScript Basics

Chapter 1

Prepare to Program in JavaScript

How to...

- Choose a development environment
- Learn what JavaScript can and cannot do
- Decide which version of JavaScript to use
- Test JavaScript programs using HTML
- Use the HTML <script> tag
- Create a JavaScript template with Microsoft Notepad
- Communicate with the user

Behind every successful movie, there is a person behind the scenes who governs the interaction of actors, camera operators, writers, and other crew members. This is the director, and although you don't usually see this person on screen, the quality of the movie rests on the success of his or her efforts.

Well, JavaScript is the behind-the-scenes "director" of many Internet web sites. Its job is to govern the interaction of objects and events so that the two interact seamlessly with one another. Generally, the more complex the web site, the more it relies on JavaScript to direct. Lights! Camera! Browser! Action!

Perhaps the first question that needs to be asked about JavaScript is, what is it? The simplest answer is that JavaScript is a simple programming language, used mainly to bring interactivity to web sites. It is often called a *scripting* language, hence the name, but it also has a nonscripting form.

A *script,* in programming terminology, is a program that does not need to be compiled in order to run. Scripts tend to perform a specific task and then exit, and do not generally have a graphical user interface (GUI) to speak of. JavaScript, Perl, and VBScript are the most common scripting languages used by Internet web sites.

Learn the History of JavaScript

JavaScript was born out of the need to coordinate HTML (Hypertext Markup Language) web pages with embedded content such as Java applets. But JavaScript is used for much more than that. It is often used to help users fill out online forms, provide web site navigation through dynamic menus, and power e-commerce shopping carts. In fact, it is said that 25 percent of all web sites today use JavaScript in one way or another.

> TIP   *Although most (99.5 percent or more) of the web browser software in use today has built-in support for JavaScript, users can choose to turn off that support. When designing web sites for everybody to see on the Internet, it's important to remember that some people won't "see" JavaScript.*

Considering how rapidly other web-related technologies have been changing to incorporate new features, JavaScript has been fairly stable. It has taken JavaScript eight years to progress from its initial 1.0 release to the next major version, 2.0. Some feel that this slow pace has been both a blessing and a curse to the language.

The blessing is that JavaScript support is fairly consistent across multiple browser makers and version numbers. Web developers can implement one JavaScript program and not have to worry too much about compatibility issues (other than avoiding certain incompatible coding techniques). JavaScript has gained such widespread adoption mainly because developers can trust that it will work.

The curse is that while JavaScript has been standing still, other languages have emerged to fill the technical void. It is far more common to see web sites that use Visual Basic Script (VBScript) or Java Server Pages (JSP) as a server-side web scripting language instead of JavaScript. In fact, a recent release of a popular web server software (iPlanet Web Server) has dropped JavaScript support altogether. This could change, however, as JavaScript 2.0 catches developers' attention.

The Origin of JavaScript

JavaScript made its first appearance in Netscape 2.0 in 1995. JavaScript was originally designed to help integrate HTML pages with *Java applets*—Java applications embedded in web pages. Developers quickly realized its true potential, though, and soon JavaScript was being used to add interactivity to web sites—most of the time without the help of Java.

Figure 1-1 shows Navigator 2.0, the first JavaScript-enabled web browser.

JavaScript Makes Its Way into Internet Explorer

Soon after Netscape Communications first introduced JavaScript in its Navigator 2.0 browser, Microsoft realized the importance of incorporating this language into its Internet Explorer browser. Since Netscape was not exactly going to mail Microsoft the source code, and even the language specification was a well-guarded secret, Microsoft was forced to reverse engineer JavaScript to create its own version. Microsoft named its version JScript, since Netscape owned the trademark on the word *JavaScript*.

Early versions of JScript did not perform certain functions in exactly the same way JavaScript did, and so JavaScript incompatibility between the browsers was something developers often had to take into account when scripting their web pages.

JavaScript Becomes an Official Standard

In the early days of the Web, cross-browser compatibility was a big issue—a lot bigger than it is today. The two main browser companies were making changes to the HTML and JavaScript languages to try to gain a competitive advantage over each other, causing massive headaches for web developers trying to create web sites that supported both browsers. Luckily for us, both companies relented.

Netscape wisely turned JavaScript standardization over to the European Computer Manufacturers Association (ECMA) in 1996. The ECMA concentrated on standardizing the core language, but left other things (such as the JavaScript Document Object Model, or DOM) to the browser makers. The result was that incompatibilities continued to exist between the browsers.

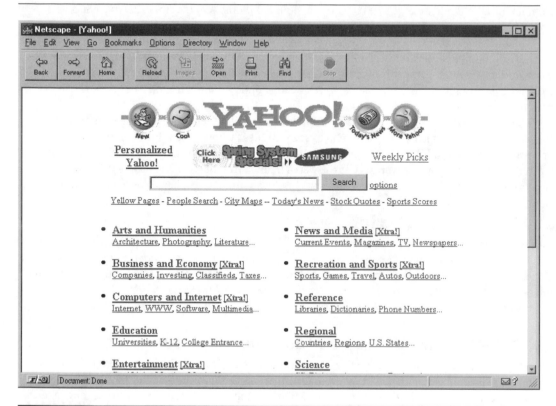

FIGURE 1-1 What the Web looked like in 1995, through the eyes of Navigator 2.0

The ECMA released their standardized scripting language known as ECMAScript in 1997. They updated the standard twice in the two years that followed, calling the updates Edition 2 and Edition 3. JavaScript 1.5 conforms to Edition 3 of the standard.

Where JavaScript Is Today

The ECMAScript Edition 4 standard will be the first update to be released in over four years. JavaScript 2.0 conforms to Edition 4 of the ECMAScript standard, and the difference between the two is extremely minor.

NOTE   *The specification for JavaScript 2.0 can be found on the Mozilla.org web site: http://www.mozilla.org/js/language/js20/index.html.*

Today, Netscape's JavaScript and Microsoft's JScript conform to the ECMAScript standard, although each language still supports features that are not part of the standard.

JavaScript Version	Date Released	Browsers	Standards Compliance
1.0	December 1995	Navigator 2, Internet Explorer 3	No
1.1	April 1996	Navigator 3	Partially, with ECMAScript 1
1.2	December 1996	Navigator 4, Internet Explorer 4	Partially, with ECMAScript 1
1.3	August 1998	Navigator 4.06, Internet Explorer 5	ECMAScript 1, ISO-16262
1.4	October 1998	Version 1.4 did not appear in any web browser	ECMAScript 1, ISO-16262
1.5	April 2000	Navigator 6 and 7, Internet Explorer 5.5 and 6, Mozilla 1	ECMAScript 3
2.0	2003		ECMAScript 4

TABLE 1-1   Chronology of JavaScript Releases

Table 1-1 contains a chronological list of JavaScript versions, including a short list of popular browsers that supported each one.

NOTE   *The exact release date of JavaScript 2.0 and version numbers of the browsers that will support it were not yet determined at the time this was written.*

Choose a Development Environment

One of JavaScript's biggest strengths is its support on many different platforms, often for different purposes. The most common type of JavaScript application today is one that runs inside a web browser, as a client-side script. JavaScript has long been supported as a web server-side language as well, in popular environments such as IIS and LiveWire. Recently, developers have had even more choices for using JavaScript in different environments.

In this section, we will take a look at how JavaScript is used in each of these environments. None of them supports JavaScript 2.0 yet, but it is still important to look at the potential environments that will, since support will probably be introduced in the near future.

Also in this section, we will discuss development environments for JavaScript developers. In the first few years of JavaScript's existence, developers had to create their JavaScript programs using only a text editor, without the aid of integrated development environments (IDEs)—and many still do. But as HTML development tools evolved, many added development support for the world's most popular scripting language. And today this support exists in all the big tools, as we will see later on in this section.

Develop JavaScript-Enabled Web Pages

Applications that are designed to run inside a browser are by far the most popular use for JavaScript. JavaScript was given very strong integration into the web browser environment through the DOM. Netscape introduced the original DOM in JavaScript 1.0.

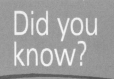

The Client-Server Analogy

In web-development terminology, the web browser and the computer it runs on are often called *the client*. Similarly, the web server software and the computer it runs on are called *the server*. Thus, the term *client-side JavaScript* refers to JavaScript programs that are embedded inside a web page and run on the client machine. JavaScript that runs on the server machine is referred to as *server-side JavaScript*.

Fairly soon thereafter, control of the DOM was handed over to the World Wide Web Consortium (W3C), a standards organization. The DOM standard has evolved from dealing with how JavaScript interacts with a browser to dealing with standard ways to create, read, and modify HTML and XML documents.

NOTE *The W3C (http://www.w3.org) specializes in web standards, including HTML, XML, DOM, and Cascading Style Sheets (CSS). The various documents related to the DOM standards can be viewed at http://www.w3.org/DOM/DOMTR. It's important to note that the original DOM (sometimes called Level 0) is not an official standard.*

JavaScript applications that are designed to run inside a browser are subject to a number of security restrictions. These applications generally do not have access to the user's hard drive or any installed applications on the user's computer. For users, this means a JavaScript application generally poses no security risk, as it cannot contain a virus or other malicious code.

Netscape Navigator 4.0 (also known as Communicator) introduced the concept of signed scripts. A script that has been signed using a secure digital key can request additional privileges within the browser environment, such as the ability to send e-mail or read a file from the hard disk. Often the browser would prompt the user to ask if they will allow the script such privilege.

The Mozilla web browser, and its cousin Navigator 6, changed the way signed scripts are handled in a way that is no longer compatible with Navigator 4. Microsoft Internet Explorer (IE) handles security completely differently (using trusted zones, for instance). As a result of these heterogeneous security solutions, there still is no standard way to write JavaScript applications that have expanded privileges. In practice, signed JavaScript is rarely used.

Client-side application development is still very much one of JavaScript's core strengths. Developers actually risk incompatibility with many operating systems and web browsers by choosing any language other than JavaScript for their client-side development!

Create Server-Based Web Applications

Although JavaScript dominates all other languages when it comes to web-client programming, that is not the case with server-side programming. JavaScript was one of the first server-side languages supported (back in 1996, when Netscape released its web server platform), but it was unable to use that head start to its advantage. Perl quickly became a popular server-side scripting tool, and several other languages have emerged (including VBScript in the ASP environment, PHP, and JSP) as popular alternatives.

One of the reasons server-side languages vary so much is that the server environment can be controlled to a certain extent by web developers. In most cases, developers have very little control over the browsers people use. So while the choice of client-side programming language is really a "lowest common denominator" decision (which language is supported by the most browsers), the choice on the server is whatever the developer wants to use.

For some developers, getting to choose the programming language is like being a kid in a candy store. There are many server-side programming languages to choose from, and no real reason to choose one over another except personal preference.

Use JavaScript in a DOS or Windows Environment

For a long time now, Microsoft has been providing the Windows Script Host (WSH) tools as a free add-on to Windows as a download from its web site. WSH includes the latest versions of Microsoft's two scripting languages—VBScript and JScript.

With WSH, you can create a small program in JScript that could be run from the DOS prompt. In fact, many virus writers took advantage of this ability (particularly with VBScript), so these macros and small scripts are less frequently used these days. In fact, many mail systems ban them altogether when sent as an attachment to e-mail, due to the potential for viruses.

NOTE   *Windows Script, including the JScript and VBScript engines, can be downloaded free from http://msdn.microsoft.com/scripting.*

Developers can still create small programs using JScript for use in a Windows environment, although it is rarely done. These JScript programs rely on the presence and enablement of the Windows scripting environment, and in these security-conscious times, that is something which you cannot rely on too heavily.

JavaScript Development Tools

One of JavaScript's strengths is that expensive development tools are not usually required. With a simple text editor such as Notepad, which is built into Windows, you can create relatively complex JavaScript code with little trouble. Since it is an interpreted language inside the context of a web browser, you don't even need to buy a compiler.

NOTE   *A* compiler *is a program that turns programming code into machine-ready form, often called a* binary *or an* executable.

But just because JavaScript can be edited in a simple text editor doesn't mean that it *should* be. Development environments offer several key resources that often make development faster and easier, such as:

- Predefined scripts that can be easily added to a web page
- Integrated help, to quickly look up the syntax of a function
- Automatic FTP uploads to a web server
- Integrated debugging tools

In this section, we will examine the top four HTML editors. Each of these editors has significant support for JavaScript development, including ready-to-use scripts, JavaScript editing tools, and embedded help.

Microsoft FrontPage

Microsoft has developed a popular HTML editor called FrontPage. FrontPage provides web developers with a number of JavaScript tools to assist in the creation of an interactive web site. FrontPage was once the undisputed leader in HTML and JavaScript development tools. Now a couple of other competitors in the field have taken a significant slice of the Microsoft market share—Macromedia and NetObjects.

FrontPage still contains many useful features, including capabilities such as designing a web site's hierarchy before creating any of the pages, configuring web site security, setting sitewide styles, and creating custom banner images. Figure 1-2 shows how FrontPage Explorer can be used to organize a web site by graphically linking pages together. Microsoft FrontPage also has a server-side component called FrontPage Server Extensions, which enables it to integrate well into Microsoft's IIS web server.

FrontPage can be purchased for $90 to $170, which makes it a very affordable tool for nonprofessional web site developers.

Microsoft offers a free 30-day trial version of FrontPage 2002 for those who are interested in trying out the software. The trial CD can be ordered from http://www.microsoft.com/frontpage.

Macromedia Dreamweaver MX

Macromedia Dreamweaver MX is a very popular HTML and JavaScript editor in the professional web development crowd. It is packed with features, including the ability to edit most of the popular web server programming languages (like ASP, JSP, and PHP), provides several handy prebuilt JavaScript components, integrates well with databases, and conforms to new standards such as XHTML and XML. In short, it includes lots of goodies that professionals will find useful but that many home users might not require.

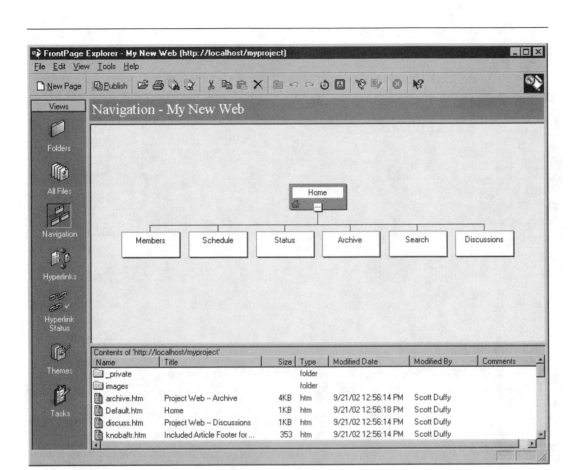

FIGURE 1-2   Using FrontPage Explorer to organize a web site

The power of the Dreamweaver MX environment is shown in Figure 1-3.

Macromedia Dreamweaver MX retails for between $200 and $400, which makes it an ideal tool for professional developers.

NOTE   *You can download a free trial of Macromedia Dreamweaver MX for either Windows or Mac at http://www.macromedia.com/software/dreamweaver.*

Macromedia HomeSite 5

Macromedia purchased Allaire Corporation and took over ownership of Allaire's flagship product, HomeSite. The most recent version is HomeSite 5, and Macromedia includes a free copy of it with each copy of Dreamweaver it sells. HomeSite appeals to the home user because of its price, although it lacks most of the sophisticated features of its sibling.

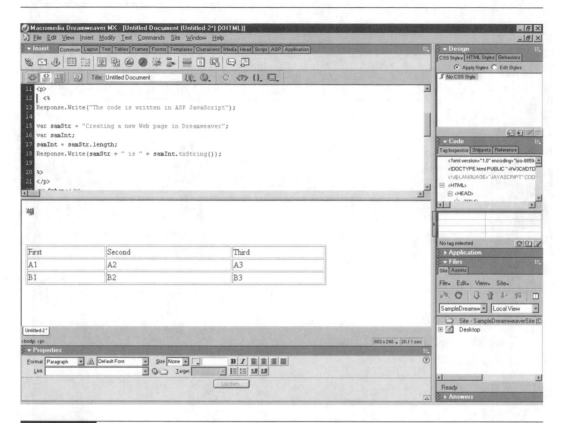

FIGURE 1-3 Dreamweaver MX is an extraordinary working environment for the professional web developer.

For $29 to $99 users receive a well-liked HTML and JavaScript editor, which will manage their personal web site just fine. Users with large sites to manage or more than one developer might want to consider investing the extra money to get Dreamweaver instead.

 *Macromedia offers a free trial version of HomeSite 5 for Windows at http://www.macromedia.com/software/homesite.*

Adobe GoLive

Adobe is best known to most surfers on the Internet for its Acrobat software, which writes and reads documents in their popular Portable Document Format (PDF). However, Adobe is also a leader in graphics, digital video, and desktop publishing software with its Photoshop, Premiere, and PageMaker products.

In fact, it is likely that all the other industry-leading tools and software packages the company produces overshadow their web publishing tool business. However, even though Adobe GoLive might be trailing the pack in many respects, for developers who regularly work with Adobe's graphics- and video-editing tools, GoLive may be an easy choice.

As with other web authoring tools, you can download a trial copy of GoLive 6.0. GoLive is available for both Windows and Mac, and can be downloaded from Adobe's web site at http://www.adobe.com/products/golive.

NetObjects Fusion

FrontPage, Dreamweaver, GoLive, and NetObjects Fusion make up the top four most popular web site development tools in use today. NetObjects, unfortunately, did not have sufficient cash or resources to stay in the race against such tough competitors. The company has been sold and the new owner, Website Pros, has been continuing development of the Fusion tool under the existing brand name.

Fusion is priced competitively in the $70 to $150 range. It includes many interesting new features, such as integration with popular online payment services, JavaScript pop-up menus, and improved support for embedded multimedia. It was once a popular tool with developers, and may become so again under new guidance.

A free trial of NetObjects Fusion 7 for Windows can be downloaded from the company's web site at http://www.netobjects.com. The full version of the software can also be purchased and downloaded online.

Learn What JavaScript Can and Cannot Do

Historically, JavaScript has differentiated itself from other languages in the following ways:

- It is easy to develop for.
- It interfaces well with other languages and environments.
- No special tools or compilers are required.
- It's flexible.

These properties made it particularly well suited for web development. Web pages can be made dynamic with as little as one line of JavaScript code, and often only a handful of lines are required to accomplish common tasks. DOM provides JavaScript access to the browser, the web page, and all the objects (Java, multimedia, etc.) embedded within it.

Despite the significant improvements, JavaScript 2.0 was not designed as an all-purpose language. Specifically, it does not intend to challenge C, C++, or Java in areas where those languages currently dominate. Rather, JavaScript 2.0 tries to improve upon the strengths of the existing language, while also adding features that developers often like to use when developing large or complex code, namely:

- The ability to write modular and object-oriented applications
- Improved ability to interface with other programming languages

- ■ The ability to write scripts that can be compiled for faster performance
- ■ The ability to restrict the way functions and code are used

The ECMA has actually designed JavaScript 2.0 with these goals in mind.

Use JavaScript as a Client-Side Language

One of the unique qualities of the core JavaScript specification is that it does not attempt to define how JavaScript interacts with its environment. There are no JavaScript methods or functions in this specification that define how to draw the user interface or how to write text to the screen. Likewise, there are no file input/output routines that allow the language access to the hard drive.

That feature can be considered both a strength and a weakness. The flexibility given by this lack of a standard I/O interface has resulted in JavaScript's use in many different environments (browsers, servers, stand-alone applications, mobile devices, etc.). This has allowed devices with different ways of storing data and different ways of displaying output to run JavaScript applications.

The downside to this flexibility is that the same JavaScript application cannot be run in each environment without some alteration. While most web browsers have standardized on a document object model, some differences remain between the DOMs of various browser makers. For example, a JavaScript application designed to run in a web browser cannot be run on a web server without taking the server's own object model into consideration.

Today, JavaScript is practically the only scripting language used inside web pages. Even though a couple of alternatives exist (most notably VBScript), JavaScript was (and still is) the only scripting language supported by all the major browser manufacturers. It is the only scripting language worth learning for client-side development.

Use JavaScript as a Server-Side Language

JavaScript also gained some popularity as a web server programming language. Both Netscape Enterprise Server and Microsoft IIS (popular web servers of the mid-1990s) supported server-side JavaScript development. Netscape supported this through the LiveWire server-side language. Microsoft allowed JScript as one of the potential languages for ASP development.

Unfortunately, Netscape Enterprise Server (now called iPlanet Web Server) no longer supports JavaScript on the server, starting with version 6. This might have something to do with the fact that iPlanet is part of Sun Microsystems, and Sun Microsystems prefers programmers to use Java.

And although Microsoft's ASP environment has been hugely successful, developers prefer to use VBScript when developing for that platform. With the introduction of Microsoft's ASP .NET platform, VB .NET and C# have become the two languages developers use most.

Microsoft did the JavaScript community a small favor when it included JScript .NET support in the Visual Studio .NET development environment. JScript .NET has access to all the classes of the .NET Framework, and was the first (albeit, extremely early) implementation supporting features of the ECMAScript Edition 4 proposal.

Although the ECMA has given JavaScript the ability to function as a full programming language, JavaScript is not necessarily suitable for every environment. You would probably not want to use JavaScript as a programming language for the following types of tasks:

- Very large applications
- Performance-critical applications
- Device drivers and other low-level programs

After all, we wouldn't want to see all those C++ programmers out of a job, would we?

Decide Which Version of JavaScript to Use

One decision that JavaScript developers must make early on in the development process is which version of the language they wish to support. Several factors go into this decision, such as:

- The size and scope of the programming task at hand
- The possibility of future enhancements to the program
- The need for the program to easily interoperate with other programs written in different programming languages
- The need to take advantage of new features only offered in JavaScript 2.0 (new built-in objects, for instance)
- The version of JavaScript supported by your favorite development tool
- The version of JavaScript supported by the vast majority of your intended audience

By far the most important consideration would be the last one. There is no point placing JavaScript 2.0 inside web pages if a significant amount of your intended audience still uses browsers that don't support it. Of course, if your program will reside only on the server (a server-side program), all that matters is the version supported by the server.

It is also important to remember one of the fundamental rules of computer programming: never write more code than is absolutely necessary for a task. So if your JavaScript program is a three-line script that converts degrees Celsius to degrees Fahrenheit, there is no need to create packages and classes in JavaScript 2.0 syntax (as discussed in Chapter 5). You may want to do it for other reasons, including future extensibility of your program. But this is also a case of *if it ain't broke…*

So as a general rule, be very cautious about developing in client-side JavaScript 2.0 code if your intended audience is likely to be running a wide variety of web browsers. Otherwise, if you know for certain what the minimum browser version will be or are developing in a server or embedded environment, feel free to use the new features and improvements in JavaScript 2.0 to your heart's content!

Test JavaScript Programs Using HTML

Before jumping into the fundamentals of JavaScript, we need to set up a way to test our code. The easiest way to test a JavaScript program is by putting it inside an HTML page and loading it in a JavaScript-enabled browser.

To run any of the code samples in this book using this HTML method, you will need a web browser. I recommend using IE 5 or Navigator 4 or later, as some examples won't work with earlier versions.

If you would like to upgrade the browser on your computer to a more recent version, you can visit Microsoft's IE web site at http://www.microsoft.com/windows/ie, or Netscape Browser Central at http://channels.netscape.com/ns/browsers.

Create a JavaScript Template

The <script> tag is the HTML element used to signify JavaScript code. It's a good idea to create this file as a template using Notepad (or your favorite web development tool) and save it on your hard drive. That way it will be much easier to start creating JavaScript-powered web pages using this HTML code as a base.

Here's how to create the template in Notepad:

1. In Windows, click the Start menu button.

2. Select Run from the pop-up menu.

3. Type in **notepad** as shown here, and press ENTER.

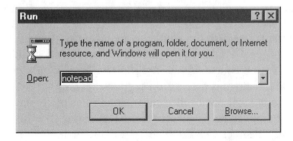

4. In Notepad, enter the following HTML code:

```
<html>
    <head>
        <title>JavaScript sample code</title>
    </head>
    <body>
        <h1>My Sample Code</h1>
        <script language="JavaScript" type="text/javascript">
```

```
          <!-- // Begin
              // NOTE:: Replace this line with JavaScript code
          // End -->
          </script>
      </body>
  </html>
```

5. Select the File menu, and choose Save As.

6. Navigate to the desired location on your hard drive. The My Documents folder is commonly used, but you can also choose to save it to any directory of your choice.

We will use this HTML file to run the JavaScript code samples throughout the book, so put it someplace handy.

7. Give the HTML file a name ending in **.htm** such as **JSTemplate.htm**.

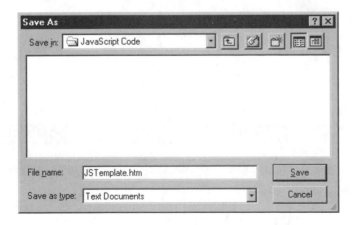

8. Close Notepad.

9. From your Windows desktop, choose My Computer. This will bring up Windows Explorer, which allows you to navigate to the directory where you saved your HTML file.

10. Double-click the HTML file. A web browser (usually Microsoft Internet Explorer) will open your HTML document.

11. You should see the words "My Sample Code" in large letters.

12. Close the browser window when you are finished with it.

Figure 1-4 shows how the HTML template looks in the browser. This is the most basic example of a <script> tag in an HTML page.

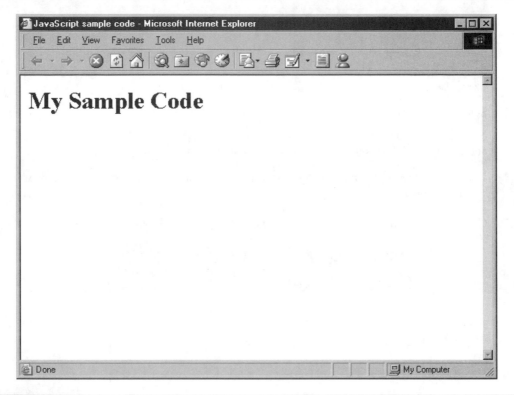

FIGURE 1-4   A simple HTML document containing a <script> tag that does nothing

Understand the JavaScript Template

Remember that HTML documents are divided into two distinct pieces: the header section and the body. HTML documents always start with the <html> tag and end with the </html> closing tag. Similarly, the HTML header section is delimited with the <head> and </head> tags, as so:

```
<head>
    <title>JavaScript sample code</title>
</head>
```

Generally, the HTML markup inside the header section is used to describe the main content that appears in the body section. Most commonly, the header section contains:

■   A mandatory title for the document (<title>)

■   Style sheet definitions (<style> and <link>)

- Meta data, such as search keywords (<meta>)
- JavaScript functions (<script>)

The bulk of the HTML document is inside the body section, delimited by <body> and </body> tags. In this section you would find text, images, forms, and embedded content. JavaScript can also be used in this section to output dynamic text to the screen. Our template's body section looked like this:

```
<body>
    <h1>My Sample Code</h1>
    <script language="JavaScript" type="text/javascript">
    <!-- // Begin
        // NOTE:: Replace this line with JavaScript code
    // End -->
    </script>
</body>
```

Our body section starts and ends with the mandatory <body> and </body> tags. The <h1> and </h1> tags indicate header text. <h1> is the predefined header with the largest font. The <h2>, <h3>, <h4>, <h5>, and <h6> tags indicate headers with decreasing font sizes.

I have included a <script> element inside the body section for later use. I've included two attributes with this tag, **language** and **type**. The **language** attribute was the original way to indicate what scripting language was used inside the tags. Although recent versions of HTML (and XHTML, its successor) have phased out the use of this attribute, it is still quite common to use it. The **type** attribute is what is now recommended to indicate the scripting language in use.

The template contains three lines inside the <script> section:

```
<!-- // Begin
    // NOTE:: Replace this line with JavaScript code
// End -->
```

All three of these lines are *comments*. In web programming, a comment is one or more lines of text that is ignored by the browser when interpreting the code. Programmers often use comments to make a program easier for humans to read, but in the preceding code, the first and last lines are used to stop browsers that don't support JavaScript from displaying the code. As time goes on, this technique becomes less and less important. But it is still quite prevalent, and there is really no reason not to include it. The <!-- and --> are markers for the start and end of HTML comments. JavaScript comments are marked with double slashes (//), which is why the browser will ignore the second line as well.

Communicate with the User

Many JavaScript programs perform their tasks quietly. A web page may use JavaScript to verify that all the fields on a form have been completed in the proper manner. When they are complete, the JavaScript program allows the form to be submitted to the web server for further processing. But if one of the form fields has not been filled out properly, JavaScript should, ideally, inform the user so that they can correct the problem and submit the form again.

There are generally two ways to bring an error like this to the user's attention. The first is to take advantage of a JavaScript alert box, which requires the user to click an OK button in order for processing to continue. This is considered a slightly intrusive technique that ensures the user reads and acknowledges the error message.

The other way is to write an informative message inside the web page directly. This is obviously a less intrusive technique, although you must be sure that the user does not accidentally overlook the message.

In this section, we will examine how to communicate with the user using both methods, as each will be important before we move on to the next chapter.

Display an Alert Message

JavaScript provides three types of pop-up dialog boxes for use in your applications:

- An alert box
- A confirm box
- A user-input prompt box

Basic alert messages are displayed using the built-in alert function:

```
alert ("This message will be displayed to the browser");
```

You can place any text string or expression inside the parentheses. The dialog box displayed looks like this in Internet Explorer.

Netscape Navigator displays a similar message box.

A confirm box acts in much the same way as an alert box, except it displays both OK and Cancel buttons to the user. The confirm box tells the program which button the user chose, allowing two different outcomes.

```
result = confirm ("Would you like a piece of chocolate cake?");
```

The result variable will contain true if the user selects the OK button, or false otherwise. This is how the confirm box appears in Internet Explorer.

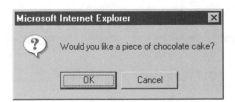

Finally, the user-input prompt box allows the program to ask for a typed response to a message. This is rarely used on Internet web pages, as HTML web forms are a more commonly accepted way to retrieve user input.

```
firstname = prompt ("What is your first name?",
    "Enter name here");
```

The result of this JavaScript code is shown here.

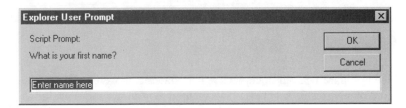

Write Text to the Browser Window

Many of the examples in this book will use the document.write() function to print text into the web browser window. This can be used for more than just error reporting. In fact, it is quite common to see web sites using document.write() to support dynamic functions such as navigation, user help, banner ad rotation, and more.

```
document.write ("<b>This text goes right into the browser</b>")
```

Notice how you can include HTML tags inside the document.write() function and the browser will process those tags. By adding a few document.write() statements into our HTML template, we can create a web page with a bit more content.

```html
<html>
    <head>
        <title>JavaScript sample code</title>
    </head>
    <body>
        <h1>Hamlet, by Bill Shakespeare</h1>
        <script language="JavaScript" type="text/javascript">
        <!-- // Begin
            // NOTE:: Replace this line with JavaScript code
            document.write
                ("To be, or not to be: that is the question:<br>");
            document.write
                ("Whether 'tis nobler in the mind to suffer<br>");
            document.write
                ("The slings and arrows of outrageous fortune,<br>");
            document.write
                ("Or to take arms against a sea of troubles,<br>");
            document.write
                ("And by opposing end them.<br>");
        // End -->
        </script>
    </body>
</html>
```

As you can see in Figure 1-5, our document.write() statements were output to the screen just as if we had entered them directly in HTML. This technique becomes more useful when we get into the next chapter, when we learn about variables, functions, and statements.

Now that we have covered the boring stuff—the history of the language, and what it is used for—we are ready to jump into a bit of real programming. The next chapter starts off by covering the basics of JavaScript, to get you ready to start coding on your own.

Learn More about Topics Discussed in this Chapter

There are several good books available to learn more about HTML and Java, namely:

- *How to Do Everything with HTML,* by James Pence (McGraw-Hill/Osborne, 2001)
- *HTML: A Beginner's Guide,* 2nd edition, by Wendy Willard (Osborne, 2002)
- *Java 2: A Beginner's Guide*, by Herbert Schildt (Osborne, 2000)
- *Learn to Program with Java,* by John Smiley (Osborne, 2001)

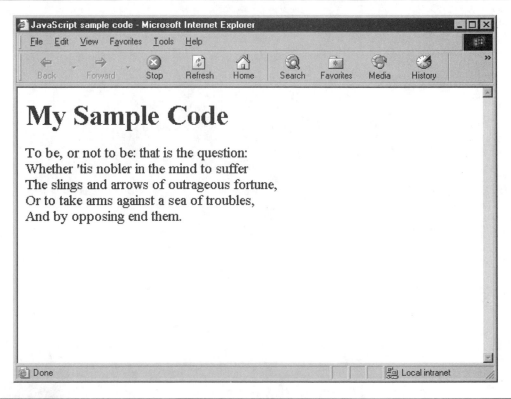

Hamlet's famous soliloquy, as delivered by JavaScript

In addition, you may want to check out some of the following web sites:

- DevGuru: http://www.devguru.com
- W3 Schools: http://www.w3schools.com/html
- Sun Microsystems' Java home page: http://java.sun.com
- JavaRanch: http://www.javaranch.com

Chapter 2

Learn JavaScript Fundamentals

How to...

- Define variables
- Define constants
- Understand program flow
- Execute code conditionally
- Repeat statements using loops
- Comment your code
- Set a default object
- Handle errors
- Understand the basics of expressions
- Organize your code into functions
- Use the improvements in JavaScript 2.0 to create more powerful functions

JavaScript is extremely dependent on other technologies for help. In fact, if you tried to write a program in JavaScript that didn't rely on anything outside of the official JavaScript specification, your program would not be able to do very much. JavaScript relies on external components for communication with the outside world, such as writing to a screen, retrieving data from a web form, and receiving notification of browser events.

In this chapter, we will examine JavaScript's fundamentals. We will learn the basics of writing a program by learning about statements, variables, and functions—the three basic building blocks of any program.

Understand Basic Terminology

Like practitioners of other specialties, computer programmers have developed their own lingo over the years. Ordinary English words such as *variable, function,* and *string* have been given computer-related meanings. Table 2-1 lists some of the programming terms you will encounter in this chapter and throughout the book.

Store Data in Variables

When it gets right down to it, there are only three places to store information in modern computing: the hard disk, a database, or memory. Sure, there are other data-storage media, such as floppy disks, CDs, Zip disks, and backup tapes upon which information can be saved, but the devices these media require are much slower than a hard drive—sometimes taking 100 times as long (or more) to record the same data. So application programmers cannot—and should not—generally rely on any of these media when storing information.

The programming term...	Refers to...
statement	One line of programming code; statements are often separated by semicolons (;) in JavaScript.
variable	A named location for storing values that can be changed during program execution.
constant	A named location for storing values that cannot be changed during program execution.
function	A named set of statements that perform some operation and can optionally return a single value.
keyword	A word that has a predefined meaning in JavaScript, and cannot be used for any other purpose.
operator	Typically a symbol (such as +, -, *, or /) that takes one or more values (called *operands*) and returns a result.
expression	A combination of keywords, operators, variables, and/or functions from which a result can be calculated.
string	A sequence of 0 or more letters, numbers, or other text characters; strings are typically enclosed in quotation marks, as in "this is a string".
Boolean	A value or expression that evaluates to either true or false.
literal	A Boolean, number, or string that is written directly in the code; for instance, the expression ((3+2)/total) contains two numeric literals, 3 and 2.
value	A number, Boolean, string, or object.

TABLE 2-1   Common JavaScript Programming Terminology

On the hard disk, information is stored in the form of files. In a database, information is stored as records. But in memory, program data is stored and retrieved using variables. *Variables* are named sections of memory.

Define Variables

In JavaScript 1.5, variables are declared using the **var** keyword:

```
var counter;
```

This code tells JavaScript that we intend to store information in a variable we'll refer to as "counter." Variables defined in such a way can contain any type of information: numbers, strings, Booleans (true and false), or objects. For convenience, you could assign the variable an initial value like so:

```
var counter = 5;
```

We have assigned the variable named counter an initial value of 5.

JavaScript 2.0 has introduced the concept of data types into JavaScript programming. Before this release of the language, programmers could not predefine the types of data that a variable could contain—all JavaScript variables could be assigned any type of data.

But with this important new release of the language, we can now restrict variables to certain types of data: integers, for example, or strings. Attempting to assign data that does not belong to the variable's predefined data type would result in an error. Data types are defined as follows:

```
var counter : Integer;
```

The counter variable defined here belongs to the Integer data type. Thus, that variable can never contain anything other than whole numbers. (We examine all the data types available in JavaScript 2.0 in Chapter 3.)

Define Constants

Variables are called variables for a reason: a program is free to change the value stored inside the variable at any time. Constants are similar to variables, but once a value has been assigned, constants cannot be changed.

 *Constants are only currently supported by Netscape 6 and later, or the Mozilla web browser. Microsoft IE has not yet incorporated support, so the use of constants should be limited to uses when you are absolutely sure they are safe.*

Constants were introduced into JavaScript starting with version 1.5, so early versions of the language do not support them. But other programming languages (most notably C) use constants very effectively, and they can be useful in your JavaScript programming as well.

Constants are defined using the **const** keyword:

```
const ERR_INVALID_USERID;
```

In the preceding code, I created a constant named ERR_INVALID_USERID. Notice how I capitalized the name. It is not mandatory, but it is a programming convention often used in C, so you will sometimes see constants capitalized in JavaScript as well.

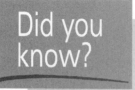 ## JavaScript Can Store Some Mighty Big Numbers

Integers in JavaScript 2.0 are double-precision floating-point numbers, which allows them to contain values in the range of approximately +/–100 *unodecillion*—1 with 38 zeros after it.

Once a value has been set, a constant cannot be altered.

```
const ERR_INVALID_USERID = 300;
ERR_INVALID_USERID = 50;      // This will cause an error!
```

Constants are often used to give human-readable names to error codes and other numbers that "mean something." It is much easier for humans to read the following code than if it just used the error numbers directly:

```
switch (returncode) {
    case ERR_INVALID_USERID:
        // do something
    case ERR_INVALID_PASSWORD:
        // do something else
    case ERR_INVALID_DOMAIN_NAME:
        // etc.
}
```

Like variables, constants can be assigned a data type in JavaScript 2.0.

Understand Program Flow

The bulk of this chapter is devoted to learning the fundamentals of the JavaScript programming language, statements, and functions. But before we get into that, it is important to spend a few moments examining *program flow*.

When I talk about program flow, I am talking about the order in which JavaScript executes a program's code. Assuming you have a program that is five lines long, JavaScript will always start by executing the first line of code. In theory, the second line is executed next, then the third, and so on until it reaches the last line (line 5 in our example). Figure 2-1 illustrates this.

In reality, that is an extreme oversimplification of what goes on. The next line to be executed depends on the task that the current line asked JavaScript to perform. If the current line calls a function, all the code inside the function will be executed first, before JavaScript continues with the next line. If the current line contains a loop, the same group of lines will be executed repeatedly. And if the current line declares a new function to be defined, JavaScript will read the function into memory without executing any of it (until it is called elsewhere in the program).

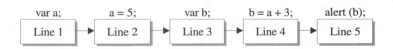

FIGURE 2-1   JavaScript executes a program from start to finish in order.

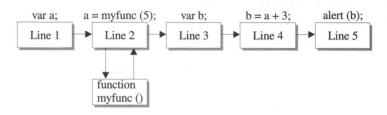

FIGURE 2-2   JavaScript will stop executing a program in order to execute the contents of a function.

But, for the most part, it is still fair to characterize a program as being executed in order from start to finish. Figure 2-2 shows how the program flow jumps around depending on the code itself. We can see that all the code inside a function is executed before the program continues where it left off.

Control Program Flow with Statements

The HTML template we defined in Chapter 1 (see "Create a JavaScript Template") didn't really do anything useful, other than displaying some header text. The only way we can get our JavaScript program to do anything is to add some statements.

A *statement* is the basic action item in any program code. In effect, each statement is telling the computer to do something. Statements can be divided up into five categories:

- Conditional
- Loops
- Object manipulation
- Comments
- Expressions

The typical JavaScript program uses statements that fall into each of those categories. Often, statements inside a program are organized into functions and classes as well, to make the program easier to manage and more efficient to develop. We will examine functions in more detail later in this chapter, and classes in Chapter 5.

Execute Code Conditionally

Computer programs almost always contain *conditional statements*. There are two conditional statements in JavaScript: **if** and **switch**. The **if** statement allows the program to choose one of two alternatives, based on some predefined factor. In real life, you might decide that, if it were not raining, you would like to go to the baseball game. Of course, if it were raining, you would then decide to stay home. You can make that same decision in a JavaScript program with the following code:

```
function stay_or_go (raining) {
    if (raining == false) {
        return "Go to baseball game!";
    } else {
        return "Got to stay home today.";
    }
}
```

So you see, conditional statements give programs a choice between two or more alternatives in much the same way we make those choices in real life.

The if Statement

Depending on how you use it, the **if** statement can be very simple or very complex. The **if** statement can be used in the following ways.

Syntax	Use
if (*expression*) {*statements*;}	If *expression* evaluates to true, execute *statements*.
if (*expression*) {*statements1*;} else {*statements2*;}	If *expression* evaluates to true, execute *statements1*. Otherwise, execute *statements2*.
if (*expression1*) {*statements1*;} else if (*expression2*) {*statements2*;} else {*statements3*;}	If *expression1* evaluates to true, execute *statements1*. Otherwise, if *expression2* evaluates to true, execute *statements2*. Otherwise, execute *statements3*.

The **if** statement evaluates an expression to determine which set of statements to execute, if any. Since the **if** statement expects a Boolean expression (one that evaluates to either true or false), it will try to convert expressions of other data types to either true or false.

JavaScript makes certain assumptions when converting from other data types to Boolean. The strings "true" and "false" evaluate to the Booleans true and false. The integers 1 and 0 are also converted to the Booleans true and false, respectively.

In computer programming terminology, an expression is a piece of code that, when evaluated, returns a value. In JavaScript, the following can be used as expressions.

Expression	Example
A variable	if (x) {*statements*;}
A function that returns a value	if (myfunc(x)) {*statements*;}
A literal	if (true) {*statements*;}
Variables, functions, and literals combined using operators	if (a > 5) {*statements*;}

Even the same **if** statement can be written in at least four different ways, all of which are valid:

- ```
  if (expression) statement;
  ```
- ```
  if (expression)
       statement;
  ```
- ```
  if (expression) {statements;}
  ```
- ```
  if (expression) {
       statements;
  }
  ```

The various preceding forms of the **if** statement are technically equivalent. The first two can include only one statement. Notice that the third and fourth forms use curly brackets, { and }, to enclose the statements. Statements enclosed in curly brackets are generally treated as a group, called a *statement block*.

The **if** statement can include an optional **else** clause, to decide between one of two alternatives. This form of the statement is sometimes called the *if-else statement:*

```
if (expression) {statements1;}
else {statements2;}
```

The **else** clause allows you to specify a statement or group of statements that will be executed if the expression does not evaluate to true. Only one **else** clause is allowed in any **if** statement. Again, the statement can be used with or without the curly brackets.

Finally, the **if** statement can be used to choose between one of three or more alternatives. With the introduction of the **else-if** clause, the **if** statement can include multiple expressions that will each be evaluated until either one of them evaluates to true or the **else** clause is encountered. Multiple **else-if** clauses can be included, but keep in mind that the **else-if** clause must always precede any **else** clause.

```
if (expression) {
    statements;
} else if (expression) {
    statements;
} else {
    statements;
}
```

TIP   *If you find yourself using more than two or three **else-if** clauses in a single **if** statement, you may want to consider using a **switch** statement instead, as described in the following section.*

The switch Statement

The **switch** statement has a very similar role to the **if** statement in JavaScript. The **switch** statement evaluates an expression and compares the value to one or more **case** clauses. If you need to compare a variable against more than two or three values, the **switch** statement is the most efficient way.

The following code shows how the **switch** statement is typically used in JavaScript programming. In this example, our program will try to determine the name of a country based on its official three-letter ISO (International Organization for Standardization) country code.

```
// ISO official country codes
switch (countrycode) {
    case "ALB":
        countrystring="Albania";
        break;
    case "DZA":
        countrystring="Algeria";
        break;
    case "ASM":
        countrystring="American Samoa";
        break;
    case "AND":
        countrystring="Andorra";
        break;
    case "AGO":
        countrystring="Angola";
        break;

    // etc.

    case "", "?":
    default:
        countrystring="Unknown code";
}
```

The same code could be written using **if-else-if** statements, but that would be both inefficient and harder to read. Let's take a look at the preceding code, to see what is going on.

The first line of the statement uses the **switch** keyword, followed by the expression that needs to be evaluated.

```
switch (countrycode) {
```

In this example, countrycode is a variable that happens to contain a string.

The next three lines in the **switch** statement contain the first **case** clause.

```
case "ALB":
    countrystring="Albania";
    break;
```

The **case** clause indicates that we would like to compare the value of countrycode (the expression the **switch** statement is acting on) with the string "ALB". If there is an exact match, JavaScript will execute the next two lines:

- Set the countrystring variable to "Albania".
- Exit the **switch** statement at the **break** statement.

Of course, if the value of countrycode does not match the string "ALB", the countrystring variable is not set and the **switch** statement continues.

The next **case** clause compares the expression against a new value:

```
case "DZA":
    countrystring="Algeria";
    break;
```

The **switch** statement evaluates each of the case statements in order, until it finds one that matches. It then executes the code that immediately follows the **case** clause until the first **break** statement is encountered.

> **TIP** *Once a match is found, JavaScript will execute all the code that follows, even inside other **case** clauses, until the **break** statement is encountered.*

In JavaScript, the **switch** statement has a special kind of **case** clause known as the **default** clause. The **default** clause executes only if JavaScript was unable to match the expression with any of the previous clauses. The **default** clause must always be the last clause in a **switch** statement.

```
case "", "?":
default:
    countrystring="Unknown code";
```

Our example includes an empty **case** clause, trying to match against the empty string ("") or a question mark (?). You can provide multiple values to match against the expression in a single **case** clause, as long as they are separated with commas. If the expression matches our empty case, the code inside the **default** clause will be executed, since there is no **break** statement to stop it.

Repeat Statements Using Loops

Loops are convenient statements for two purposes:

- When you want to repeat a set of statements a specific number of times
- When you want to repeat a set of statements an unknown number of times

There are four loop statements in JavaScript: **while**, **do-while**, **for,** and **for-in**. JavaScript also provides the **break** and **continue** statements to give programmers more control over how loops execute. In this section, we will examine each of the statements related to looping and see how they can be applied in our programs.

The while Loop

The **while** loop evaluates an expression before executing a group of statements. It will execute the statements repeatedly, until the expression no longer evaluates to true.

```
while (expression) {
    statements;
}
```

JavaScript processes the **while** loop in the following manner. The expression is first evaluated, and its value is interpreted as a Boolean (true or false) value. If the expression evaluates to true, the statements contained inside the curly brackets are executed once. The expression is then evaluated again, and if it still evaluates to true, the statements are executed a second time. This continues indefinitely until the expression evaluates to false.

A common programming trap is the *infinite loop*. An infinite loop is a loop statement that never ends, and this is most like to happen with the **while** statement. Most browsers will inform the user when a script takes too long to execute, which allows them to force an infinite loop to end.

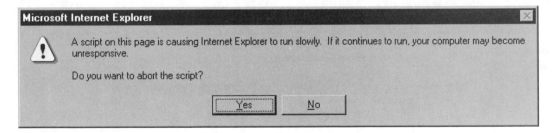

To avoid infinite loops, it is common programming practice to make sure the expression always has a chance to evaluate to false. The following **while** statement is guaranteed not to cause an infinite loop:

```
var counter = 1;

while (counter < 101) {
    document.write ("This is line number " + counter + "<br>\n");
    counter++;
}
```

This code will execute exactly 100 times. We know this because the counter variable starts off at 1, and after every successive **while** loop iteration, it is incremented by one. (We will learn about operators, such as the ++ operator, later in this chapter. In this code, the ++ operator takes the counter variable and increments it by 1.) When it reaches 101, the loop will exit, since "counter < 101" would evaluate to false.

If we paste this **while** loop into our HTML template from Chapter 1, we get the following HTML code:

```
<html>
    <head>
        <title>JavaScript sample code</title>
    </head>
    <body>
        <h1>My Sample Code</h1>
        <script language="JavaScript" type="text/javascript">
        <!-- // Begin
        var counter = 1;

        while (counter < 101) {
            document.write ("This is line number " + counter + "<br>\n");
            counter++;
        }
        // End -->
        </script>
    </body>
</html>
```

Loading this HTML code into a web browser gives you something similar to Figure 2-3. The browser window has been scrolled all the way to the bottom to demonstrate exactly how many lines were printed.

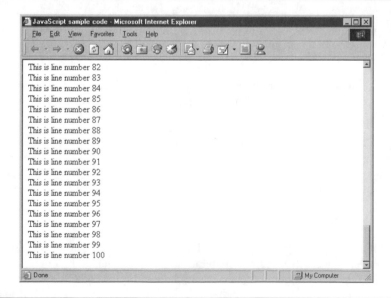

FIGURE 2-3   The **while** loop prints exactly 100 lines.

The do-while Loop

The **do-while** loop acts exactly like the **while** loop, with one exception. The expression is evaluated after the end of each iteration in a **do-while** loop. That means the loop is guaranteed to execute at least one time. A **while** loop evaluates its expression prior to each iteration, which means that it's possible that the contents of the loop will never be executed.

```
do {
    statements;
} while (expression);
```

Even though the expression is evaluated after each iteration of the loop, the following loop still executes exactly 100 times. So the only iteration that is affected by choosing **do-while** instead of a **while** loop is the first run through the loop.

```
var counter = 1;

do {
    document.write ("This is line number " + counter + "<br>\n");
    counter++;
} while (counter < 101);
```

You can look at the **while** and **do-while** loops as two versions of the same statement. Everything you can do with **do-while**, you can do with **while**. As a result, **do-while** loops are less commonly seen "in the wild" than **while** loops.

The for Loop

In discussing **while** loops just now, we used the following example:

```
var counter = 1;

while (counter < 101) {
    document.write ("This is line number " + counter + "<br>\n");
    counter++;
}
```

That **while** loop can be rewritten using a **for** loop. In fact, this type of loop (one that employs a counter variable) is better suited to a **for** loop.

```
for (var counter = 1; counter < 101; counter++) {
    document.write ("This is line number " + counter + "<br>\n");
}
```

As you can see, the **for** loop version is a more efficient way of looping a predefined number of times. The **for** loop syntax has four components:

```
for (initializer; expression; incrementor) {
    statements;
}
```

The *initializer section* is traditionally used to define variables and give them an initial value. In our example, we defined a new variable named counter and set it to the value 1. The JavaScript code contained in the initializer section gets executed only once—before the loop begins.

The *expression* is evaluated before every loop. Whether or not the statements are executed depends on the Boolean results of this expression.

The *incrementor section* contains code that gets executed following each run through the loop. Traditionally, this is where any counters are incremented or decremented. In our example, we add 1 to the counter variable using this section.

Each of these sections is optional. If the variables being used are already defined and have a value set, the initializer can be empty. But don't forget that the semicolon in between is mandatory. In fact, the following code is an infinite loop using a **for** statement:

```
for (;;) {
    // do nothing
};
```

 *Although this is another example of an infinite loop (which is generally a bad idea in programming) this loop is a valid technique if you have code inside the loop that executes a **break** statement when a certain condition is met.*

The for-in Loop

I only want to talk about the **for-in** loop here for the sake of context. You will see a proper discussion of it in Chapter 5, when we talk about classes and objects.

For now, think of an object as a tool chest that contains a bunch of tools. The **for-in** loop will extract each tool individually from that tool chest, and allow you to examine and manipulate it on its own.

In the following code, we create a simple object (compatible with JavaScript 1.5) and retrieve each of its properties using the **for-in** loop.

```
<html>
    <head>
        <title>JavaScript Test</title>
```

```
    </head>
    <body>
        <h1>for-in Loop</h1>
        <script language="JavaScript" type="text/javascript">
        <!-- // Begin
            // We define the tool chest object
            var toolchest = {tool1:"Wrench",
                tool2:"Hammer",
                tool3:"Cordless drill",
                tool4:"Needlenose pliers"};

            // for-in iterates over its properties
            for (var tool in toolchest) {
                document.write(toolchest[tool] + "<BR>");
            }

        // End -->
        </script>
    </body>
</html>
```

This program creates an object named toolchest. The object is created using an object literal, as discussed in Chapter 5.

```
// We define the tool chest object
var toolchest = {tool1:"Wrench",
                tool2:"Hammer",
                tool3:"Cordless drill",
                tool4:"Needlenose pliers"};
```

The code that we're interested in is the **for-in** loop:

```
// for-in iterates over its properties
for (var tool in toolchest) {
    document.write(toolchest[tool] + "<BR>");
}
```

This code picks loops through the contents of the toolchest object—tool1, tool2, tool3, and tool4. When executed, the program outputs the value of each property, like so.

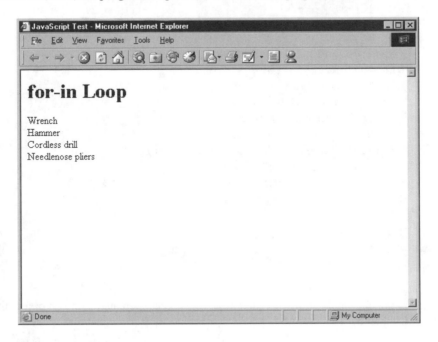

The break and continue Statements

We already saw the **break** statement in action when we looked at the **switch** statement. When JavaScript encounters a **break** statement inside a **switch**, it stops executing code inside the **switch** and continues execution at the first statement that follows it.

The **break** statement works in a similar fashion with loops. When JavaScript encounters a **break** statement, it stops executing the code inside the loop and starts again at the first statement outside the loop. The **break** statement is not valid outside a loop or a **switch** statement.

The **continue** statement causes JavaScript to stop executing code inside the loop as well, but execution continues at the next iteration of the loop instead. In effect, the **break** statement says, "Exit the loop," while the **continue** statement says, "Skip this iteration and move on to the next." The **continue** statement is also not valid outside of a loop.

```
var Fahrenheit, Celsius;
for (Celsius = -70; Celsius <= 70; Celsius += 10) {
    Fahrenheit = (Celsius * 9/5) + 32;
    document.write ("Celsius = " + Celsius);
    document.write (", Fahrenheit = " + Fahrenheit + "<br>");

    if (Fahrenheit > 100) {
        // It's getting hot in here
        break;
    }
}
```

The **for** loop in this code is designed to run through all of the degrees Celsius starting at –70, incrementing by 10 degrees per iteration, until Celsius reaches +70 degrees (–70, –60, –50, –40, etc.).

But if you examine the code inside the loop, it tells JavaScript to break out of the loop when the temperature exceeds 100° Fahrenheit. Since 100° Fahrenheit is approximately 37° Celsius, the loop will actually exit when Celsius hits 40, and not 70. The **break** statement causes the loop to exit prematurely.

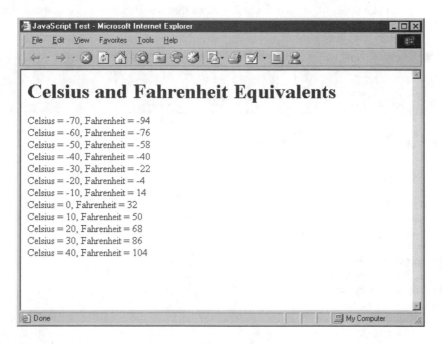

The **continue** statement is very useful when you want to loop through a range of values, ignoring some that don't meet certain criteria. But when you find some that do, you have a lot of code to execute inside the loop. Instead of surrounding dozens of lines of code with a giant **if** statement, the **continue** statement can be used to skip on to the next iteration.

```
// Which numbers are evenly divisible by 23?
var iNumber;
for (iNumber = 1; iNumber <= 1000; iNumber++) {
    if (iNumber % 23 > 0) {
        // Not divisible by 23
        continue;
    }
    document.write("<b>" + iNumber + "</b>");
    document.write(" is evenly divisible by 23!<br>");
}
```

In this code, the loop is designed to execute 1,000 times, running through the numbers from 1 to 1,000. The **if** statement inside the loop checks to see whether the number is evenly divisible by 23, using the modulus (%) operator. If it is not evenly divisible by 23, the **continue** statement is executed—the rest of the current loop is skipped and the next iteration of the loop starts.

Every 23 numbers (it's odd how it works out like that), we will run into a number that is evenly divisible by 23. The **continue** statement is not executed, and the rest of the loop has a chance to run. In our example, we output the happy news that we finally found a number that matches, using the document.write() function.

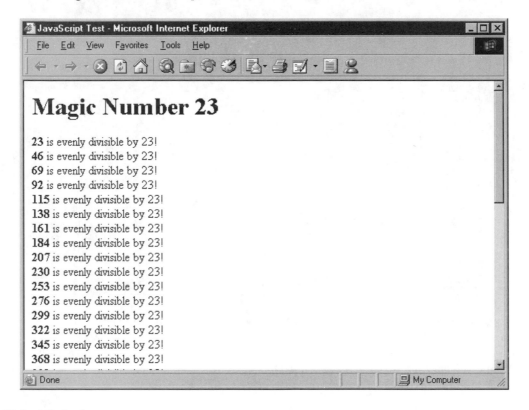

Using Labels

A *label* is a named line of code. Since their only purpose is related to loops—nested loops in particular—labels are rarely used in real life, although it is important to know they exist.

In programming terminology, you have created a nested loop *when you place one loop completely inside another—for instance, if you have a **for** loop inside a **while** loop. In this situation, the **for** loop is known as the* inner loop, *and the **while** loop is called the* outer loop. *Loops can be nested many levels deep.*

Labels are fairly easy to create.

1. Open your JavaScript program using a text editor, such as Notepad.

2. Pick the line of code that you would like to name. Labels must appear at the beginning of a valid statement.

3. Type a label name, using only letters or numbers. No spaces or other special characters are allowed in the name.

4. End the label with a colon (:).

For instance, in the following code, we have a set of nested loops, which are also labeled.

```
var x, y, z;
outer: for (x = 1; x < 20; x++) {
    middle: for (y = 1; y <= x; y++) {
        inner: for (z = 1; z <= y; z++) {
            document.write
                ("x = " + x + "; y = " + y + "z = " + z + "<br>");
        }
    }
}
```

In this code, we have three loops. The innermost loop, acting on the variable z, is labeled "inner." The middle loop, which encloses the loop named "inner," is called "middle." And the outermost loop is named "outer" and encloses both the middle and inner loops.

The only reason to label a loop is because the **break** and **continue** statements are designed to work with labels. By adding the following code immediately after the document.write function call inside the innermost loop, you could cause all three loops to exit prematurely:

```
break outer;
```

This is convenient when you have a condition inside an inner loop (it doesn't have to be the innermost one, however) that would make you want to stop processing all the loops—or even just stop processing the two innermost and continue with the outer loop. For instance, the following code placed inside the innermost loop in the preceding code would cause the variables y and z to never get past the value of 1, while x is allowed to increment to 20:

```
break middle;
```

Comment Your Code

We discussed comments briefly in Chapter 1. Comments are not really a type of statement, although they are often lumped in with the other JavaScript statements for the sake of convenience. There are two ways to add comments inside a JavaScript program.

You can add a single line of comments by starting your comments with two slashes.

```
// Everything after the slashes will be ignored by JavaScript
```

It is also possible to include comments on the same line with valid code.

```
var Students = 3;      // There will be three students in the class
```

Another way to comment code is with block comments. Block comments start with a slash and an asterisk (/*).

```
/* This is the start of block comments
```

Block comments continue until an asterisk and slash (*/) are encountered, even if the comments extend over several lines.

```
/* This is the start of block comments
   Even this will be ignored
   document.write ("This will not be executed either!");
   Because it is still considered a comment */
```

When you are developing small JavaScript programs for yourself, you may not wish to spend much time commenting your code. That is fine—it's called programmer's prerogative. You may find, however, that comments are useful for the following reasons:

- You can include a copyright notice with your program.
- You can describe what a program or function does in "plain English."
- In the development stage, or when debugging, sometimes you would like code not to execute, but you don't want to delete it.
- Comments can also be placeholders for code you want to add some time in the future.

If you create programs professionally, you may be required to include a copious amount of comments to make it easier for others to understand your code.

Set a Default Object

We have not yet spent any time looking at the concept of programmable objects in this book and I'm going to defer most of that discussion to Chapters 3 and 5, when we get to built-in objects and user-defined classes. But in order to understand the **with** statement and its ability to specify a default object for a set of statements, let's spend a moment looking at what objects, methods, and properties are.

To understand the concept of objects in programming, it is helpful to draw an analogy to the real world. Almost anything in real life can be thought of as programmable object—a car, a television, a coffee cup, or even a person. In programming, objects can have both *methods* and *properties*. An object's methods are actions it can take, while an object's properties describe the object. For instance, let's assume we have created a Person object in JavaScript. In real life, a person typically has certain unique features, such as a name, hair color, eye color, and height. These features would be defined as properties of the Person object. In real life, a person can take actions such as eating, sleeping, talking, and listening. These actions would translate into methods of the Person object.

The with Statement

The **with** statement allows you to access the methods and properties of an object without having to specify the name of the object on every line. Without the **with** statement, you will always need to specify the name of the object you are working on next to every property or method you wish to access:

```
person.fullname = "Bob Jones";
person.haircolor = "Black";
person.eat();
person.sleep();
```

But when statements are surrounded by the **with** statement, the object name is implied, as in:

```
with (person) {
    fullname = "Bob Jones";
    haircolor = "Black";
    eat();
    sleep();
}
```

When JavaScript first encounters the reference to fullname inside the **with** statement, it will first check to see if a variable called fullname exists. If not, it will check to see if the person object has a property called fullname. As you can see, when you need to access the same object repeatedly over many lines, it may make sense to surround your code in a **with** statement.

The **with** statement can be a convenient statement for the programmer to use—anything that saves typing is convenient. But some developers feel using the **with** statement also makes your program a bit harder to read. With the technique of copy-and-paste in most text editors, there may not be many reasons you would need to use this statement in your programs.

```
with (document) {
    write("99 bottles of beer on the wall<br>");
    write("99 bottles of beer<br>");
    write("If one of the bottles happens to fall<br>");
    write("98 bottles of beer on the wall<br><br>");

    write("98 bottles of beer on the wall<br>");
    write("98 bottles of beer<br>");
    write("If one of the bottles happens to fall<br>");
    write("97 bottles of beer on the wall<br><br>");
}
```

In the preceding code, we start off by declaring that we would like document to be the default object. Notice how we can then start using the write() method without referring to document at all.

 *The default object set using the **with** statement applies only to code within the curly brackets. Outside the curly brackets, the object will need to be explicitly used once again.*

Handle Errors

Perhaps the most difficult programming challenge most developers face on a regular basis is intelligently handling errors. In JavaScript programming, an *error* is a problem that the browser encounters when it is trying to run a program. Errors can be triggered by something the browser saw and didn't like, called a *system error*. Or it can be triggered by something your program saw and didn't like, called an *application error*.

A JavaScript program could easily be doubled in size with the addition of a reasonable amount of error-handling code. Error-handling code is typically additional code a programmer has to write to check for the existence of errors and do something with them. In JavaScript, if the program contains no error-handling code, the default action is often for the browser to present the problem to the user.

The problem with error-handling is that it often takes as much work (or more) to create good error-handling code as it took to create the rest of the program. So frequently, for a variety of reasons, programmers skip that step.

It is all too easy to write a program (in any language) without any error-handling code. You can tell the computer to go to the database, read in some values, ask the user for some input, add the user's input into the existing data, and put it back into the database. That can be done in a programming language such as Visual Basic in about 30 lines of code. But that assumes nothing could ever go wrong. If you think about it, lots of things can go wrong:

- The database is not available.
- The database is available but you are unable to log in.
- You can log in to the database, but the data is not available.
- The data you retrieve from the database contains invalid values.
- The user enters invalid values.
- Adding the user's data into the database data causes an error.
- You are unable to save the data back to the database.

So by the time you add code to your program to handle all those errors, you are suddenly looking at a 120-line program, instead of a 30-line program. So you see, it is certainly easier to avoid worrying about this type of stuff.

But when you are writing programs professionally, you *must* worry about how errors are handled. Should the program crash when the user types in a wrong value? Or should you simply

2

continue on, writing the bad data to the database, causing errors the next time the program is run? Or is the best solution to inform the user of their mistake and ask them to try again? This is why errors such as these need to be caught and properly handled.

The try-catch Statement

Web browsers are designed to handle errors differently depending on the browser type and version, and to some degree on the user's browser settings. In some cases, if you include some bad JavaScript code inside a web page the browser would simply not run it, with no error message or other indication that something went wrong. In other cases, the browser pops up a message box with details of the error it encountered, asking the user what to do next. The JavaScript error message usually looks something like this.

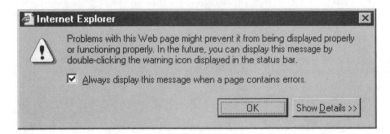

For JavaScript developers, neither of the default error-handling methods is ideal. Ignoring an error completely stops the program from executing. And displaying an ugly error message to the user can be embarrassing for the programmer—not to mention frustrating to the user.

> **NOTE** *There are some minor differences between the ways Netscape and Microsoft use this statement and what the official ECMA specification defines. In this section, I am using the statement as supported by most web browsers.*

The **try-catch** statement is used to allow programs to handle the error themselves, instead of allowing the browser to do it. It is often used to wrap a statement or set of statements that are likely to fail. The statement has the following syntax:

```
try {
    statements;
}
catch (variable) {
    // error handling code
    statements;
}
```

> **NOTE** *The **try-catch** statement was only added in JavaScript 1.4, so only recent browsers (such as IE 5.5 and Netscape 6) support it.*

For example, you can surround a function call using the **try-catch** statement, and report a more friendly error message to the user if it fails.

```
try {
    open_database();
}
catch (err) {
    // error handling code
    alert("An error occurred connecting to the database." +
        " Please try again in a few minutes.");
}
```

So instead of receiving the ugly-looking JavaScript error message (or none at all, depending on the browser settings), your user will receive a friendlier message asking them to try again in a few minutes:

The official system error message that occurred is still passed to the statement as a parameter of the catch clause. In our example, the err variable contains the description of the error that occurred. So if you needed to determine what happened inside the catch clause, you can. You can even display the original error message text to the user.

The **try-catch** statement is not only used for catching system errors; you can also use this construct to catch errors generated by your own program.

It is a good idea to use a **try-catch** statement when your program is attempting to do something that could cause an error, for instance, if your program is attempting to connect to an embedded Java applet. It is possible for an applet to encounter a problem and be unable to load, or for a browser's security settings not to permit certain Java applets to run. If you surrounded such code in a **try-catch** statement, you could detect this problem and redirect the user to a non-Java version of the application.

There are also plenty of errors that your application could detect programmatically, including:

- Invalid user input in a form
- Unsupported browser maker or version
- Missing or invalid browser cookies

The throw Statement

The **throw** statement allows a JavaScript program to declare an error in the exact same manner as it would use for system errors. That means these errors can be caught using a **try-catch** statement.

It also means that user-declared errors that are not caught are displayed to the user in a JavaScript pop-up dialog box.

NOTE   *Like the **try-catch** statement, the **throw** statement was only added in JavaScript 1.4, so only recent browsers (such as IE 5.5 and Netscape 6) support it.*

The following is an example of a program that throws its own errors.

```
try {
    var errors = 0;
    // Do something
    errors++;
    if (errors > 0) {
        throw "Could not find the file.";
    }
}
catch (errorstring) {
    alert("The following error occurred:\n\n" +
        errorstring);
}
```

Understand the Basics of Expressions

Many of the programming statements that we have been examining in this chapter use an expression to make some sort of decision. An *expression* is anything that returns a value. Table 2-2 lists the common types of expressions, along with an example of their use.

Expression	Example
Numeric literal	47
String literal	"Hello"
Boolean literal	true
Object literal	{make : "Toyota"}
Program-defined variable	x
Program-defined function	get_toast()
Null	null
Assignment expression	x = 5
Mathematical operations	x + y
Boolean operations	x == y
Conditional operator	x == 5 ? "yes" : "no"
Combination	x = "You have " + messagecounter + " new messages"

TABLE 2-2   Common Types of Expressions

Some statements, such as the **if** statement or **while** statement, specifically require expressions that return a Boolean value (true or false). JavaScript does its best to automatically convert strings and integers to the appropriate Boolean value. Expressions are also often used as parameters to functions, and can also be used as statements themselves.

```
x = 5;
```

This code is an expression, but it is also a statement. It assigns the value 5 to the variable x.

Use Operators to Create Complex Expressions

JavaScript provides a number of operators to perform mathematical and other functions within your code. Some operators modify the variables they operate on, although most do not. All operators return a value, and thus can be used to create complex expressions.

There are 12 types of operators in JavaScript, and several dozen individual operators. Most operators are represented by symbols (like +), while some operators are represented by words (like **new**). Most operators require two operands, while some operators only require one (particularly the unary operators).

Table 2-3 lists the operators available in JavaScript 1.5.

Operator Type	Operators
Member	dot (.) square bracket ([])
Unary	new delete typeof instanceof void ++ -- negation (-) logical not (!) bitwise not (~)
Multiplicative	multiply (*) divide (/) modulus (%)
Additive	add (+) subtract (-)
Bitwise Shift	shift left (<<), unsigned shift right (>>>), signed shift right (>>)

TABLE 2-3   Operators Available in JavaScript

2

Operator Type	Operators
Relational	less-than (<) greater-than (>) less-than-or-equal (<=) greater-than-or-equal (>=) in
Equality	equal (==) not equal (!=) strictly equal (===) strictly not equal (!==)
Bitwise Logical	bitwise and (&) bitwise or (|) bitwise exclusive or (^)
Logical	logical and (&&) logical or (||) logical exclusive or (^^)
Conditional	conditional (?:)
Assignment	equals assignment (=) shortcut assignment (*=, /=, +=, -=, %=, <<=, >>=, >>>=, &&=, ||=, ^^=, &=, |=, and ^=)
Special	comma (,) function this

TABLE 2-3   Operators Available in JavaScript *(continued)*

JavaScript 2.0 adds two new operators to the language, and they are both considered relational:

■   is

■   as

We have already seen a few of these operators in action so far in this chapter, such as equals (==), greater-than (>), increment (++), in, and equals assignment (=). Most of these operators have their origin in mathematics. Additional operators exist to deal with logical Booleans (such as logical and and logical or), plus binary operators to deal with the ones and zeros of binary math.

Organize Your Code into Functions

There may be the occasional instance when you can sit down and write an entire JavaScript program without functions, but believe it or not, that type of JavaScript program is rare. Most JavaScript programs contain at least one function.

Functions allow you to predefine a group of JavaScript statements before you actually need to call that code. Since functions can be called repeatedly, with varying parameters, they are also convenient time-savers.

Define Functions

Functions are defined using the **function** keyword. Functions must be assigned a name and can optionally take one or more parameters. Parameters are contained in brackets, and separated by commas.

```
function name(parameter1, parameter2, …, parameterN) {
    statements;
}
```

This is the JavaScript 1.5 format for defining functions. JavaScript 2.0 introduces some powerful extensions to this basic format, by allowing parameters to have a data type, the function itself to have a data type, parameters to be optional, named parameters, and more. We will examine the JavaScript 2.0 functions later in this chapter.

The parameters specified inside the function definition are treated as variables inside the function. Parameter names must be unique, in that two parameters of the same function cannot have the same name.

From the basic function syntax, we can define a basic function:

```
function add_two(x, y) {
    if (x > 7) {
        x = x - 7;
    } else {
        x = x + 7;
    }
    if (y > 18) {
        y = y - 18;
    } else {
        y = y + 18;
    }
    return x + y;
}
```

The preceding code creates a function called add_two(). This function accepts two parameters, named x and y. The function's name and the parameters it accepts are defined in the first line of code:

```
function add_two(x, y) {
```

The function's code defines a somewhat complicated way to add two numbers together. First, the contents of both x and y are examined, and depending on their values something is added or subtracted from each.

```
if (x > 7) {
    x = x - 7;
} else {
    x = x + 7;
}
if (y > 18) {
    y = y - 18;
} else {
    y = y + 18;
}
```

Then the two numbers are added together and the result is returned. With the addition of a **return** statement that returns a result, this function can act as an expression, by returning a value.

```
return x + y;
```

Now the code just defines a function. If you were to add this into our HTML template and try to execute it in a web browser, it would actually do nothing. Functions need to be called in order to run. And if a function defines one or more parameters, values must be given for those as well.

In order to call a function, you must do the following:

1. Type its function name followed by an open parenthesis:

```
add_two(
```

2. Provide a list of parameters, if required, separated by commas:

```
add_two(12, 2
```

3. Followed by a close parenthesis and a semicolon:

```
add_two(12, 2);
```

4. Of course, in the case of our function, we need to assign its return value to a variable, or use it in a context that expects a value:

```
var result = add_two(12, 2);
```

We can combine the function definition, our HTML template, and a bit of code that calls our function with various parameters as follows:

```
<html>
    <head>
        <title>JavaScript sample code</title>
    </head>
    <body>
        <h1>Defining JavaScript Functions</h1>
        <script language="JavaScript" type="text/javascript">
```

```
<!-- // Begin
function add_two(x, y) {
    if (x > 7) {
        x = x - 7;
    } else {
        x = x + 7;
    }
    if (y > 18) {
        y = y - 18;
    } else {
        y = y + 18;
    }
    return x + y;
}

document.write("add_two(2, 17) = " +
    add_two(2, 17) + "<BR>");
document.write("add_two(14, 9) = " +
    add_two(14, 9) + "<BR>");
document.write("add_two(100, 200) = " +
    add_two(100, 200) + "<BR>");
// End -->
</script>
</body>
</html>
```

In this code, we have inserted our add_two() function definition into the <script> section of our HTML template. For the code inside that function to be executed, we need to call that function. In our code, we call the function three times, with three different sets of parameters.

When we load this code into a browser, we see something similar to Figure 2-4. Since we are calling the functions inside the document.write() function call, the output of the function is written to the screen. This is also a good example of how functions can themselves be passed as parameters to other functions—the value of add_two has to be executed to come up with the value that gets passed to document.write.

Accept Parameters

Of course, a function can be defined without any parameters.

```
function print_header() {
```

The parentheses are still required when defining and calling such a function.

```
print_header();
```

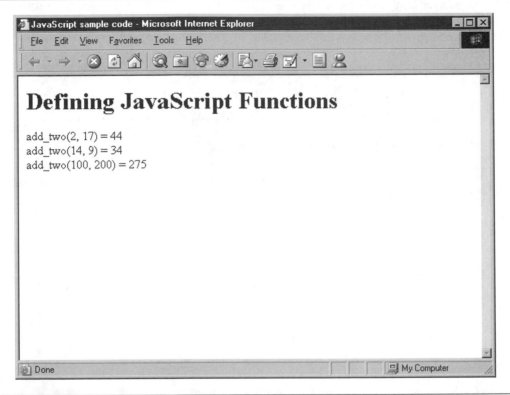

FIGURE 2-4   Defining a function and calling it repeatedly

Another important consideration when using functions is how variables and even parameters are treated. Consider the following bit of JavaScript code:

```
var counter;
counter = 5;
function add2(input) {
    input = input + 2;
    document.write("input = " + input + "<br>");
    return;
}
add2(counter);
document.write("counter = " + counter + "<br>");
```

What value will be written to the screen at the end of that program? We start off by defining a variable named counter, and assigning it a value of 5. We then define a function named add2()

which appears to add the value 2 to the parameter that is passed to it. We then call this function with our counter variable and print its value to the screen.

The answer is that counter will still have a value of 5 at the end of the program.

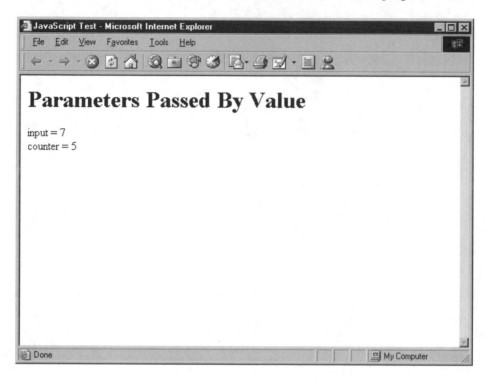

Why? Well, that has to do with how parameters are handled inside functions. JavaScript does not pass the actual counter variable into the add2() function. It actually makes a *copy* of counter, and passes the copy into add2(). Therefore, any changes add2() makes to the parameter are lost when the function exits.

NOTE *JavaScript passes parameters by value, which means the value of any parameters cannot be permanently altered inside a function.*

Understand Variable Scope

Another important rule concerning functions is one of variable scope. In programming, when and where a variable can be used is determined by where you define it. If you declare a variable inside

2

a function, it can only be used inside that function. When you exit the function, the variable is no longer defined and its value is lost.

```
// get_factors() returns all the numbers that divide into
//     the parameter evenly
function get_factors(inputValue) {
    var counter;
    var factorString = "";
    for (counter = 1; counter <= inputValue; counter++) {
        if ((inputValue % counter) == 0) {
            factorString = factorString + counter + " ";
        }
    }
}
get_factors(6777214);
document.write (factorString);
```

For instance, in this code, a function named get_factors() is defined. We then call it using the value 6,777,214 as its parameter. We would like to print out the string that results using document.write(), but by that time it is too late. The factorString variable is only valid inside the function, because that is its scope. When we attempt to run this program, an error message attributed to the final line of our program is displayed. The variable factorString cannot be used outside the function in which it is defined.

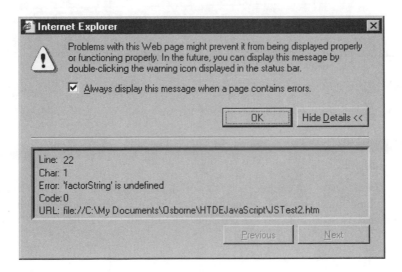

If we were to move the document.write() statement inside the function call, we would see a better result.

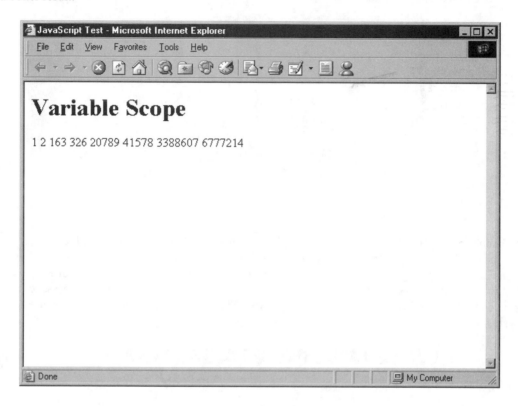

Return Values

Inside a function, the **return** statement serves two purposes:

- It causes the function to exit.
- It optionally passes a value back to the line of code that called it.

Much as the **break** statement causes a loop to exit, the **return** statement causes a function to exit as well. Since functions can act as expressions by returning a value to the code that called it, the **return** statement can accept the value returned as an optional parameter.

- `return;`
- `return "Hello";`
- `return 32;`
- `return true;`

All four of these are valid uses of the **return** statement inside a function.

Use the Improvements in JavaScript 2.0 to Create More Powerful Functions

JavaScript 2.0 brings a number of improvements to the language. The European Computer Manufacturers Association (ECMA) has added a number of features that increase the power and flexibility:

- Classes
- Packages
- Namespaces
- Data types
- More powerful and flexible data arrays
- Access controls, such as public and private

With this added functionality, JavaScript can now be used for tasks that used to require a more complex language like C++ or Java, while still retaining the simplicity that has made JavaScript so popular with web developers for all these years.

If you've worked with JavaScript before, one of the first changes you will notice is the addition of data types to the language. Data types allow you to restrict the range of values a variable can contain or a function can return. We can modify the add_two() function we defined earlier in this chapter with JavaScript 2.0 syntax to use data types for all its variables, parameters, and the function itself:

```
function add_two(x : Number, y : Number) : Number {
    if (x > 7) {
        x = x - 7;
    } else {
        x = x + 7;
    }
    if (y > 18) {
        y = y - 18;
    } else {
        y = y + 18;
    }
    return x + y;
}
```

Now that we have added the Number data type to our x and y parameters, JavaScript will report an error if something other than a number is passed. It is also clearer to other developers what data types we expect for each of the parameters.

Use Named Optional Parameters

Another change to the way parameters are used in JavaScript 2.0 is the ability to define named optional parameters. The **named** keyword allows us to identify some parameters as optional when defining the parameter list of a function.

For instance, let's say we have a function that expects a person's name to be passed to it in three parts:

```
function sayHello
    (first : String,
     initial : String,
     last : String) : String {

    var fullname;
    if (initial <> "") {
        initial = initial + ". ";
    }
    fullname = first + " " + initial + last;
    return fullname;


}
```

If we define it using the preceding syntax, we have no choice but to call it in the following way:

```
sayHello ("Scott", "", "Duffy");
```

But by using the **named** modifier on the middle initial parameter, we can allow the function to be called without the middle initial.

```
function sayHello
    (first : String,
     last : String,
     named initial : String = "") : String {
    var fullname : String;
    if (initial <> "") {
        initial = initial + ". ";
    }
    fullname = first + " " + initial + last;
    return fullname;
}
document.write (sayHello ("Scott", "Duffy") + "<br>");
document.write (sayHello ("Bobby", "Jones", initial:"H") + "<br>");
```

By defining the middle initial parameter as named, we can then call the sayHello() function with only the first and last name specified. Named parameters must always specify an initializer in case a value is not specified for that parameter, so one can be assigned. If you want to provide a value for a named parameter, you have to refer to that parameter by name.

Accept Any Number of Parameters

Functions in JavaScript 2.0 can be defined so that they can accept an unlimited number of parameters. You would want to do this when your function needs to accept a large number of identical parameters but you do not want to create lots of named optional parameters.

The rest parameter must always appear at the end of any unnamed parameters that are defined, using three periods (...). Named parameters, those defined using the **named** keyword, can still be listed after the rest parameter. Of course, there can only ever be one rest parameter for a single function.

The following code defines a function that can accept an unlimited number of parameters. The first four arguments passed will be assigned to the first four parameters defined: name, address, phoneNum, and spouseName. Any arguments passed beyond those four will be assigned to an array called childName. We can use a **for-in** loop to get the list of names out of that variable. (We will look at arrays in depth in Chapter 4.)

```
function printform (name : String,
    address : String,
    phoneNum : String,
    spouseName : String,
    ... childName : Array) {

    // An unlimited number of children can be provided
    with (document) {
        write ("Name: " + name + "<br>");
        write ("Spouse: " + spouseName + "<br>");
        write ("Address: " + address + "<br>");
        write ("Phone: " + phoneNum + "<br>");
        for (child in childName) {
            write ("Child " + childName[child] + "<br>");
        }
    }
    return;

}
```

In the next chapter, we will focus on some of JavaScript's most powerful features—its built-in objects and functions.

Chapter 3

Use Built-in JavaScript Classes

How to...

- Master objects in JavaScript
- Understand JavaScript's built-in classes and data types
- Create a String object in JavaScript
- Perform mathematical functions
- Apply JavaScript's date-handling functions
- Convert strings into numbers
- Prepare text before sending to web server
- Decide when to use regular expressions
- Use JavaScript 2.0's powerful new data types
- Decide when to use JavaScript 2.0's special data types

JavaScript has always contained a number of built-in classes that programmers could employ when developing programs. These *classes*—self-contained data and code—provide useful functionality for handling dates, mathematical functions, and arrays. For instance, if you wanted to retrieve the current date and time in JavaScript, you would create an instance of the Date class, as so:

```
var today = new Date();
```

The today variable in this code is actually an object. Not only does the today object contain a value (today's date in fact), but it also contains a number of built-in functions for retrieving and setting individual parts of the date and converting it into a number of different formats (a string, for instance). The Date class, and all of its functionality, is explored in the section "Apply JavaScript's Date-Handling Functions," later in the chapter.

JavaScript 1.5 contains nine such classes, but only three are used in common practice (Array, Date, and Math). JavaScript 2.0 has expanded the list to more than 18 classes, and almost all of them are useful. In this chapter, we will examine most of these classes and learn to apply them in our JavaScript programs.

Learn about Objects in JavaScript

We are approaching the 50th anniversary of the development of Fortran, the first high-level programming language, which was developed in 1956. Since that time, computer scientists have developed several programming methodologies. Table 3-1 lists the most common methods of designing programs.

It's important to remember that no methodology is perfect for every situation. In JavaScript programming, you are likely to use any of the four methodologies listed in Table 3-1, depending on the task at hand.

Methodology	Description
Unstructured	Sequence of statements acting on global data
Procedural	Main program that calls functions to perform certain tasks
Modular	Main program that uses modules to group related functionality
Object-oriented	Main program that uses objects to group related data and functionality

TABLE 3-1   Common Programming Methodologies

Write Unstructured Programs

Unstructured programming is usually best used for short, simple scripts, since they would not benefit from many functions and objects. An unstructured program is simply a set of JavaScript statements that does not use user-defined functions or objects.

The following is an example of an unstructured program, in the context of an HTML web page. Notice that there are only three lines of JavaScript code in the program.

```
<html>
    <head>
        <title>JavaScript sample code</title>
    </head>
    <body>
        <h1>Unstructured Program</h1>
        <script language="JavaScript" type="text/javascript">
        <!-- // Begin
        for (var counter = 1; counter < 101; counter++) {
            document.write ("This is line number " + counter + "<br>\n");
        }
        // End -->
        </script>
    </body>
</html>
```

Organize Code into Procedures

Procedural code is also quite common in JavaScript programming. We could easily rewrite the unstructured code in the preceding program using the procedural approach.

```
function printline(value) {
    document.write ("This is line number " + value + "<br>\n");
}


for (var counter = 1; counter < 101; counter++) {
    printline(counter);
}
```

This program creates a function named printline(), whose sole job is to write text to the screen that includes the value passed to it as a parameter. Later on in the program, we can repeatedly call that function.

The benefits of this type of programming practice are twofold:

- The same function can be called from multiple locations in a program, thereby removing the code duplication of an unstructured approach.

- Dividing a program into functions makes it easier to test, which generally results in fewer bugs.

Separate a Program into Modules

If a program gets sufficiently big (in size and scope), it gets increasingly difficult to manage and maintain. Programmers require an additional technique (besides using procedures and functions) to separate their programs into smaller, more manageable pieces. The next logical step up from the procedural approach is the modular approach.

Modular programming generally involves separating one large program into two or more separate files. These files, or *modules,* as they are called, are not necessarily self-contained, but they do group related code and functions together. Typically, a modular program consists of a main program plus one or more modules, such as:

- Main program
- Database module
- User interface module
- Error-handling module

We can infer from the preceding modular configuration that the main program does most of the work, but it calls functions that exist in the database module whenever it needs to talk to the database. Similarly, it uses the user interface and error-handling modules to do their own tasks, as needed. This type of program is much easier for a programmer to manage when broken up into modules, as opposed to one large single module.

To create a modular program using JavaScript, you need to create one or more JavaScript files. When you import those external code files into an HTML page using a property of the <script> tag, your main program has access to all the functions defined in those external modules. We will learn more about creating and importing JavaScript files in Chapter 6.

Use the Object-Oriented Approach

The next progression from modular programming is to object-oriented programming. The concept of objects can be a little bit intimidating at first, but that should not stop anyone from attempting to at least understand how using objects can make the job of a programmer much easier.

In programming, an object is simply a "thing" that has its own attributes (known as *properties*) and related functions (known as *methods*). You can think of objects in programming just as you would think of objects in real life. Let me give you an example.

My car is an object that has certain attributes and can perform certain actions. The unique attributes of my car distinguish it from most others on the road. Even if I encounter another vehicle that is the same make and model as my own, they are still separate vehicles. The following is a list of some common properties of my car:

Property	Value
Year	2001
Make	Toyota
Model	4Runner SR5
Tires	4
Doors	4
Color	Thundercloud
Speedometer (mph)	Ranges from 0 to 70
Gas gauge (volume, in gallons)	Ranges from 0.0 to 16.0
Etc.	

What I have just listed are, in fact, the programming variables that will go into my Car object. In fact, the first five properties (Year, Make, Model, Tires, and Doors) are permanent—in programming parlance they're *constants*. The rest of the properties can be changed, thus they are variable. Remember, we examined constants and variables in Chapter 2. If I were to turn the list of properties related to my car into JavaScript 2.0 code, it would look something like this.

```
const Year  : Integer;
const Make  : String;
const Model : String;
const Tires : Integer;
const Doors : Integer;
var Color : String;
var CurrentSpeed : Number;
var CurrentGas : Number;
```

Besides having several properties, my car also has several actions it can perform:

If I do this...	The car does this...
Step on the gas pedal	Increases its speed; increases fuel consumption
Step on the brake pedal	Decreases its speed; decreases fuel consumption

If I do this...	The car does this...
Turn the steering wheel right or left	Turns its front wheels right or left
Press the center of the steering wheel	Honks its horn
Add gasoline into the gas tank	Increases its gas volume

Again, from a programmer's perspective these are functions of the car. Many of the functions are related to the car's properties. For instance, both the gas pedal and the brake pedal affect the car's speed and gasoline usage.

If my car were a programmable object, it would have the following JavaScript 2.0 function definitions.

```
function depressGasPedal (howMuch : Integer) {}
function depressBrakePedal (howMuch : Integer) {}
function turnSteeringWheel (degrees : Integer) {}
function beepHorn () {}
function addGas (volume : Number) {}
```

Turn Properties and Functions into a Class

Simply defining the collected constants, variables, and functions of a car does not make it an object. Before a collection of code can become an object, it must first become a class.

A class is a self-contained grouping of variables and functions. The variables and functions of a class, also called its *members*, cannot be used to store data or perform actions. Classes are merely the blueprints from which objects are created. There will only ever be one Car class in our computer program, but there could potentially be several Car objects. There could also be no Car objects, if we do not choose to create any.

TIP *There is one exception to the rule that classes cannot store data or perform actions. If a class member is defined as* static, *it can be used without the existence of an object. Static class members are discussed in more detail in Chapter 5.*

We will examine user-defined classes in Chapter 5. There is a different syntax for creating this class definition in JavaScript 1 and JavaScript 2, and it is important to understand the difference. Without getting into more detail, this is how our Car class would look in JavaScript 2.0 syntax.

```
class Car {
    const Year : Integer;
    const Make : String;
    const Model: String;
    const Tires : Integer;
    const Doors : Integer;
```

```
    var Color : String;
    var CurrentSpeed : Number;
    var CurrentGas : Number;

    function depressGasPedal (howMuch : Integer) {
        // Gas pedal JavaScript code
    }
    function depressBrakePedal (howMuch : Integer) {
        // Brake pedal JavaScript code
    }
    function turnSteeringWheel (degrees : Integer) {
        // Steering wheel JavaScript code
    }
    function beepHorn () {
        // Horn JavaScript code
    }
    function addGas (volume : Number) {
        // Gas tank JavaScript code
    }
}
```

We can create a Car object by calling the **new** operator with the name of the Car class. We will examine the **new** operator in more detail in the section "Instantiate an Object with the **new** Operator," later in this chapter.

```
var myAuto = new Car();
myAuto.Year = 2001;
myAuto.Make = "Toyota";
// etc.
```

Finally, classes in JavaScript 2.0 are also automatically defined as data types, so variables can be defined that can only contain the specified object.

```
var Ferrari : Car = new Car();
```

JavaScript's Built-in Classes and Data Types

Despite the lack of true data types in previous versions of the language, JavaScript has always had the concept of classes. Developers could use a number of built-in classes, which provided useful methods and functions for manipulating certain types of data.

Table 3-2 lists the classes that exist in JavaScript 1.5, along with a brief description of the functionality each class provides.

The most significant improvement in JavaScript 2.0 is that the language has evolved to become more object-oriented than it ever was before. JavaScript 1.5 was object-based, but did

Class Name	Description
Array	Allows lists of data to be stored in a single variable
Boolean	A wrapper for Boolean values
Date	Lets you work with dates and times
Function	Allows you to define a function programmatically
Math	Contains convenient mathematical constants and functions
Number	A wrapper for primitive numeric values
Object	All objects derive from this data type
RegExp	Provides support for regular expressions in JavaScript
String	A wrapper for string values

TABLE 3-2 Predefined Core JavaScript 1.5 Classes

not meet several of the key attributes of object-oriented programming languages. JavaScript 2.0 meets most of the key attributes.

Table 3-3 lists the classes supported by JavaScript 2.0. The list is obviously much longer than that in Table 3-2.

Class Name	Description
Array	Allows lists of data of type Object to be stored in a single variable; is equivalent to the Array[Object] data type
Array[*type*]	Allows lists of data of type *type* to be stored in a single variable
Boolean	Supports variables that can only store true and false
char	Supports variables that can only store a single character
ConstArray	Allows lists of data of type Object to be stored in a single constant; is equivalent to the ConstArray[Object] data type
ConstArray[*type*]	Allows lists of data of type *type* to be stored in a single constant
DynamicArray[*type*]	Allows resizable lists of data of type *type* to be stored in a single variable
Function	The "data type" of functions
Integer	Supports variables that can only store integers
Never	Supports variables that cannot contain any value
Null	Supports variables that can only store "null"
Number	Supports variables that can only store numbers
Object	Supports variables that can contain any value
Prototype	Supports variables that contain prototype-based objects (JavaScript 1.5's way of handling objects)

TABLE 3-3 Predefined Data Types in JavaScript 2.0

Class Name	Description
StaticArray[*type*]	Allows writable lists of data of type *type* to be stored in a single variable
String	Supports variables that can only store strings
Type	The "data type" of data types
Void	Supports variables that can only store "undefined"

TABLE 3-3 Predefined Data Types in JavaScript 2.0 *(continued)*

NOTE *All classes in JavaScript 2.0, even ones you create yourself, can be used as data types. Consequently, the list of classes in Table 3-3 is also a partial list of data types.*

In addition to the list of predefined classes that can be used as data types in Table 3-3, there are a number of *machine types* in JavaScript 2.0. These machine types (listed in Table 3-4) are low-level data types that can be used in JavaScript, although not all JavaScript environments will support them. They are provided for compatibility with other languages—for instance, when your JavaScript program needs to exchange data with an external C-language application.

NOTE *NaN (Not a Number) is a defined constant in JavaScript that is, effectively, a number representing that an error occurred when processing that variable.*

Machine types can be used just like data types derived from classes, although they are not classes themselves. For instance, in the following JavaScript 2.0 code listing, we create a handful of variables defined as machine types.

```
var counter : short = 14;
var account_balance : int = 1701330222;
var bigNumber : long = 74440000000000;
var anotherBigNumber = 312L;
```

SHORTCUT *The machine type suffixes listed in Table 3-4 are convenient shorthand notation for assigning a machine type to a value. The three suffixes—L, UL, and F—indicate to JavaScript that you wish to treat a number as either a long, unsigned long (ulong), or float number respectively. So the expression "0L" tells JavaScript to treat the value 0 as a long, due to the L machine-type suffix.*

In the preceding code, the variable anotherBigNumber will be treated as a long integer, since we are assigning the value 312L to it. The L suffix forces the value 312 to be treated as a long integer. This works only when assigning numeric literals to a variable, and will not work with other types of expressions such as variables.

Type	Suffix	Range of Values
sbyte		Integers between −128 and +127
byte		Integers between 0 and +255
short		Integers between −32768 and +32767
ushort		Integers between 0 and +65535
int		Integers between approximately −2.1 billion and +2.1 billion
uint		Integers between approximately 0 and +4.3 billion
long	L	Integers between approximately −9 quintillion and +9 quintillion (9 followed by 18 zeros)
ulong	UL	Integers between approximately 0 and +18 quintillion (18 followed by 18 zeros)
float	F	Single-precision floating point numbers, including positive and negative zeros, infinities, and NaN

TABLE 3-4   Machine Types Defined in JavaScript 2.0

Instantiate an Object with the new Operator

The procedure to create an object from either a user-defined or system-defined class is basically the same. JavaScript provides a special operator called **new** for this purpose, also called *object instantiation*.

```
var myAuto = new Car();
```

When the **new** operator is called with the name of an existing class (in this example, Car), it calls the class's constructor and returns an instance of the object. By assigning that object instance to the variable myAuto, we are keeping a reference to that object so we can use it in our program.

A *constructor* is a special function defined in some classes that makes the object ready for use. The initialization code is placed in the constructor. Classes can have more than one constructor or none at all. We examine creating your own classes, and constructors for those classes, in Chapter 5.

Any parameters included in our **new** operator are passed to the constructor as parameters as well. If we had defined a constructor to our Car class, we would probably want to allow the user to pass in most of the relevant properties (Make, Model, Year, etc.) as parameters, so that the constructor can make the object completely ready for use. Otherwise, we would have a Car object with no predefined properties and our program would have to manually set each relevant one.

```
var myAuto = new Car (2001, "Toyota", "4Runner SR5", "Thundercloud");
```

This technique of object initialization using the constructor is a recommended programming technique.

Access an Object with the . Operator

Once an object has been created using the **new** operator, we can access all its public properties and methods using the *dot operator* (.). The dot operator is placed between the object name (not the class name) and the name of the property or method you wish to access.

```
document.write ("Your car was created in " + myAuto.Year);
```

In this code example, we actually use the dot operator twice. We use it to access the write() method of the built-in document object and also to access the Year property of our user-defined myAuto object, which is an instance of the Car class.

You can define properties and methods as private, which restricts the ability to access them using the dot operator. We will examine private properties and methods in Chapter 5.

Access an Object with the [] Operator

JavaScript also allows access to an object's properties using the *square brackets operator* ([]). The one advantage this operator has over the dot operator is that you do not need to know the name of the property you wish to look up. For instance, let's look at the following **for-in** loop.

```
for (var tool in toolchest) {
    document.write(toolchest[tool] + "<BR>");
}
```

In this code example, we are passing a variable named tool to the square brackets operator, which is then able to extract the value of the property from the toolchest object. The public properties of any class defined in JavaScript 2.0 can be accessed using the square brackets operator. This even works for JavaScript's built-in DOM objects for version 1.5.

```
for (var prop in document) {
    document.write
        ("document." + prop + " = " + document[prop] + "<BR>");
}
```

This code results in the entire contents of the DOM document object being written to the web browser window, as you can see in Figure 3-1. Since the DOM is slightly different between different browser makers and even versions of the same browser, your own test will probably reveal different properties and values.

Create a String Object in JavaScript

A *string* is simply a sequence of zero or more Unicode characters. The following are all valid strings:

- ■ "" (an empty string)
- ■ "How was work today, Sofia?"

- "32" (numeric characters)
- "Êtes-vous prêt pour l'examen?" (non-English characters)

There are two ways to create strings in JavaScript:

- A string literal
- Using the String object

The vast majority of strings are created using the string literal, since it is by far the quickest and easiest technique.

Create a String Object Using a String Literal

A *string literal* in JavaScript is simply a sequence of zero or more characters surrounded by either single or double quotation marks, like so:

```
var myString = "This is a string literal";
var myOtherString = 'So is this, using single quotation marks.';
```

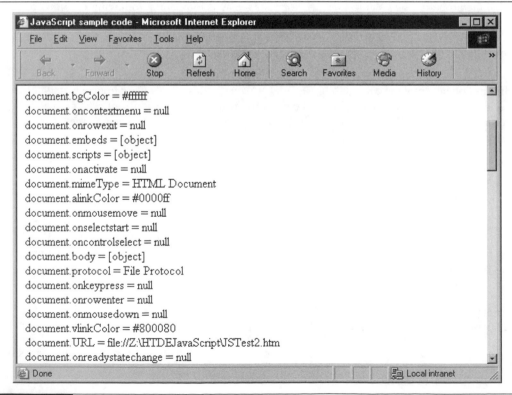

```
document.bgColor = #ffffff
document.oncontextmenu = null
document.onrowexit = null
document.embeds = [object]
document.scripts = [object]
document.onactivate = null
document.mimeType = HTML Document
document.alinkColor = #0000ff
document.onmousemove = null
document.onselectstart = null
document.oncontrolselect = null
document.body = [object]
document.protocol = File Protocol
document.onkeypress = null
document.onrowenter = null
document.onmousedown = null
document.vlinkColor = #800080
document.URL = file://Z:\HTDEJavaScript\JSTest2.htm
document.onreadystatechange = null
```

FIGURE 3-1 The contents of the document object in Internet Explorer 6.0

NOTE *The string literal can be used with any version of JavaScript.*

In JavaScript 2.0, you can even go so far as to assign the variable a String data type, while using a string literal to create the object.

```
var title : String = "How To Do Everything with Paper Clips";
```

It's important to remember that creating a String object using a string literal still allows you to use all the properties and methods provided by the object.

```
var myString = "This is a string literal";
var myOtherString = 'So is this, using single quotation marks.';
document.write ("\"" + myString + "\" = " +
    myString.length + " characters<br>");
document.write ("'" + myOtherString + "' = " +
    myOtherString.length + " characters<br>");
```

Length is a property of the String object. Accessing the length property results in the actual length of the string, as we can see in the following browser output.

Create a String Object Using the String Data Type

JavaScript 1.1 introduced the ability to create strings using the String class constructor.

```
var hometown = new String("Chicago");
```

By passing the text of the string to be created into the constructor, we end up with the hometown variable being a String. There are almost no advantages to creating strings like this, and you will very rarely see it done.

Use the String Object's Built-in Functionality

String objects are given a number of predefined functions, which allow you to perform all sorts of manipulations on them. Table 3-5 lists the most common String methods.

 Four of the methods listed in Table 3-5 work with regular expression patterns. We examine regular expressions in the section "Understand the Basics of Regular Expressions," later in this chapter.

Method	Purpose
charAt (*index*)	Returns one character from the string
charCodeAt (*index*)	Returns the ASCII code of one character from the string
concat (*string*)	Joins two strings together
indexOf (*string, index*)	Finds the first occurrence of one string inside another
lastIndexOf (*string, index*)	Finds the last occurrence of one string inside another
match (*regexp*)	Searches the string for the regular expression pattern, and returns any matches
replace (*regexp, newString*)	Searches the string for the regular expression pattern, and replaces any matches with the string provided
search (*regexp*)	Searches the string for the regular expression pattern, and returns the index of the first match
split (*separator, limit*)	Splits a single string into an array of substrings, based on a separator character or regular expression
substring (*start, end*)	Returns a part of a string
toLowerCase ()	Returns the string as lowercase characters
toString ()	Same as valueOf (); returns the string
toUpperCase ()	Returns the string as uppercase characters
valueOf ()	Returns the string

TABLE 3-5   Common String Object Methods

Each of the methods listed in Table 3-5 can be accessed from any String object using the dot operator.

```
var msg = "ERROR: Invalid User ID or Password<br>";
document.write ( "<b>Original message:</b> " +
    msg.valueOf() );
document.write ( "<b>Upper case:</b> " +
    msg.toUpperCase() );
document.write ( "<b>Lower case:</b> " +
    msg.toLowerCase() );
document.write ( "<b>Partial string:</b> " +
    msg.substring(20, 22) + "<br>" );
document.write ( "<b>Single character:</b> " +
    msg.charAt(17) + "<br>" );
document.write ( "<b>Search from beginning:</b> " +
    msg.toLowerCase().indexOf("sword") + "<br>" );
document.write ( "<b>Search from end:</b> " +
    msg.lastIndexOf("User ID") + "<br>" );
```

As you can see from the following screenshot, all the String properties can be applied to the msg object, since msg is of type String.

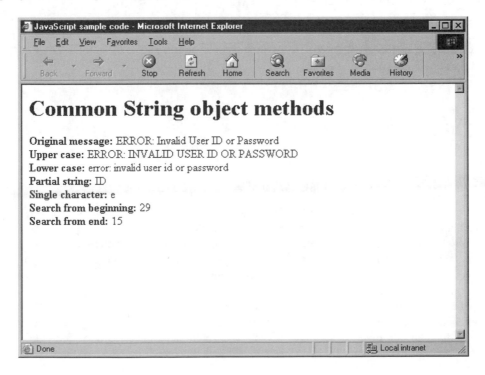

 *More than one dot operator can appear in a single expression. Take the expression "msg.toLowerCase()"—this expression will return the msg string as all lowercase characters. You can apply another String method to that expression, such as "msg.toLowerCase().indexOf("sword")". Since the indexOf() method returns an integer, you could add a third dot operator to perform one of the Integer object methods.*

Perform Mathematical Functions

JavaScript provides one built-in class that cannot actually be used to create an object—Math. The purpose of the Math class is to provide all sorts of mathematical functions and constants. Since all the members of the Math class are defined as static, you can call them directly using the Math object.

Attempting to create an object based on the Math class results in an error in JavaScript. You call Math's static members using the dot operator, just as you would with the instance members of any other class. Table 3-6 lists the names of all the predefined constants provided by the Math class.

The Math class also provides a number of methods that are useful for performing complex mathematical calculations, as shown in Table 3-7.

For example, if we wanted to create some JavaScript code that took advantage of the mathematical constants and functions provided by the Math object, we could do the following:

```
// area of a 12-inch circle, (PI * r^2)
var area = Math.PI * Math.pow (12/2, 2);

// length of the long side of a right angle triangle
//     assume, 5 inch base and 7 inches high, (a^2 + b^2 = c^2)
var longside = Math.sqrt( Math.pow(5,2) + Math.pow(7,2) );
```

Did you know?

Instance Members Versus Static Members

By default, properties and methods of a class will be defined as *instance members*. This means that they can only be accessed within the instance of an object based on that class. These objects are created using the **new** keyword, and a new copy of the class's instance members will be created for each new object created. If you create 100 objects based on a class, you have 100 separate copies of each method and variable. Changing the value of one of the copies does not affect the others.

Properties and methods of a class can optionally be defined as *static members*. Static members can only be accessed directly from the class and are not part of instances created based on that class. In essence, static class members are global, since only one version of that member ever exists, regardless of how many objects have been created from it.

Constant	Purpose
E	Euler's constant, 2.7183
LOG2E	The base 2 logarithm of E
LOG10E	The base 10 logarithm of E
LN2	The natural logarithm of 2
LN10	The natural logarithm of 10
PI	Pi, 3.1416
SQRT2	The square root of 2
SQRT1_2	The square root of one-half (0.5)

TABLE 3-6   A List of the Static Constants Provided by the Math Class

Apply JavaScript's Date-Handling Functions

We already took a quick look at the Date class at the beginning of this chapter, but it is worth looking at it again in more detail. The Date class allows you to create Date objects containing any date you specify, or today's date if you specify none. With a Date object, you can:

- Retrieve specific parts of the date (the month, for instance)
- Change or modify parts of the date
- Convert the date between different string formats
- Convert the date between different time zones

Method	Purpose
abs (x)	The absolute value of x
acos (x), asin (x), atan (x), atan2 (y, x), cos (x), sin (x), tan (x)	Trigonometry functions
ceil (x)	Returns the next largest integer larger than x (or x, if it is an integer)
exp (x)	Returns the constant E to the power of x
floor (x)	Returns the next lower integer less than x (or x, if it is an integer)
log (x)	Returns the natural logarithm of x
max (x, y)	Returns x or y, whichever is highest
min (x, y)	Returns x or y, whichever is lowest
pow (x, y)	Returns x to the power of y

TABLE 3-7   Static Methods of the Math Object

Method	Purpose
random ()	Returns a pseudorandom number between 0 and 1
round (x)	Rounds x to the nearest integer
sqrt (x)	Returns the square root of x

TABLE 3-7   Static Methods of the Math Object *(continued)*

> **TIP** *Early versions of JavaScript restricted the Date object so that it could not handle dates before January 1, 1970. This was corrected in version 1.3 of the language. Dates can now range between −100 million and +100 million days of January 1, 1970, which is approximately 270,000 years into the past and future.*

There are no such things as date literals in JavaScript, so a Date object can only be created out of the Date class. The constructor for the Date class accepts a number of different input parameters.

```
var holiday = new Date ("July 4, 2010");
var newyears = new Date (2010, 12, 31);
var today = new Date ();
var midnight = new Date (2010, 12, 31, 23, 59, 59, 999);
```

As we can see in the code, the Date constructor can attempt to interpret a date written as a string literal. You can also pass in the year, month, and day as integers. You can even specify the date and time down to the millisecond. If no parameters are provided, the object is set to today's date by default.

Table 3-8 lists all the methods supported by the Date object. Using these methods, you can extract specific parts of a date, change the date, or convert it to different formats.

Method	Purpose
getDate ()	Returns the day of the month (1–31) according to local time
getDay ()	Returns the day of the week (1–7) according to local time
getFullYear ()	Returns the four-digit year according to local time
getHours ()	Returns the hour component of the time according to local time
getMilliseconds ()	Returns the milliseconds component of the time according to local time
getMinutes ()	Returns the minutes component of the time according to local time
getMonth ()	Returns the month (0–11) according to local time; 0 is January, 1 is February, and so on
getSeconds ()	Returns the seconds component of the time according to local time

TABLE 3-8   Methods of the Date Object

3

Method	Purpose
getTime ()	Returns the numeric value corresponding to the time
getTimezoneOffset ()	Returns the number of hours the current time is offset from Universal time (Greenwich mean time)
getUTCDate ()	Returns the day of the month (1–31) according to Universal time
getUTCDay ()	Returns the day of the week (1–7) according to Universal time
getUTCFullYear ()	Returns the four-digit year according to Universal time
getUTCHours ()	Returns the hour component of the time according to Universal time
getUTCMilliseconds ()	Returns the milliseconds component of the time according to Universal time
getUTCMinutes ()	Returns the minutes component of the time according to Universal time
getUTCMonth ()	Returns the month (0–11) according to Universal time; 0 is January, 1 is February, and so on
getUTCSeconds ()	Returns the seconds component of the time according to Universal time
getYear ()	Returns the year according to local time
parse (*string*)	Parses a date string and returns the number of seconds since January 1, 1970
setDate ()	Sets the day of the month (1–31) according to local time
setFullYear ()	Sets the four-digit year according to local time
setHours ()	Sets the hour component of the time according to local time
setMilliseconds ()	Sets the milliseconds component of the time according to local time
setMinutes ()	Sets the minutes component of the time according to local time
setMonth ()	Sets the month (0–11) according to local time; 0 is January, 1 is February, and so on
setSeconds ()	Sets the seconds component of the time according to local time
setTime ()	Sets the numeric value corresponding to the time
setUTCDate ()	Sets the day of the month (1–31) according to Universal time
setUTCFullYear ()	Sets the four-digit year according to Universal time
setUTCHours ()	Sets the hour component of the time according to Universal time
setUTCMilliseconds ()	Sets the milliseconds component of the time according to Universal time
setUTCMinutes ()	Sets the minutes component of the time according to Universal time
setUTCMonth ()	Sets the month (0–11) according to Universal time; 0 is January, 1 is February, and so on
setUTCSeconds ()	Sets the seconds component of the time according to Universal time
setYear ()	Sets the year according to local time
toDateString()	Returns a string representing the date portion of the specified Date object
toGMTString ()	Converts a date to a string, using the Internet GMT conventions

TABLE 3-8   Methods of the Date Object *(continued)*

Method	Purpose
toLocaleDateString()	Converts the date portion of a date to a string, using the current locale's conventions
toLocaleString ()	Converts a date to a string, using the current locale's conventions
toLocaleTimeString()	Converts the time portion of a date to a string, using the current locale's conventions
toString ()	Returns a string representing the specified Date object
toTimeString()	Returns a string representing the time portion of the specified Date object
toUTCString ()	Converts a date to a string, using the Universal time convention
UTC ()	Returns the number of milliseconds in a Date object since January 1, 1970, 00:00:00, Universal time
valueOf ()	Returns the primitive value of a Date object

TABLE 3-8   Methods of the Date Object *(continued)*

The constructor for the Date class accepts four formats. The actual date the object represents depends on the number and type of parameters passed.

To create a date based on...	Use this...
A date string	new Date ("January 1, 2008")
Date components	new Date (2008, 0, 31)
Date and time components	new Date (2008, 0, 31, 12, 0, 0, 0)
Milliseconds since January 1, 1970	new Date (1034214221530)
Current date and time	new Date ()

NOTE   *JavaScript expects numbers in the range of 0 to 11 to represent months of the year. January is month 0, February is month 1, and so forth.*

Convert Strings into Numbers

JavaScript contains two built-in ways to convert numbers embedded in strings (like "32") into actual numbers that can be used in mathematical equations (like 32)— parseInt () and parseFloat ().

As their names imply, the parseInt function will return an integer (a number without a decimal portion), and parseFloat will return a floating-point number (including any decimal portion).

Use the parseInt and parseFloat Functions

JavaScript provides parseInt and parseFloat to help you convert numbers inside strings into actual number data types. This is an important technique when it comes to Internet web pages, since data read in from URLs and forms usually arrives as strings. Here is how they work:

1. Start by defining a variable to contain your string.

```
var myString;
```

2. Assign a string that contains a valid number to that variable. This number does not have to be an integer.

```
var myString;
myString = "3.14159265358979323846";  // The value of Pi...
```

3. Define a variable to contain your integer.

```
var myString, myInteger;
myString = "3.14159265358979323846";  // The value of Pi...
```

4. Call the parseInt () function on the string, and assign the value to the integer.

```
var myString, myInteger;
myString = "3.14159265358979323846";  // The value of Pi...
myInteger = parseInt (myString);
```

5. The parseInt () function should return the value 3 from the string defined in this example. We can verify this with a call to the alert message box.

```
var myString, myInteger;
myString = "3.14159265358979323846";  // The value of Pi...
myInteger = parseInt (myString);
alert (myInteger);
```

6. What would happen if myString were not a valid number? Let's modify it and find out.

```
var myString, myInteger;
myString = "Madrid, Spain";  // The value of Pi...
myInteger = parseInt (myString);
alert (myInteger);
```

The parseFloat () function works in a similar fashion to parseInt (), except the digits after the decimal place are included. We can verify this by changing the function name.

```
var myString, myInteger;
myString = "3.14159265358979323846";  // The value of Pi...
myInteger = parseFloat (myString);
alert (myInteger);
```

Prepare Text Before Sending to Web Server

Every web page on the Internet has a unique URL (uniform resource locator). Even web pages stored on your hard drive have their own unique URL. The following are a few examples of URLs:

URL	URL Description
http://www.amazon.com/	Default web page of Amazon.com
news:comp.infosystems.www.servers.unix	Usenet newsgroup
file:///C:/temp/test.html	File residing on user's hard drive

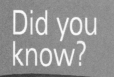

Uniform Resource Locator (URL) Limitations

The URL format only accepts the following characters in the URL string:

- Letters—a to z
- Numbers—0 to 9
- Marks—$ - _ + ! * ' ( ) ,
- Special characters reserved for special purposes—; / ? : @ = &

No other characters can appear in a URL. And the special characters can only be used in their designated roles. Characters that fall outside these rules must be properly escaped, as described in "Use the escape and unescape Functions."

Imagine a file with a long and uniquely creative name, such as We're #1 & proud of it; no ifs ands or buts!.htm. Windows does allow such a name for a file. But when it comes to accessing this file through a browser, we're going to have problems. The space, #, &, !, and ; characters are not allowed in the URL naming scheme. In order to access the file, it will first have to be escaped, as described in the following section.

Use the escape and unescape Functions

Escaping a file is the process of converting all the invalid characters into specially encoded symbols before sending the URL to the server to process. To escape a filename, we must use the escape function built into JavaScript.

1. Start with a string that has some invalid characters inside it.

```
var filename;
filename =
    "We're #1 & proud of it; no ifs ands or buts!.htm";
```

2. Define a variable to contain the escaped character sequence.

```
var filename, newFilename;
filename =
    "We're #1 & proud of it; no ifs ands or buts!.htm";
```

3. Assign the result of the escape function on the string to the new variable.

```
var filename, newFilename;
filename =
    "We're #1 & proud of it; no ifs ands or buts!.htm";
newFilename = escape(filename);
```

4. To examine the results of the escape() function, we should display it to the user using an alert box.

```
var filename, newFilename;
filename =
    "We're #1 & proud of it; no ifs ands or buts!.htm";
newFilename = escape(filename);
alert (newFilename);
```

Decide When to Use Regular Expressions

Regular expressions are a powerful search-and-replace technique that is widely used in other environments (such as Unix and Perl), but rarely used in JavaScript. Perhaps if more programmers knew about the existence of regular expressions in JavaScript, their use would catch on.

 *JavaScript only started supporting regular expressions in version 1.4 of the language, which means they will only work in Netscape 4 or Internet Explorer 4 web browsers, or subsequent releases.*

A *regular expression* is a sequence of characters written using a special regular expression language, which can be used to match patterns in other strings. To give you an idea of how powerful the regular expression pattern matching capability is, I wrote a little JavaScript program (primarily using the String object's substring() method) that checks to see if a string matches the standard telephone number format—(XXX) XXX–XXXX, where X represents any number from 0 to 9. That program contained 69 lines of JavaScript code, just to check a phone number.

Fortunately, the program can be rewritten using regular expressions, as follows:

```javascript
var phonenum = "(415) 555-1212";
var pattern = /^\(\d{3}\) \d{3}-\d{4}$/;
document.write ("Trying to match \"" + phonenum + "\" with pattern " +
    pattern.toString() + "...<br><br>");
if (pattern.test (phonenum)) {
    document.write ("This is a valid phone number.");
} else {
    document.write ("This is NOT a valid phone number.");
}
```

Running this JavaScript results in this output to the browser window.

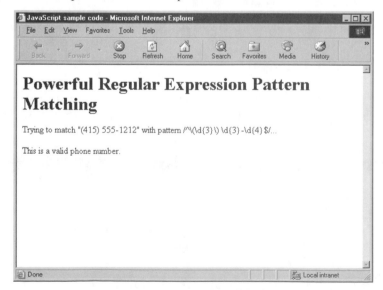

As you can see, substantial time and effort can be saved by using regular expressions to check a string against a pattern. We'll look at the workings of this code in the next section.

Understand the Basics of Regular Expressions

Regular expressions in JavaScript deal with pattern matching. Other programming languages allow regular expressions to search and replace text, but JavaScript programmers do not have that luxury. Despite this, regular expressions are still a powerful way to search for complex patterns. For instance, you can use them to

- Validate telephone numbers in more than one format
- Extract all the numbers from a string
- Ensure a date is entered in the valid format
- Verify an e-mail address has the proper format

As we saw in the preceding code example, the regular expression pattern is quite complex and can be a little bit intimidating.

```
var pattern = /^\(\d{3}\) \d{3}-\d{4}$/;
```

As I mentioned, regular expressions have their own language. There are many, many symbols and special characters to represent different things. The following are some general rules:

1. We start with defining a variable for our regular expression pattern.

   ```
   var pattern;
   ```

2. The forward slash (/) signifies the start and end of a regular expression literal in JavaScript. Regular expression literals allow us to create a regular expression object without having to use the RegExp class.

   ```
   var pattern = //;
   ```

3. The caret (^) and dollar sign ($) represent the start and end of a line. They also represent the start and end of a string. If we only wanted to match the pattern to part of the string, we would omit them. Similarly, if we wanted to test specifically for a pattern at the beginning of a long string, we could just use the caret (^) by itself. The following pattern only matches an empty string ("") so far.

   ```
   var pattern = /^$/;
   ```

4. The \d represents a single digit. If we add the \d to our pattern, it would only match a one-character string containing a number from 0 to 9.

   ```
   var pattern = /^\d$/;
   ```

5. If we want to match more than one number (as we do with a phone number), we can put multiple \d tokens together; \d\d\d would represent three numbers. We can also specify the number in curly braces: \d{3}.

```
var pattern = /^\d{3}$/;
```

6. Other characters in the pattern, such as spaces and hyphens, represent only themselves. So the following pattern would match 999-999-9999, which is one way to represent a telephone number.

```
var pattern = /^\d{3}-\d{3}-\d{4}$/;
```

7. Since the parentheses characters have special meaning in regular expression syntax, to include them we will need to escape them with a backslash: \(and \). That gives us a pattern that matches (999) 999-9999, which is what we want.

```
var pattern = /^\(\d{3}\) \d{3}-\d{4}$/;
```

There are many special tokens in the regular expression syntax to match different sets of characters. The tokens listed in Table 3-9 are the basic set.

Character	Meaning
\	Either denotes the start of a special token (for example, \d matches a digit) or indicates a special character is to be treated literally (* matches an asterisk)
^	Matches the beginning of a line; also matches the beginning of every string
$	Matches the end of a line; also matches the end of every string
*	A special quantifier, meaning the preceding token or group of tokens must match zero or more times
+	A special quantifier, meaning the preceding token or group of tokens must match one or more times
?	A special quantifier, meaning the preceding token or group of tokens must match zero or one time only
.	Matches any single character except the newline character (\n)
(abcd)	Matches "abcd" and remembers the match
car|bus	Matches either "car" or "bus"
{3}	Matches exactly three occurrences of the preceding token or group of tokens
{3,}	Matches three or more occurrences of the preceding token or group of tokens
{4,8}	Matches four to eight occurrences of the preceding token or group of tokens
[abcdef]	Matches any one of the characters a through f
[a-f]	Matches any one of the characters a through f
[a-zA-Z0-9]	Matches any single alphanumeric character

TABLE 3-9   Regular Expression Syntax in JavaScript

Character	Meaning
[^aeiou]	Matches everything except *a, e, i, o,* and *u*
\d	Matches a digit; identical to the pattern [0-9]
\D	Matches a nondigit; identical to the pattern [^0-9]
\s	Matches a space character (there are eight defined space characters)
\S	Matches a nonspace character
\t	Matches a tab
\n	Matches a new line
\r	Matches a carriage return
\w	Matches any alphanumeric (word) character (*a–z* and 0–9), including underscore (_); identical to the pattern [a-zA-Z0-9_]
\W	Matches any nonword character; identical to the pattern [^a-zA-Z0-9_]
\0	Matches null

TABLE 3-9   Regular Expression Syntax in JavaScript *(continued)*

Create Patterns with a RegExp Object

We've already seen how to create patterns with a regular expression literal. A regular expression literal starts and ends with a forward slash (/), as follows:

```
var zipCodePattern = /^\d{5}(-\d{4})?$/;
```

JavaScript also provides a class named RegExp to create these patterns as well. We can rewrite the pattern using this class's constructor, as follows:

```
var zipCodePattern = new RegExp ("^\\d{5}(-\\d{4})?$");
```

NOTE   *The backslash (\) character needs to be escaped anytime it is included in a string, and the RegExp constructor is no exception. The double backslash (\\) represents the escaped backslash character.*

The RegExp object provides two main methods for performing its search and match functions: test() and exec(). Table 3-10 lists the most common methods of the RegExp object.

Method	Purpose
compile ()	Compiles a regular expression
exec ()	Searches a string for a pattern and returns all the matches
test ()	Compares a string to a pattern and returns true or false based on the result

TABLE 3-10   Methods of the RegExp Object

Once a RegExp object has been created, JavaScript makes it very easy for you to test that pattern against any string.

```
var myPattern = new RegExp ("hat.*hat");
document.write ("Pattern 1: \"hat.*hat\"<br>");
document.write (myPattern.test ("That is a nice hat.") + "<br>" );
document.write (myPattern.test ("I love your hat!") + "<br><br>" );

var myPattern2 = new RegExp ("\\w+\\s\\w+");
document.write ("Pattern 2: \"\\w+\\s\\w+\"<br>");
document.write (myPattern2.test ("Jackie Gleason") + "<br>" );
document.write (myPattern2.test ("Cher!") + "<br>" );
```

The results of this pattern checking can be seen in Figure 3-2.

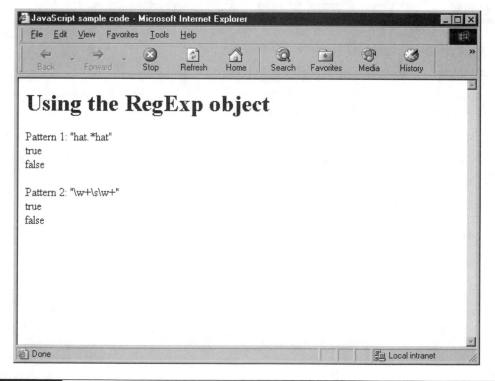

FIGURE 3-2   Creating and testing patterns using the RegExp object

Understand JavaScript 2.0's Powerful New Data Types

Up until this point, we have been examining the classes supported by the vast majority of web browsers used today. JavaScript 2.0 introduced a number of new classes, which were listed earlier, in Table 3-3. The way objects are created and accessed remains virtually the same from previous versions of JavaScript, with the **new** and dot (.) operators doing most of the work.

In this section, we will examine some of these new data types and learn how their powerful functionality can be applied in JavaScript programs.

 NOTE *The rest of the code in this chapter is designed to work in environments that support JavaScript 2.0 and will not work elsewhere.*

Use the Boolean, Integer, and Number Data Types

There are three basic data types in JavaScript known as *primitives:* numbers, strings, and Boolean values. All other data types are built on these three basic building blocks.

We already examined the String data type earlier in this chapter. The String object provides many methods to assist in manipulating strings, including searching (indexOf), extracting a portion of a string (substring), and determining the length of a string (length).

The Boolean data type is very simple compared to String. You can use it to store a Boolean value (true or false), and you can retrieve that Boolean value. That's pretty much it. There is really no reason to use the Boolean class in your programming, as the Boolean literals are easier to create and just as useful.

```
var isFinished : Boolean = false;
var paidToll : Boolean = true;
```

The number primitive is actually represented by two JavaScript data types: Number and Integer. The only difference between the two is that an Integer data type cannot contain a decimal portion. Other than that, the two classes are identical. Again, for the most part I will continue to use numeric literals to create simple numbers, for the sake of convenience.

```
var counter : Integer = 0;
var invoice_amount : Number = 12363.22;
```

Use the char Data Type

Perhaps the one thing that distinguishes the char data type more than anything else is the odd way it was named. This data type does not capitalize its initial letter and its name is not a complete word. (In fact, the ECMA technical committee wanted to call it the "Character data type" at one point during the language's development, which would have been more in line with how other classes were named.)

The char data type represents only single 16-bit Unicode characters. Some languages call this a *byte,* and it is normally used when allocated memory space is a prime consideration. It exists for compatibility with other languages, and does not have much practical purpose in modern-day web programming.

Use the Object Data Type

Every class in JavaScript—both user-defined and system-defined—is a member of this data type. If you wanted to create a variable that could hold any object in the system, this would be the data type to use.

```
var myObject : Object = new Date ();
myObject = new String ("This is a string");
myObject = new Car (2002, "Ferrari", "Testarosa", "Cherry red");
```

The myObject variable, once defined as a member of the Object data type, can act as an object for any other class in the system. This ability, where one class can act as an object for another related class, is known in object-oriented programming as *polymorphism*. Inheritance and polymorphism are discussed in Chapter 5, when we create our own classes.

Understand Special Data Types

JavaScript 2.0 also contains some data types that you may not use in everyday programming— or may not ever use. As you learned in the previous chapter, functions can return a value. And in JavaScript 2.0, you can assign a data type to that value.

```
function addTwo (num1 : Number, num2 : Number) : Number {
    return num1 + num2;
}
```

Use the Void Data Type

Well, you may sometimes need to define a function that does not return any result. The following program does its task and exits without returning a value.

```
function errorMessage (msg : String) {
    alert ("A serious error occurred\n" + msg +
            "\nPress OK to continue.");
    return;
}
```

Defining a function without any return value, as in this code, is certainly valid. But by doing so you have left the return value type ambiguous. Your function can either return a value or not, neither of which is an error. Leaving off the data type from the function only tells the system that the type of the return value is unknown.

If you want to explicitly state that your function does not return a value, you can use the Void data type. A function defined as type Void is not allowed to return a value—it is an error condition if it does.

```
function errorMessage (msg : String) : Void {
    alert ("A serious error occurred\n" + msg +
           "\nPress OK to continue.");
    return;
}
```

Use the Never Data Type

Or perhaps your function reports the error and then stops running completely. You can't do
this in a web browser environment, but you can in other environments, such as on the server.
Functions that cause the program to exit should have the data type of Never, as in "This function
will never return." The following code example is written using JavaScript in an IIS web server
environment.

```
function errorMessage (msg : String) : Never {
    response.write ("A serious error occurred\n" + msg +
           "\nPress OK to continue.");
    response.end;
}
```

Use the Null Data Type

Finally, the Null data type can only contain one valid value—null. I honestly cannot think of
a reason why you would wish to do this.

```
var useless : Null = null;
```

Well, we have looked at every object and data type that JavaScript allows us to use—almost,
that is. We haven't talked about arrays yet. JavaScript 2.0 has introduced five new array classes.
In the next chapter, we will examine arrays and see how they can be used to store tons of easily
accessible data.

Chapter 4

Organize Data into Arrays

How to...

- Create an Array object
- Set and retrieve values in an array
- Use multidimensional arrays
- Use JavaScript 2.0's enhanced arrays

In Chapter 2, we examined how our programs could use variables to store data for later retrieval. There is almost no limit to the number of variables a program can define. The number is limited only by the programmer's ability to remember what each variable does.

But you may sometimes be faced with the task of having to store dozens, or even hundreds, of related values into variable names for later use. For instance, how would you store the following?

- The names of the 50 U.S. states
- The names of the months of the year
- The album titles of the CDs in your collection
- The list of products in your store inventory

You may be able to come up with ways to store the first two lists (state and month names) in JavaScript code, perhaps by assigning each name its own variable (for example, var Nebraska = "Nebraska"). But while this is possible, it's not that practical. What's the point of having variables (or even constants) whose value won't ever change and whose value matches the variable name?

So then, how could you store those types of lists (album titles and products in inventory)? After all, these lists could get quite large (your store could carry hundreds of products), the values can (and do) change, and even the length of the list will be different over time.

JavaScript provides *Array objects* to handle lists of data. Arrays can handle long lists of data whose values can be easily retrieved or modified. Arrays can also grow or shrink as required.

```
for (counter = 0; counter < 50; counter ++) {
    document.write ("State #" + counter + ": " +
        statesArray[counter]);
}
```

In the code, the variable statesArray contains an array of the 50 U.S. state names. We can access this array using its index (which ranges in value from 0 to 49) using the square brackets ([]) operator.

```
statesArray[counter];
```

Of course, the code neglects to show how the Array object was created. There are two ways to create Array objects:

- The Array class
- The Array literal

Unfortunately, there is a little inconsistency between the official specifications and the way each of the major browser manufacturers has implemented arrays in JavaScript. In this chapter, we will examine how arrays are created and how to create code that works across all browsers. We will also take a look at some of the exciting improvements in arrays in JavaScript 2.0.

Create an Array Object

There are three ways to create an Array using the JavaScript Array class:

- `new Array ()`
- `new Array (size)`
- `new Array (element1, element2, ..., elementN)`

Create an Empty Array

Passing no arguments to the constructor of the Array class creates an *empty array,* also called an array of zero length. (In JavaScript, the number of items inside an array is known as its length.) We can then populate the array manually, as follows.

1. We start by defining a variable to contain our array.

```
var months;
```

2. We then create a new Array object using the **new** operator.

```
var months = new Array();
```

3. We manually assign a value to the first index of the array. Indexes start at value 0.

```
var months = new Array();
months[0] = "January";
```

4. Now our array has a length of 1. We can then populate the rest of the values for our array.

```
var months = new Array();
months[0] = "January";
months[1] = "February";
months[2] = "March";
months[3] = "April";
months[4] = "May";
months[5] = "June";
months[6] = "July";
months[7] = "August";
months[8] = "September";
months[9] = "October";
months[10] = "November";
months[11] = "December";
```

5. We now have an array that can be accessed by the rest of our program using only its numerical index.

```
var months = new Array();
months[0] = "January";
months[1] = "February";
months[2] = "March";
months[3] = "April";
months[4] = "May";
months[5] = "June";
months[6] = "July";
months[7] = "August";
months[8] = "September";
months[9] = "October";
months[10] = "November";
months[11] = "December";

for (var i = 0; i < 12; i++) {
    document.write (months[i] + "<br>");
}
```

6. As you can see here, JavaScript is able to store a list of related values (months of the year) into a single variable, and then easily access each of those values for later use.

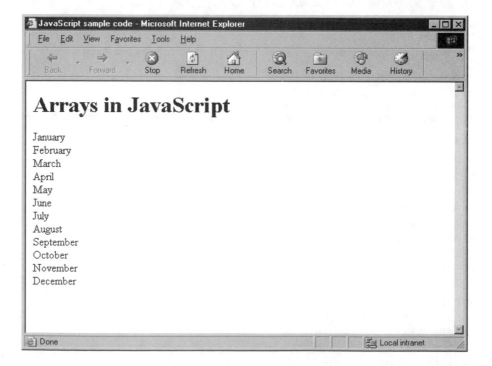

7. A list such as this (months of the year) is convenient if you want your program to convert a numerical month into its string equivalent. Luckily, the Date object's getMonth() function returns the month in a range of 0 to 11, so we do not even have to adjust the value before using it.

```
var today = new Date();
var monthnum = today.getMonth();
document.write ("Today is a lovely " +
    months[monthnum] + " day.");
```

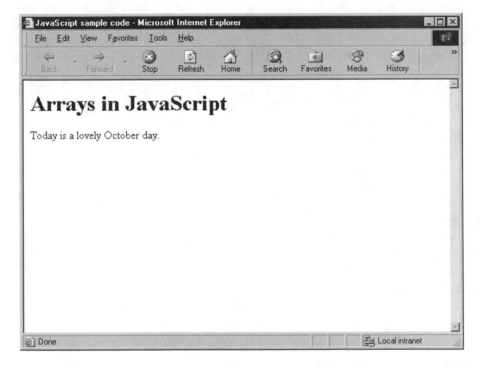

Specify an Initial Array Length

JavaScript allows you to specify an initial length for your array by passing a single integer as a parameter.

```
var months = new Array(12);
```

Setting the length of an array in advance like this provides few advantages in JavaScript 1.5, since arrays grow automatically. Perhaps the one benefit it does provide is to remind you how large an array you intended to define.

The length of an array can also be set within the program by altering the length property of the Array object.

```
var months = new Array();
months.length = 12;
```

Create and Initialize an Array in One Line of Code

Looking at the months array defined earlier, we ended up writing 13 lines of code just to create and initialize the array. It would be nice if we could create this same array using only one line of code.

Of course, I wouldn't have mentioned it if JavaScript couldn't do it...

```javascript
var months = new Array ("January", "February", "March", "April",
    "May", "June", "July", "August",
    "September", "October", "November", "December");
```

The constructor of the Array class also accepts a comma-separated list of the initial values of the array. The first item listed is assigned the index 0, the next item becomes index 1, and so on.

This is especially helpful for long lists of items. For instance, if we needed an array containing the 50 U.S. states, it would be much easier to create it in one line of code, as opposed to 51 or more.

```javascript
var USStates = new Array ("Alabama", "Alaska", "Arizona",
    "Arkansas", "California", "Colorado", "Connecticut",
    "Delaware", "Florida", "Georgia", "Hawaii", "Idaho",
    "Illinois", "Indiana", "Iowa", "Kansas", "Kentucky",
    "Louisiana", "Maine", "Maryland", "Massachusetts",
    "Michigan", "Minnesota", "Mississippi", "Missouri",
    "Montana", "Nebraska", "Nevada", "New Hampshire",
    "New Jersey", "New Mexico", "New York", "North Carolina",
    "North Dakota", "Ohio", "Oklahoma", "Oregon", "Pennsylvania",
    "Rhode Island", "South Carolina", "South Dakota", "Tennessee",
    "Texas", "Utah", "Vermont", "Virginia", "Washington",
    "West Virginia", "Wisconsin", "Wyoming");
```

Use Array Literals

Just as JavaScript provides ways to create numbers, strings, and regular expressions without having to manually create an object, you can do the same thing with arrays.

```javascript
var months = ["January", "February", "March", "April",
    "May", "June", "July", "August",
    "September", "October", "November", "December"];
```

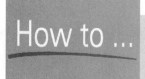 **Break Long Lines of Code into Several Lines**

To make long lines of code more readable (to yourself and other programmers looking at your code), it is a wise idea to include a carriage return before the text scrolls off the right side of the screen. JavaScript supports code written over several lines, as long they are placed in the proper places. JavaScript will ignore extra spaces and new line characters, as it considers the semicolon (;) the actual end of the statement.

The square brackets in the preceding code cause JavaScript to interpret their contents as the contents of a new array. It is equivalent to creating an array using the proper constructor syntax.

```
var months = new Array("January", "February", "March", "April",
    "May", "June", "July", "August",
    "September", "October", "November", "December");
```

All the properties and methods of the Array object are available to objects created using the Array literal.

Call the Properties and Methods of the Array Object

The Array object in JavaScript exposes only three properties. Two of those properties are only set when the array being called is the result of a regular expression pattern match, as discussed in Chapter 3. The length property (which is available to all arrays) is the only one of the three that can be modified, as it indicates the current length of the array.

Property	Description
index	Related to regular expression pattern matching; contains the index of the matching substring (read-only)
input	Related to regular expression pattern matching; contains the original string against which the match was made (read-only)
length	Retrieves or sets the length of the array

TIP   *Not every element in an array has to contain a value. You could just as easily create an array that skips every second index number, or skips an arbitrary number of index numbers.*

The length property takes into account the number of empty (unused) indexes in an array as well as the number of elements an array contains. So if you skip a large amount of index numbers, the length property will be much larger than the number of elements.

```
var employee = new Array();
employee[127756] = "Tom Jones";
alert(employee.length);
```

This code returns 127,757 as the length of the array, since that is the number of elements (including empty ones) from 0 through 127,756.

The Array object also contains a number of helpful methods to make managing the contents of the array easier for the programmer, as we can see in Table 4-1.

Using the methods of the Array object listing in Table 4-1 provides several advanced modification functions on the contents of arrays. Four of the methods allow us to treat arrays like either a *call stack* or a *queue*.

In programming, a call stack is similar to a stack of pancakes. The last pancake added to the top of stack has to be the first pancake taken off (or eaten). This arrangement is sometimes called the *last in, first out* (LIFO) method.

A queue is much like a line at a bank, where the first person to enter the line is the first person served. Not surprisingly, this arrangement is sometimes called the *first in, first out* (FIFO) method.

Method	Description
pop() and push()	Last in, first out (LIFO); similar to a call stack
shift() and unshift()	First in, first out (FIFO); similar to a queue

There are several other interesting methods that allow you to convert an array into a single string, split arrays into subarrays, or even concatenate two or more arrays together.

In the following code, we create a number of arrays using the Array class.

```
var MainMenu = new Array("File", "Edit", "View",
    "Window", "Help");
var FileMenu = new Array("New", "Open", "Close", "Save", "Exit");
var EditMenu = new Array("Undo", "Repeat", "Cut", "Copy", "Paste");
var ViewMenu = new Array("Normal", "Web Layout", "Outline");
var WindowMenu = new Array("New Window", "Arrange All", "Split");
var HelpMenu = new Array("Contents", "About", "Contact Us");
```

Method	Description
concat (*array1, array2...arrayN*)	Joins two or more arrays into a single array
join (*separator*)	Joins all the elements of an array into a single string, separated by the separator indicated or a comma if none is specified
pop ()	Returns the last element of an array and removes it
push (*element1, element2...elementN*)	Adds one or more elements to the end of an array and returns its new length
reverse ()	Reverses the order of the elements in an array
shift ()	Similar to pop (); returns the first element of an array and removes it

TABLE 4-1 Methods of the Array Object

Method	Description
slice (*begin*, *end*)	Creates a new array from a subsection of the existing array, as defined by the start and end indexes
splice (*index*, *howMany*, *element1*, *element2...elementN*)	Used to add or remove elements from an array
sort (*functionName*)	Used to sort the elements of an array
unshift (*element1*, *element2...elementN*)	Similar to push (); adds one or more elements to the beginning of an array and returns its new length

TABLE 4-1   Methods of the Array Object *(continued)*

These arrays represent a menu of a hypothetical web site. We can use some of the methods of the Array object on each of these arrays to modify it or extract bits of information.

```
//Creates a string of all elements of an array
// The array itself is unaffected
var MenuItemsStr = MainMenu.join(" | ");
document.write (MenuItemsStr + "<br><br>");


// Creates a new array that contains all elements of all arrays
// The existing arrays are all unaffected
var AllMenuItems = MainMenu.concat(FileMenu, EditMenu, ViewMenu,
    WindowMenu, HelpMenu);
document.write (AllMenuItems.join(", ") + "<br><br>");


// Reverses the order of elements in an array
// Modifies the existing array
MainMenu.reverse();
document.write (MainMenu.join(" | ") + "<br><br>");


// Creates a new array that contains a subset of an existing array
// The existing arrays are all unaffected
var ChildMenuItems = AllMenuItems.slice(MainMenu.length);
document.write (ChildMenuItems.join(" <font size=+3>||</font> ")
    + "<br><br>");
```

4

The results from these array manipulations can be seen in the following screenshot.

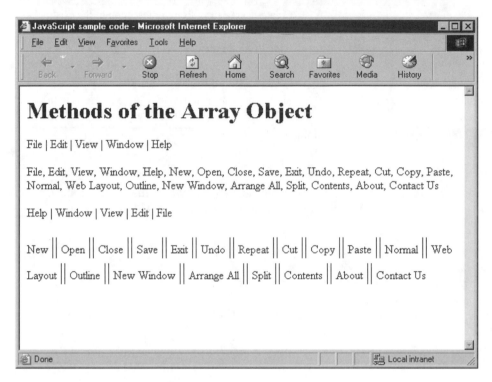

Set and Retrieve Values in an Array

Elements inside the JavaScript Array object are accessed using the square brackets operator.

```
var myArray = new Array();
myArray[16] = "Some value";
document.write (myArray[16]);
```

The number inside the square brackets is called the *index*. You can think of an array as a series of parking spaces, numbered from 0 up to infinity. When the valet parks your car in one of those spaces, he has to keep note of the spot number in order to be able to find your car again.

JavaScript arrays support using strings as indexes. When a string is used as an index, this is called a *hash table*.

```
var FruitColors = new Array();
FruitColors["Apple"] = "red";
FruitColors["Banana"] = "yellow";
FruitColors["Grape"] = "purple";
```

Here, the string "Apple" is being used as the index to store the value "red". The string "Apple" can be referred to as the *key*. Values stored in hash tables can be retrieved using the key, just as they can with numerically indexed arrays.

```
document.write ("Apples are " + FruitColors["Apple"] + ".<br>");
document.write ("Bananas are " + FruitColors["Banana"] + ".<br>");
document.write ("Grapes are " + FruitColors["Grape"] + ".<br>");
```

As we saw in Chapter 2, arrays can also be accessed using the **for-in** statement. The **for-in** statement will loop through each of the elements in an array, returning the indexes or keys.

```
var FruitColors = new Array();
FruitColors["Apple"] = "red";
FruitColors["Banana"] = "yellow";
FruitColors["Grape"] = "purple";

for (var fruit in FruitColors) {
    document.write (fruit + "s are " + FruitColors[fruit]
        + ".<br>");
}
```

Here, the **for-in** loop iterates over the document.write() function three times, once for each of the items in the array. The resulting output can be seen in Figure 4-1.

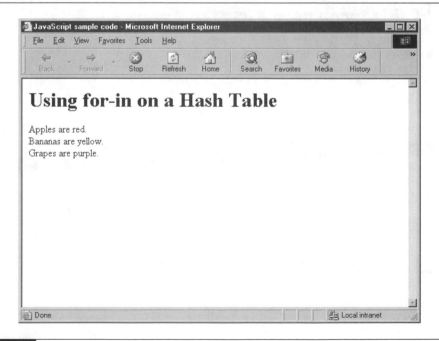

FIGURE 4-1   The **for-in** loop iterates over a hash table.

The same technique can be used for arrays with numerical indexes:

```
var Players = new Array();
Players[0] = "Jaime";
Players[1] = "Mom";
Players[2] = "Bart";
Players[3] = "Liez'l";

// Who do we have playing bridge?
for (var name in Players) {
    document.write (name + ": ");
    document.write (Players[name] + " is playing bridge.<br>");
}
```

As you can see from the output in Figure 4-2, the **for-in** loop was able to iterate over each of our bridge players as well.

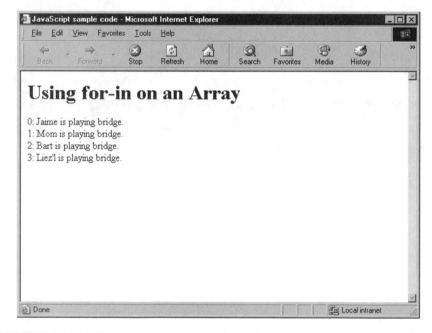

FIGURE 4-2   The **for-in** loop iterates over an array.

Use Multidimensional Arrays

The arrays that we have seen thus far in this chapter are sometimes called *one-dimensional arrays*. If you think of an array as a graphical table containing rows and columns, these one-dimensional arrays would only have one column, as shown in Figure 4-3.

A two-dimensional array is an array that would contain more than one column when displayed as a graphical table. Two-dimensional arrays are used when you need to store more than one value for each item in your list. Figure 4-4 shows a graphical representation of a two-dimensional array.

A three-dimensional array would look more like a cube, as an element of depth is added to the graph. Believe it or not, there are such things as four-dimensional arrays and higher. We live in a three-dimensional world, though, and it gets increasingly difficult to graphically display these complex sets of data.

Some programming languages allow the definition of multidimensional arrays as a core feature of the language. Unfortunately, JavaScript is not one of them. If you want to define a multidimensional array in your JavaScript application, you will have to work within the limitations of the one-dimensional array.

There are two techniques you can use to simulate a multidimensional array in JavaScript:

- You can create parallel one-dimensional arrays.

- You can create arrays of arrays.

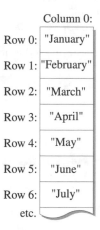

FIGURE 4-3   A graphical representation of a simple (one-dimensional) array

	Column 0:	Column 1:	Column 2:	Column 3:
Row 0:	"January"	"Garnet"	"Red"	"Constancy"
Row 1:	"February"	"Amethyst"	"Purple"	"Sincerity"
Row 2:	"March"	"Bloodstone"	"Blue"	"Courage"
Row 3:	"April"	"Diamond"	"White/Clear"	"Innocence"
Row 4:	"May"	"Emerald"	"Green"	"Love"
Row 5:	"June"	"Pearl"	"Cream"	"Health"
Row 6:	"July"	"Ruby"	"Red"	"Contentment"
etc.				

FIGURE 4-4   A two-dimensional array contains multiple columns.

One of the first arrays we looked at in this chapter was a listing of the months of the year. Let's continue with that example. We started with the following one-dimensional array:

```
var months = new Array ("January", "February", "March", "April",
    "May", "June", "July", "August",
    "September", "October", "November", "December");
```

Let's say we wanted to make a list of the following four items:

- The months of the year
- The birthstone related to each month
- The color of each birthstone
- The meaning associated with each birthstone

Right now our array only contains months; if we were to arbitrarily add the three other things we wish to list, it would only add confusion to the array and make it harder to use.

```
var months = new Array ("January", "February", "March", "April",
    "May", "June", "July", "August",
    "September", "October", "November", "December",
    "Garnet", "Amethyst", "Bloodstone or Aquamarine",
    "Diamond", "Emerald", "Pearl, Moonstone, or Alexandrite",
    "Ruby", "Sardonyx or Peridot", "Sapphire",
    "Opal or Tourmaline", "Topaz", "Turquoise or Lapis lazuli",
    "Red", "Purple", "Green/Red or Blue", "White/Clear",
    "Green", "Cream", "Red", "Light Green",
```

```
    "Blue", "Many Colors", "Orange/Brown", "Blue",
    "Constancy", "Sincerity", "Courage", "Innocence",
    "Love and success", "Health and longevity", "Contentment",
    "Married happiness", "Clear thinking", "Hope",
    "Fidelity", "Prosperity");
```

As you can see from this code, simply adding the extra lists to the existing array is not the best solution. Not only is it difficult for humans to read and understand, the programmer will also have to be careful when creating the program so that things don't get mixed up.

We can rewrite that messy array using four parallel arrays, as follows.

```
var months = new Array ("January", "February", "March", "April",
    "May", "June", "July", "August",
    "September", "October", "November", "December");

var stones = new Array ("Garnet", "Amethyst",
    "Bloodstone or Aquamarine", "Diamond", "Emerald",
    "Pearl, Moonstone, or Alexandrite", "Ruby",
    "Sardonyx or Peridot", "Sapphire", "Opal or Tourmaline",
    "Topaz", "Turquoise or Lapis lazuli");

var colors = new Array ("Red", "Purple", "Green/Red or Blue",
    "White/Clear", "Green", "Cream", "Red", "Light Green",
    "Blue", "Many Colors", "Orange/Brown", "Blue");

var meaning = new Array ("Constancy", "Sincerity", "Courage",
    "Innocence", "Love and success", "Health and longevity",
    "Contentment", "Married happiness", "Clear thinking",
    "Hope", "Fidelity", "Prosperity");
```

The elements in each of the arrays match exactly to the same indexes in the other arrays, so let's say I want to find out something about the seventh month of the year. (Remember that the arrays start at index 0, so the seventh month of the year is described at element number 6.)

```
document.write ("The seventh month is <b>" + months[6]);
document.write ("</b>. Its birthstone is <b>");
document.write (stones[6] + "</b>. The " + stones[6]);
document.write (" is a <b>" + colors[6] + "</b> colored stone, ");
document.write ("and it means <b>" + meaning[6] + "</b>");
document.write (" traditionally.<br>");
```

In this manner, we are able to store several columns of information about each month, by defining them in their own arrays. We can see the results of this code in our web browser screenshot in Figure 4-5.

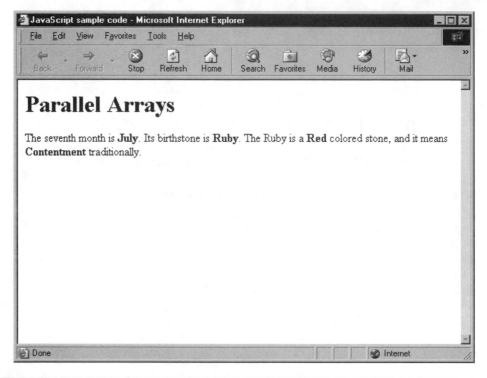

FIGURE 4-5 The use of parallel arrays can simulate two-dimensional arrays.

The other method of creating a multidimensional array is to create an array that contains other arrays—*an array of arrays,* as this is called.

To create an array of arrays, you would go through the following steps.

1. First, define the four arrays, just as you would if you were defining parallel arrays.

```
var months = new Array ("January", "February", ...);
var stones = new Array ("Garnet", " Amethyst", ...);
var colors = new Array ("Red", "Purple", ...);
var meanings = new Array ("Constancy", "Sincerity", ...);
```

2. Next, define a master array that will hold all four arrays.

```
var marray = new Array();
```

3. Then, assign each of the four arrays that contain the data to this master array.

```
var marray = new Array();

marray[0] = months;
```

```
marray[1] = stones;
marray[2] = colors;
marray[3] = meanings;
```

4. You should then modify your program to access the subarrays using the name of the master array with the appropriate index to the array.

```
var marray = new Array();

marray[0] = months;
marray[1] = stones;
marray[2] = colors;
marray[3] = meanings;

document.write ("The fourth month is <b>" + marray[0][3]);
document.write ("</b>. Its birthstone is <b>");
document.write (marray[1][3] + "</b>. The " + marray[1][3]);
document.write (" is a <b>" + marray[2][3] + "</b> "
     + "colored stone, ");
document.write ("and it means <b>" + marray[3][3] + "</b>");
document.write (" traditionally.<br>");
```

As you see, instead of referring to the array as months[3], we must now refer to it using the name and index of the master array, as in marray[0][3]. As you can see in Figure 4-6, this technique is also a valid way to create two-dimensional arrays.

Use JavaScript 2.0's Enhanced Arrays

JavaScript 2.0 has added three distinct subclasses to the traditional Array class. Each subclass is very similar to the way arrays have always worked in JavaScript, with some unique differences. Table 4-2 lists the traditional Array class and the three new classes, and describes the different classes.

Array Object Name	Description
Array [*datatype*]	This (the original Array class) is an abstract class. When called, it returns a DynamicArray object. If no data type is specified, it defaults to type Object.
StaticArray [*datatype*]	This new subclass does not automatically grow when new elements are added. It cannot contain empty elements and cannot be called without a data type.
DynamicArray [*datatype*]	This new subclass is the traditional JavaScript Array object. It cannot be called without a data type.
ConstArray [*datatype*]	This new subclass creates an array of constants whose value cannot be changed once set. It cannot contain empty elements. If no data type is specified, it defaults to type Object.

TABLE 4-2   Array Classes in JavaScript 2.0

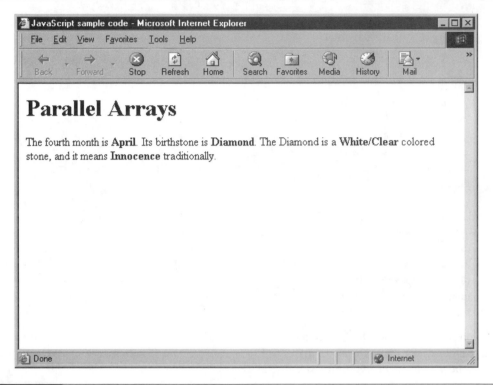

FIGURE 4-6   The array of arrays technique closely simulates true two-dimensional arrays.

Each of the Array types is usually instantiated with a data type. Both Array and ConstArray provide defaults for the data type, while the others do not. The data type provided when defining an array restricts the contents of the array to objects of that data type only.

In this section, we will examine each of the three new array types and see how they can be used in JavaScript programs.

The StaticArray Class

The StaticArray class creates arrays of predetermined length whose values can be modified at any time. There are two ways to create a new StaticArray:

- new StaticArray [*datatype*] ()
- new StaticArray [*datatype*] (*size*)

The JavaScript 2.0 specification says that StaticArrays must be defined with a data type. To create an array that can accept any data type, we can define the array to accept values of type

Object. Since Object is the parent data type of all classes in JavaScript, including those that you create yourself, Object arrays can accept any value.

Creating a StaticArray without passing in a data type results in an array that can contain any object. Recall from the last chapter that Object is the data type of every class in the system, including those that you define yourself.

```
var myArray : StaticArray = new StaticArray[Object]();
myArray.length = 4;
myArray[0] = "This is the first element";
myArray[1] = 3.141;
myArray[2] = new Car(2001, "Toyota", "4Runner", "Thundercloud");
myArray[3] = new Date();
```

This code creates a new StaticArray variable of type Object. We take advantage of this by storing a string, a number, a user-defined Car object, and a Date object into this array.

Since the StaticArray has to have a predefined length, we started by initializing the length property of the array to the value 4, the number of items we intended to store. Attempting to add an additional item would cause a JavaScript error, unless we manually increased the value of the length.

```
var myArray : StaticArray = new StaticArray[Object]();
myArray.length = 5;
myArray[0] = "This is the first element";
myArray[1] = 3.141;
myArray[2] = new Car(2001, "Toyota", "4Runner", "Thundercloud");
myArray[3] = new Date();
myArray[4] = "This is a new element.";
```

Providing a more specific data type, such as Number, would restrict the elements of the array to only that type.

```
var mySecondArray : StaticArray = new StaticArray[Number](6);
mySecondArray[0] = 14.2;
mySecondArray[1] = 13;
mySecondArray[2] = 21.9999;
mySecondArray[3] = 2141330119;
mySecondArray[4] = 0.0000003;
mySecondArray[5] = 1.0121E26;
```

 NOTE   *Arrays of type StaticArray cannot have missing elements; that is, you cannot skip index numbers as you can with DynamicArrays.*

Attempting to add a string to a StaticArray that accepts only numbers will cause a JavaScript error.

```
mySecondArray[5] = "This is not allowed.";
```

The DynamicArray Class

A DynamicArray is similar to a StaticArray, except that the size of the array will adjust itself automatically based on the elements you try to add to it. There are two ways to create a DynamicArray:

- new DynamicArray [*datatype*] ()
- new DynamicArray [*datatype*] (*size*)

This means that you can create an empty array and add elements to it without regard for the existing array length.

```
var Nieces : DynamicArray = new DynamicArray[String]();
Nieces[0] = "Sofia";
Nieces[1] = "Monica";
Nieces[2] = "Tiffany";
Nieces[3] = "Liz";
Nieces[4] = "Elke";
Nieces[5] = "Christine";
Nieces[6] = "Leah";
```

This DynamicArray, Nieces, can continue to grow to almost an unlimited size, limited only by the amount of computer memory. Another difference between DynamicArrays and the other types of arrays is that you are not obligated to fill every element. The following is valid code using DynamicArrays:

```
var emps : DynamicArray = new DynamicArray[String]();
emps[9931] = "John H. Smith";
```

Even though we have not provided values for indexes 0 through 9930, we can skip ahead to 9931 and provide a value for that element of the array.

The ConstArray Class

The third new array type supported by JavaScript 2.0 is ConstArray. ConstArrays are very similar to DynamicArrays, with three notable differences:

- They can be defined without specifying a data type.
- Their value cannot be changed once set.
- They do not support skipped elements.

There are four ways to create a new ConstArray:

- new ConstArray ()
- new ConstArray (*size*)

- new ConstArray [*datatype*] ()
- new ConstArray [*datatype*] (*size*)

The ConstArray class takes its cue from the JavaScript constant variable type. (We looked at constants in Chapter 2.) Once set, the value of a constant cannot be changed.

```
var months : ConstArray = new ConstArray[String](12);
months[0] = "January";
months[1] = "February";
months[2] = "March";
months[3] = "April";
months[4] = "May";
months[5] = "June";
months[6] = "July";
months[7] = "August";
months[8] = "September";
months[9] = "October";
months[10] = "November";
months[11] = "December";
```

Since the names of the months of the year are not likely to change during the execution of our program, we can define them as constants. We are then free to access those strings later in our program using the same square brackets syntax described earlier in the chapter.

The last two chapters have focused on the built-in classes provided by JavaScript, and in particular the new classes and data types provided by JavaScript 2.0. The next chapter is all about creating your own classes, in both JavaScript 1.5 and 2.0.

4

Chapter 5

Create Your Own JavaScript Classes

How to...

- Create objects in JavaScript 1.x
- Use an object literal
- Create objects in JavaScript 2.0
- Organize classes using inheritance

The last couple of chapters discussed how JavaScript's built-in classes could be used to store many types of data (Dates, Numbers, Booleans, etc.). JavaScript also provides a way for you to create your own classes, so that you can design your own data types.

In this chapter, we will examine the methods a JavaScript program can use to define objects for its own use. We will also examine the difference between objects created in JavaScript 1.x and those created in JavaScript 2.0.

Learn about Classes in JavaScript

In some ways JavaScript is an object-oriented programming language, and in some ways it is not. JavaScript has always had the ability to create and use objects. And in fact it is practically impossible to design a JavaScript program that does not, in some way, use the Document Object Model or any of the object-based data types JavaScript provides.

But JavaScript programs are not normally designed around the object-oriented programming model, as Java and C++ programs are. JavaScript does not mandate the use of classes, which would force programmers to use the object-oriented programming model discussed in Chapter 3. JavaScript programmers are free to write unstructured or procedural programs to fit the task at hand.

Nonetheless, support for user-defined classes and objects is one aspect of the language that will gain in acceptance over the coming months and years. Support for classes in JavaScript 1.x is limited, but it does exist. Class support in JavaScript 2.0 has been vastly improved. We will see the use of classes grow as programmers begin to discover the benefits of organizing their code into stand-alone, reusable objects.

Create Objects in JavaScript 1.x

There are four ways to create your own objects in JavaScript 1.x:

- Call a constructor function
- Use an object literal
- Extend an existing class
- Extend an existing object

In the following sections, we will examine each of these methods.

Call a Constructor Function

One way to create an object in JavaScript is to create a special function called an *object constructor*. It is the job of this constructor to initialize the object for use—essentially to perform all the necessary setup tasks. The constructor function starts off looking just like a regular function, but uses a special object—the *this object*—to add properties to itself.

To create a constructor, follow these steps:

1. Define an empty function, with the name of the class you wish to create.

```
function Car () {
}
```

2. The special this object is what a class uses to refer to itself. We can use the this object to add a new property inside the constructor function.

```
function Car () {
    this.Make = "Toyota";
}
```

3. Since we want the constructor to be flexible and support many different types of Car objects, it would be better to define any properties using parameters of the function.

```
function Car (make) {
    this.Make = make;
}
```

4. We can then add many more properties to make our Car object complete.

```
function Car (make, model, year, color) {
    this.Make = make;
    this.Model = model;
    this.Year = year;
    this.Color = color;
}
```

5. Of course, we can add a property that does not rely on any parameters.

```
function Car (make, model, year, color) {
    this.Make = make;
    this.Model = model;
    this.Year = year;
    this.Color = color;
    this.FullName = this.Year + " " +
        "<b>" + this.Make + "</b> " +
        this.Model;
}
```

5

6. Now that we have defined a constructor for the Car class, our program can call it to create a Car object.

```
function Car (make, model, year, color) {
    this.Make = make;
    this.Model = model;
    this.Year = year;
    this.Color = color;
    this.FullName = this.Year + " " +
        "<b>" + this.Make + "</b> " +
        this.Model;
}

var mySUV = new Car("Toyota", "4Runner SR5",
    2001, "Thundercloud");
```

7. With the mySUV object created, we can access any of the properties of the Car class.

```
var mySUV = new Car("Toyota", "4Runner SR5",
    2001, "Thundercloud");
document.write ("I drive a " + mySUV.FullName);
```

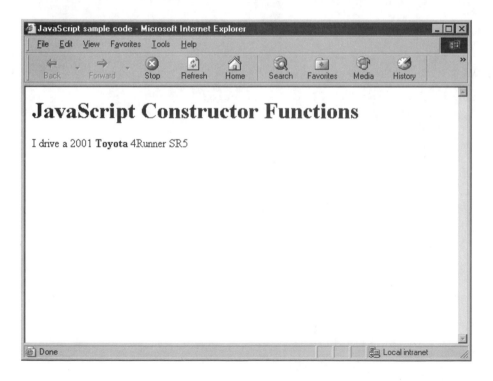

8. In fact, we can create several objects from this one constructor, all with their own independent properties. Changing the value of one object's property does not affect the value of the same property inside other objects.

```
var mySUV = new Car("Toyota", "4Runner SR5",
    2001, "Thundercloud");
var mySportsCar = new Car("Acura", "NSX-T",
    1999, "Red");
var myDreamCar = new Car("Ferrari", "F355 F1",
    2000, "Ferrari Red");

mySportsCar.Color = "Black";
document.write (mySUV.FullName + " = " +
    mySUV.Color + "<br>");
document.write (mySportsCar.FullName + " = " +
    mySportsCar.Color + "<br>");
document.write (myDreamCar.FullName + " = " +
    myDreamCar.Color + "<br>");
```

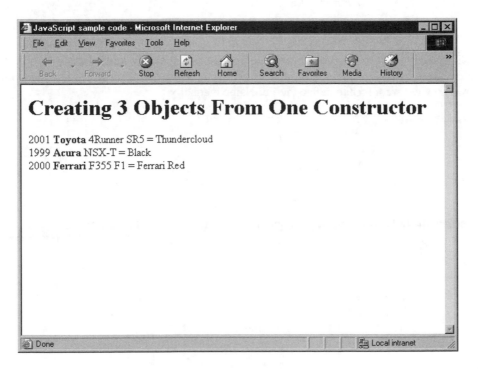

This method of creating objects will work in JavaScript using all browsers dating back to Internet Explorer 3.0 and Netscape Navigator 3.0.

NOTE *Property names are case-sensitive in JavaScript. The property myCar.color is not the same as myCar.Color.*

Use an Object Literal

The JavaScript object literal is a convenient way to create an object without having to predefine a constructor function. It is, in effect, an unnamed constructor. One of JavaScript's greatest strengths is that it allows programmers to create programs quickly, and the object literal is a prime example of how it does this. The tradeoff to creating objects quickly using the object literal is that you lose out on the ability to reuse code for other objects or other programs.

The object literal consists of a number of property-value pairs enclosed in a pair of curly brackets. Colons separate the properties and values, and commas separate the property-value pairs.

```
{ property1 : value , property2 : value , ... , propertyN : value }
```

We can create the same mySUV object we created in the last section using an object literal as follows:

```
var mySUV = {Make:"Toyota",
            Model:"4Runner SR5",
            Year:2001,
            Color:"Thundercloud"};
```

We will have to use a bit of a trick in order to define the FullName property using an object literal. Within the object literal itself, you cannot refer to any of the other properties. The following code shows how we are forced to define the FullName manually:

```
var mySUV = {Make:"Toyota",
            Model:"4Runner SR5",
            Year:2001,
            Color:"Thundercloud",
            FullName:"2001 Toyota 4Runner SR5"};
```

When it comes to defining the other two objects from the last section (mySportsCar and myDreamCar), the only way to reuse the code from the mySUV object is to copy and paste, which most people would agree is not the best way to reuse code.

```
var mySportsCar = {Make:"Acura",
            Model:"NSX-T",
            Year:1999,
            Color:"Red",
            FullName:"1999 Acura NSX-T"};
```

```
var myDreamCar = {Make:"Ferrari",
            Model:"F355 F1",
            Year:2000,
            Color:"Ferrari Red",
            FullName:"2000 Ferrari F355 F1"};
```

As you can see, object literals are best used when you do not anticipate needing to create other objects of the same type.

Extend an Existing Class

JavaScript allows you to extend the capabilities of a class by assigning your own methods and properties to it. This includes adding new methods and properties to any of the predefined system classes. It does this through a system called *prototyping*.

JavaScript automatically gives each class a property called prototype that can be used to extend the functionality at the class level.

ClassName.prototype.*member1 = value1*;

A new member (member1) can be assigned a default value (value1) and added to the class specified (ClassName). This new member is static, in that its value is shared by all objects derived in that class. Changing the value inside one object changes it for all.

Let's start with an example. In the following code, we have defined a function that accepts a Date object as its parameter and will return a string that represents the name of the season ("Spring", "Summer", "Fall", or "Winter") that the date belongs to.

```
function getSeason (obj) {
    var mon = obj.getMonth();
    var day = obj.getDay();
    if (mon < 2 || (mon == 2 && day < 20)) {
        return "Winter";
    } else if (mon < 5 || (mon == 5 && day < 21)) {
        return "Spring";
    } else if (mon < 8 || (mon == 8 && day < 23)) {
        return "Summer";
    } else if (mon < 11 || (mon == 11 && day < 22)) {
        return "Fall";
    } else {
        return "Winter";
    }
}
```

Thus, we can call the preceding function using a Date object and get the correct season that the date falls into.

```
var today = new Date();
document.write(getSeason(today));
```

You might think that it would be more convenient if the getSeason() function was a method of the Date object, instead of an external piece of code. To attach the getSeason() function to the Date class, we first need to modify it to work on the special this object, as all methods inside classes should.

```
function getSeason () {
    var mon = this.getMonth();
    var day = this.getDay();
    if (mon < 2 || (mon == 2 && day < 20)) {
        // Covers Jan 1 through Mar 19
        return "Winter";
    } else if (mon < 5 || (mon == 5 && day < 21)) {
        // Covers Mar 20 through June 20
        return "Spring";
    } else if (mon < 8 || (mon == 8 && day < 23)) {
        // Covers June 21 through Sept 22
        return "Summer";
    } else if (mon < 11 || (mon == 11 && day < 22)) {
        // Covers Sept 23 through Dec 21
        return "Fall";
    } else {
        // Covers Dec 22 through Dec 31
        return "Winter";
    }
}
```

We must then attach the getSeason() function to the Date object as follows:

```
Date.prototype.getSeason = getSeason;
```

We can then call the getSeason() method right from any and all Date objects we create.

```
var today = new Date();
document.write("The season is currently " + today.getSeason());
```

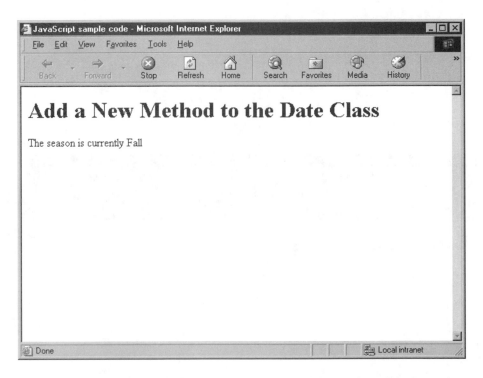

Even though the getSeason() method is still not technically a member of the Date class, JavaScript is smart enough to check to see if it exists inside the list of prototype members, which is where we created it.

Extend an Existing Object

Just as a class can be extended using the prototype property, objects themselves can have new properties and methods attached to them.

```
function Car (make, model, year, color) {
    this.Make = make;
    this.Model = model;
    this.Year = year;
    this.Color = color;
    this.FullName = this.Year + " " +
        "<b>" + this.Make + "</b> " +
        this.Model;
```

```
}

var mySUV = new Car("Toyota", "4Runner SR5",
    2001, "Thundercloud");
mySUV.mileage = 12323;
document.write(mySUV.FullName + " has traveled " +
    mySUV.mileage + " miles.<br><br>");
```

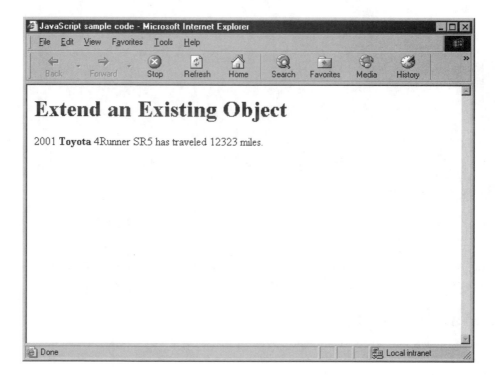

Even though the Car class does not define a property named mileage, we were able to create one for the mySUV object simply by assigning a value to it. Since we applied this property to the mySUV object and not the Car class, other objects derived from the Car class will not have a mileage property.

Create Objects in JavaScript 2.0

JavaScript 2.0 has totally redesigned the way classes are defined. Although most JavaScript environments will still support the old way for the sake of backward compatibility, it is hard to compare the two techniques. Prototypes and manually added properties are no longer the preferred method for generating user-defined classes and objects in JavaScript.

Define Your Own Classes

In JavaScript 2.0, classes are defined using the following syntax:

```
class className { statements; }
```

As you can see, this syntax is quite simple. In practice, classes are quite easy and straightforward to define. We can take the Car class defined earlier in the chapter and define it using the JavaScript 2.0 syntax.

1. Define a class named Car using the class definition syntax.

```
class Car {
}
```

2. Then define all the properties our Car class will possess.

```
class Car {
    var Make;
    var Model;
    var Year;
    var Color;
    var FullName;
}
```

3. Remember that JavaScript 2.0 supports data types for variables, so let's make our definition more specific.

```
class Car {
    var Make : String;
    var Model : String;
    var Year : Integer;
    var Color : String;
    var FullName : String;
}
```

4. We will need to add a constructor function to the Car class to initialize these variables. The constructor usually has the same name as the class, although it is possible to define constructors with different names using a special syntax. The this object is still used to refer to the current object.

```
class Car {
    var Make : String;
    var Model : String;
    var Year : Integer;
    var Color : String;
    var FullName : String;
```

```
function Car (make, model, year, color) {
    this.Make = make;
    this.Model = model;
    this.Year = year;
    this.Color = color;
    this.FullName = this.Year + " " +
        "<b>" + this.Make + "</b> " +
        this.Model;
    }
}
```

5. The Car class can be instantiated in the exact same manner as classes defined under JavaScript 1.x were, using the **new** keyword.

```
var mySUV = new Car("Toyota", "4Runner SR5",
    2001, "Thundercloud");
```

6. With the mySUV object created, we can access any of the properties of the Car class.

```
var mySUV = new Car("Toyota", "4Runner SR5",
    2001, "Thundercloud");
document.write ("I drive a " + mySUV.FullName);
```

It is easier to create methods using JavaScript 2.0 classes, as functions can be defined inside of the body of the class.

```
class Book {
    var title : String;
    var author : String;
    var chapters : Array[String];
    function print_title () {
        document.write ("Title: " + this.title + "<br>");
    }
    function print_author () {
        document.write ("Author: " + this.author + "<br>");
    }
    function print_all () {
        var counter = 0;
        print_title();
        print_author();
        for (chapter in this.chapters) {
            counter++;
            document.write ("Chapter " + counter + ": " +
                this.chapters[chapter] + "<br>");
        }
```

```
    }
}
```

Once the Book class is defined, we can create a Book object using the **new** keyword. Since our class does not have a constructor, we can then manually set each of the properties. Calling a method of that new object results in the behavior we expect.

```
var thisBook = new Book();
thisBook.title = "How To Do Everything with JavaScript";
thisBook.author = "Scott Duffy";
thisBook.chapters = new Array(15);
thisBook.chapters[0] = "Prepare to Program in JavaScript";
thisBook.chapters[1] = "Learn JavaScript Fundamentals";
thisBook.chapters[2] = "Use Built-In JavaScript Classes";
thisBook.chapters[3] = "Organize Data into Arrays";
thisBook.chapters[4] = "Create Your Own JavaScript Classes";
// etc.

thisBook.print_all();
```

This results in the following browser output.

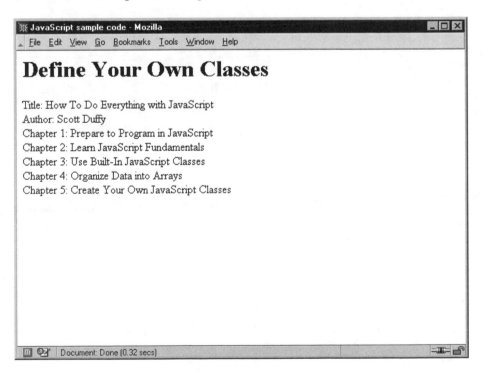

Organize Classes Using Inheritance

One of the benefits of organizing your program into classes is that you can establish relationships between classes using *inheritance.* Inheritance allows you to do two things:

- Save programming time, because related classes can share code
- Enforce a standard set of common properties and methods for related classes

JavaScript 2.0 enables one class to inherit from another using the **extends** keyword.

```
class ClassName extends ParentClass { statements; }
```

This establishes a parent-child relationship between the ParentClass and the ClassName classes. The best way to understand inheritance is to think of the class structure like a hierarchical tree.

At the top of the tree is the Object class, the parent of all classes in the system. All the classes in the system that do not have an explicit parent object derive from the Object class by default. Those that do have an explicit parent class defined, inherit from that class instead.

Note: All classes in JavaScript 2.0 (both system and user-defined) have the Object class as either a direct or indirect ancestor, even those that extend from another class.

We can define the parent class in the normal way.

```
class Vehicle {
    var Maker;
    var Price;
    var Color;

    function Vehicle (maker, price, color) {
        this.Maker = maker;
        this.Price = price;
        this.Color = color;
    }
    function Vehicle () {
        this.Maker = "Default";
        this.Price = 0.0;
        this.Color = "Transparent";
    }
}
```

This code defines a Vehicle class, although there are only three properties. This class represents any generic vehicle, whether it is a boat, or a plane, or a car. That class should be able to handle any object that can be considered a vehicle.

> **TIP** *A class can contain multiple constructors, as long as the number and type of parameters (known as the* function signature) *are unique for each constructor.*

We can then be a bit more specific by defining classes that break down the type of vehicle. By extending the Vehicle class, our child classes automatically inherit the properties and methods of the Vehicle class.

```
class LandVehicle extends Vehicle {
    // Land specific code
    var Speed;
    var xPosition;
    var yPosition;
}
class WaterVehicle extends Vehicle {
    // Water specific code
    var Speed;
    var WaterDisplacement;
    var xPosition;
    var yPosition;
    var zPosition;
}
class AirVehicle extends Vehicle {
    // Air specific code
    var AirSpeed;
    var LandSpeed;
    var xPosition;
    var yPosition;
    var zPosition;
}
class SpaceVehicle extends Vehicle {
    // Space specific code
    var Thrust;
    var DistanceFromEarth;
}
```

We can continue to define classes that inherit from these child classes (LandVehicle, AirVehicle, WaterVehicle, and SpaceVehicle). The idea is that each child class is a more specific version of the parent class. So LandVehicle would have the following child classes:

- Car
- Train
- Bus
- Truck

Did you know?

The Story of Interfaces

The ECMA, the designers of the JavaScript 2.0 specification, originally planned to include an object-oriented programming concept called *interfaces* in the specification, but it was dropped at the last minute. Interfaces allow you to define a set of standard method names and parameter lists without having to provide code for them. A class could then declare, "I support the following interfaces..."; this would provide a reliable way to know what methods are supported by the class.

   Let's say you define an interface named DoorLock, which contains two methods, Lock() and Unlock(). We know that the Car class implements the DoorLock interface, so we can be sure that a Car object has Lock() and Unlock() methods as well. Notice that a Car is not a type of DoorLock, so a parent-child relationship (one created by inheritance) should not be established.

   By defining a DoorLock interface, we have created a standard set of methods for classes that need to define door lock activity, such as the Car class and the House class.

A Car is a more specific type of LandVehicle, which is a more specific type of Vehicle. If we wanted to further define Car, for instance, we could create SUV and SportsCar classes that inherit from it, and so on.

There are obviously two major benefits to having classes inherit in such a manner. The first is the ability to reuse code. We defined a constructor all the way back in the Vehicle class.

```
function Vehicle (maker, price, color) {
    this.Maker = maker;
    this.Price = price;
    this.Color = color;
}
```

Assuming none of the child classes defined a constructor for itself, all the descendants of the Vehicle class can use the original Vehicle constructor.

```
class Vehicle {
    var Maker;
    var Price;
    var Color;

    function Vehicle (maker, price, color) {
        this.Maker = maker;
```

```
        this.Price = price;
        this.Color = color;
    }
}

class LandVehicle extends Vehicle {
    // Land specific code
    var Speed;
    var xPosition;
    var yPosition;
}

class Car extends LandVehicle {
    // Car specific code
    var Model;
    var Year;
}

// Car inherits the Vehicle constructor
var myCar : Car = new Car ("Ford", 19500, "Blue");
myCar.Model = "Focus";
myCar.Year = 2002;
myCar.Speed = 32;

// Car inherits the properties of Vehicle
document.write ("Vehicle class properties: " + myCar.Maker + "<br>");

// Car inherits the properties of LandVehicle
document.write ("LandVehicle class properties: " + myCar.Speed + "<br>");

// Car has its own properties as well
document.write ("Car class properties: " + myCar.Model + "<br>");
```

As you can see from Figure 5-1, even though the Car class itself has only two properties, it does inherit all of the properties from its parents.

Another benefit of using inheritance is what computer geeks like to call *polymorphism.* Essentially, a variable defined as the Vehicle data type can contain any of the objects derived from Vehicle (like LandVehicle or Car). This allows a program to act on an object without having to know or care what the exact type of the object is. If it can act on the parent object, the same actions can be performed on any of the child objects.

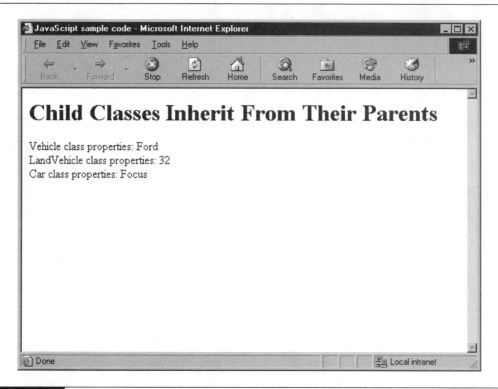

FIGURE 5-1 Classes inherit the properties and methods of their parents.

Perhaps the best demonstration of this would be with our own type of number, which we will call SuperNumber.

```
class SuperNumber extends Number {
    override function toString() {
        return super.toString() + " !!!!";
    }
}
```

The only difference between a regular Number class and a SuperNumber class is that the SuperNumber will return four exclamation marks appended to the end of the number when a user calls the toString() function.

Once we have defined a SuperNumber, we can use it just like we would use a number. Any function that works on Numbers will be able to handle SuperNumbers, due to the inheritance relationship. Even the existing arithmetic operators will be able to handle these variables without modification.

```
var x : SuperNumber = new SuperNumber(13);
var y : SuperNumber = new SuperNumber(22);
```

```
var z : Number = x + y;
alert (z);
```

We can see the result of the program here.

This illustration depicts the result we would expect to see when JavaScript 2–compatible browsers are eventually released.

Choose Between Static and Instance Members

We examined the concept of static class members when we discussed the built-in Math method in Chapter 3. Basically a *static member* is any property or method that is defined only in the class itself, and not in any of the objects derived from that class. You do not even have to have an object of a particular class defined in order to access its static members.

Static members are defined using the **static** keyword.

```
class Books {
    static const MAX_WIDTH = 8.5;
    static const MAX_HEIGHT = 11;
    static const MAX_WEIGHT = 10;
    var title;
    var author;
    var page_count;
}
```

In the Books class defined here, we have defined three static members. They happen to be defined as constants, but variables and even functions can be defined as static. In order to access them, we call them through the Books class, and not through any object created based on Books.

```
alert (Books.MAX_HEIGHT);
```

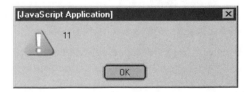

NOTE *This illustration depicts the result we would expect to see when JavaScript 2–compatible browsers are eventually released.*

Instance members are any members that are not static. Instance members are accessed through objects that have been created, and they cannot be accessed using the class directly.

```
var myBooks = new Books();
myBooks.title = "How To Do Everything With a Pencil";
myBooks.author = "Mary Major";
```

In this code, both title and author are instance members, and they can be accessed only by using an object (myBooks) based on the class Books, and not the class itself.

Make Class Members Public or Private

Another common task in object-oriented programming is to define members that cannot be accessed from outside the class. This is primarily used for security and data integrity.

Members are made private using the **private** keyword, and made public using the **public** keyword. By default, members that are not explicitly defined as either are public.

```
class Car {
    private var Make : String;
    private var Model : String;
    private var Year : Integer;
    private var Color : String;

    public function setMake (value) : Void {
        this.Make = value;
    }
    public function setModel (value) : Void {
        this.Model = value;
    }
    public function setYear (value) : Void {
        this.Year = value;
    }
    public function setColor (value) : Void {
        this.Color = value;
    }
}
```

In this code, all the properties of the Car class are defined as private. This means that they cannot be accessed from outside the class. Attempting to do the following will cause an error.

```
var myCar = new Car();
myCar.Make = "Mercedes";
```

To set the properties, we have to call the public methods we created for ourselves. The following code will work.

```
var myCar = new Car();
myCar.setMake ("Mercedes");
```

Notice how we created a Car class that has made it impossible to read the values of the properties. In the real world, the class would also contain a number of functions to retrieve the values as well.

Obviously, there is more to learn about classes in JavaScript, including getters and setters, packages, and namespaces. But these topics go beyond the scope of this chapter, and of this book. For more information on classes, consult the official JavaScript 2.0 specification on the Mozilla web site, located at http://www.mozilla.org/js/language/js20/core/classes.html.

In the next chapter, we will start to learn how to apply the concepts learned in the previous four chapters, as we use JavaScript inside web pages. We will learn about some of the key HTML tags and where JavaScript should be placed in the web page.

5

Part II

Build JavaScript-Enabled Web Sites

Chapter 6

Embed JavaScript in a Web Page

How to...

- Understand basic HTML structure
- Use <script> to add JavaScript to a web page
- Use <noscript> for browsers that don't support scripting
- Load an external JavaScript file
- Call JavaScript using hyperlinks

Up until this point in the book, we have been concentrating on JavaScript's programming syntax—the statements and definitions that are the nuts and bolts of the language. As you've seen, JavaScript has many features that make it an ideal language for many tasks, and one of its strongest features is its ability to integrate into a wide variety of other environments.

Versions of JavaScript exist in many different environments:

- An Application Server Pages (ASP) language for Microsoft IIS web servers (one of several supported languages)
- Server-Side JavaScript (SSJS) for Netscape/iPlanet web servers
- A server-side programming language for other web servers
- An embedded language for Adobe Acrobat PDF documents
- An embedded language for Macromedia Flash files (ActiveScript)

But even today, almost 10 years after it was first introduced, JavaScript's biggest success remains as an embedded programming language for web pages. It is supported by virtually every web browser in use today—it is installed on hundreds of millions of PCs worldwide. In this chapter, we will examine how to embed JavaScript in HTML pages and some basic text formatting techniques.

Understand Basic HTML Structure

Hypertext Markup Language, or HTML for short, is the language that web pages are written in. HTML is known as a markup language, because it uses a set of predefined tags, or *markup,* to provide formatting and other instructions to the web browser.

For instance, the following example contains a number of HTML markup tags:

```
<font size="2"><b>Now is the time</b> for all
good men <u>to come to the aid</u> of <i>their party</i>.</font>
```

As you can see, the HTML markup tags are always enclosed in angle brackets (< and >). Most HTML tags have both a starting tag (the bold text tag, , for instance) and a closing tag (like), although there are some exceptions to this rule.

The following shows how an HTML document with the preceding markup would appear in a standard web browser.

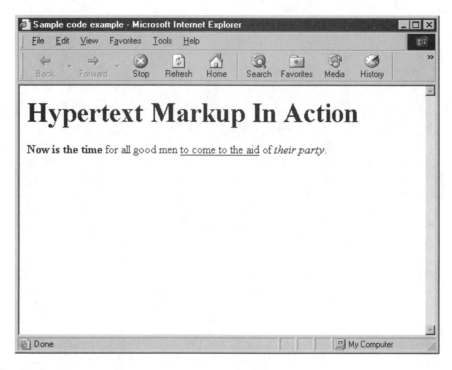

NOTE *Closing tags always start with a forward-slash character (/) followed by the name of the related start tag. For instance, if the start tag is <font>, the end tag must be called </font>.*

Entire books have been written on the subject of HTML. Actually, to be truly accurate, you could say enough books to fill more than a few bookshelves (or even bookcases) have been written on the topic. My goal, in this chapter and the ones that follow, is not really to teach the ins and outs of HTML. But since JavaScript programs rely so much on what's happening inside the browser (frames, forms, browser events, etc.), it is impossible to understand what is going on with JavaScript without first understanding the HTML it relates to. For reference, Appendix A lists each of the HTML 4.01 tags and gives a brief description of their use.

NOTE *The major browser makers (Microsoft and Netscape) have in some cases added their own tags, so their lists might not match the official list in Appendix A.*

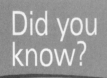

Why XML and XHTML Are the Coming Thing

Although humans can easily read HTML documents using a web browser, computers themselves have a difficult time finding specific data to extract from a web page. For instance, it would be very difficult to create an application that can reliably download daily flight schedules from all the airline web sites.

XML (Extensible Markup Language) is an ideal language for transmitting computer data over the Internet. Whereas HTML is an extremely flexible markup language, with very few mandatory elements or attributes, XML has a strict set of formatting rules. Programmers can impose additional rules on individual types of documents by creating an XML schema or DTD. XML is the new standard language for data formatting over the Internet, and it is the foundation of many of the Web Services initiatives, including Sun ONE and Microsoft .NET.

A new version of HTML has been created that allows web documents to be valid XML as well, called XHTML. In fact, the World Wide Web Consortium (W3C) has stopped developing the HTML standard (version 4.01) and has been hard at work at XHTML standards—versions 1.0 and 1.1 have already been released.

For more information on the XHTML standard, visit the W3C web site at http://www.w3c.org/markup.

In addition, as mentioned in Chapter 1, a special set of tags denotes comments in HTML: <!-- indicates the start of commented text, and --> indicates the end. Comments serve as useful documentation or author notes, such as the following:

```
<!-- Survey.html
    Purpose: To gather visitor opinions on this site
    Author: John Q. Doe
-->


<!-- Copyright 2003, Scott J. Duffy Incorporated
    All rights reserved. -->
```

As you can see, comments can extend over several lines. All text that appears inside HTML comment markup is ignored by the browser and not displayed to the user in the main display.

 *Don't forget that the user can see the underlying HTML code in most browsers by selecting View | Source from the menu bar, so your comments won't be entirely private.*

What "Officially Deprecated" Means

The World Wide Web Consortium (W3C), the group that creates and maintains several important specifications dealing with the Internet including HTML, has indicated a number of HTML tags are *deprecated*.

Indicating that a tag is deprecated is a polite way of saying support for it in the specification will likely be dropped in a future release. The W3C would like to encourage web developers to employ another method instead, such as using Cascading Style Sheets (CSS) for defining fonts.

However, given the widespread use of such tags as <font>, <center>, and <u>, it is highly unlikely that the major browser makers are going to drop support for them anytime soon.

Build an HTML Document

One of the strengths of HTML is simplicity: it is very easy to build a web page using just a few basic tags. There are three essential elements to building a web page:

1. Every HTML document must begin with the HTML start tag (<html>) and end with the HTML end tag (</html>). The only exception is for <!DOCTYPE> or <?xml?> declaration statements, which are then placed before the HTML tags. (The <?xml?> declaration is used to define documents that conform to XHTML, which is beyond the scope of this book. However, we will look at <!DOCTYPE> in the following section.)

```
<html>
</html>
```

2. The HTML document is then divided into two sections, a head and a body. The head section is where a document title, descriptive keywords, style sheets, and JavaScript functions are defined.

```
<html>
    <head>
        <title>How to Do Everything with JavaScript</title>
    </head>
</html>
```

3. The body section is where the contents of the document are placed. Often this will be plain text (sentences and paragraphs), marked up with some formatting HTML tags like <b>, <i>, and <p>.

```
<html>
    <head>
```

```
        <title>How to Do Everything with JavaScript</title>
    </head>
    <body bgcolor="white">
        <h1>A typical document header</h1>
        <p>The start of a paragraph.</p>
        <p><b>Our second paragraph.</b></p>
    </body>
</html>
```

Granted, the web page in our example is fairly simple, but even web pages with hundreds of lines of code start with three simple tags: <html>, <head>, and <body>.

Get in the habit of creating all your HTML documents using lowercase tag names, properly nested tags, and properly quoted attribute values. It will pay off when you want to start creating XHTML 1.0 documents, because XHTML has very strict rules.

You are probably already familiar with the basics of HTML. If not, since it's not feasible to compress a tutorial on HTML into one chapter, I have included a list of useful web sites at the end of this chapter.

Indicate the Document Type with <!DOCTYPE>

There is only one way to indicate to a browser (or any other application reading your HTML file) which version of HTML your web page is written for: <!DOCTYPE>. Up until a few years ago, this tag was ignored entirely by web browsers. But recent versions of browsers look for this code to determine which set of rules to use in interpreting the web page.

An HTML document that conforms to the HTML 4.01 specification would have the following <!DOCTYPE> as the very first line of the page, even before the <html> tag:

```
<!DOCTYPE HTML PUBLIC "-//W3C//DTD HTML 4.01 Transitional//EN"
    "http://www.w3.org/TR/html4/loose.dtd">
```

If a browser encounters a web page that uses this <!DOCTYPE> tag, the browser will expect valid HTML 4.01 Transitional code in the rest of the document. *Transitional* HTML includes all the deprecated tags (such as <font>). There is also a version of HTML called *Strict* that does not include deprecated tags, and another called *Frameset* that allows browser frames to be created. (We will look at browser frames in Chapter 10.)

If we wanted to use a different version of HTML, like XHTML (the XML compliant version of HTML), we would use a different <!DOCTYPE>, like so:

```
<!DOCTYPE html PUBLIC "-//W3C//DTD XHTML 1.0 Transitional//EN"
    "http://www.w3.org/TR/xhtml1/DTD/xhtml1-transitional.dtd">
```

When a browser encounters this <!DOCTYPE>, it knows to treat the contents as XHTML 1.0 Transitional. Depending on the browser, this may be slightly different from the way it treats HTML 4.01 code.

Add a Title and Define Document Keywords

The HTML head element contains information about the current document, such as its title, keywords, and other data that is not considered content. The HTML <title> tag is used to specify a title for the document, and it is mandatory in HTML 4.01.

```
<html>
    <head>
        <title>This is the document title</title>
    </head>
    <body></body>
</html>
```

The contents of the <title> tag are usually displayed in the title bar of the window, as you can see here:

Optionally, you can specify a number of keywords, which will make it easier for Internet search engines to find your web site. Keywords and a brief description of the web page can be specified using the <meta> tag. For instance, if you had a page focused on exotic pets, you might have the following <meta> tags:

```
<meta name="description" content="Articles, pictures, and stories
    about exotic pets">
<meta name="keywords" content="exotic pets, reptiles, amphibians,
    frog, toad, salamander, newt, siren, lizard, iguana, gecko,
    monitor, chameleon, dragons, turtles, tortoises, leopard,
    butterfly, butterflies, moth, bees, flies, stick insects,
    beetles, wasps, hornet, roaches, ants, cricket, grasshopper,
    tarantula, scorpion, centipede, millipede">
```

When used to specify web page descriptions and keywords, the <meta> tag takes two attributes: name and content. In the preceding code, the first <meta> tag sets the description for the web page—usually a sentence or two that is often displayed by Internet search engines to give potential visitors an accurate description of what to expect from this page.

The second <meta> tag in the example defines a number of *keywords*—words or phrases separated by commas that give search engines help in indexing the page. Some Internet search engines rank web pages with these <meta> tags higher than they would the same page without the <meta> tags.

Format Text with HTML Elements

HTML provides a number of elements to help web page developers format and style text. These tags fall into two broad categories: *phrase elements* and *font style elements*. Phrase elements are tags that structure text. The way these elements are presented to the user depends on the browser. Font style elements are tags that specify specific font properties for text. Since font style properties are fairly specific, developers can be more confident about the way browsers will present text to the user.

The following are the phrase elements in HTML 4.01:

- **<abbr>** indicates an abbreviated form
- **<acronym>** indicates an acronym
- **<cite>** indicates a citation or reference to other sources
- **<code>** designates a fragment of computer code
- **<dfn>** indicates the defining instance of a term
- **<em>** indicates emphasis; usually displayed as italic text
- **<kbd>** indicates text to be entered by the user
- **<samp>** indicates sample output from programs, scripts, and so forth
- **<strong>** indicates stronger emphasis; usually displayed as bold text
- **<var>** indicates an instance of a variable or program argument

Again, each of these elements indicates the type of text it contains, but gives only a hint as to how the browser should handle them.

The following tags are the font style elements of HTML 4.01:

- **<b>** bold text
- **<big>** larger than normal text
- **<i>** italic text

■ **<s>** strikethrough text (officially deprecated)

■ **<small>** smaller than normal text

■ **<strike>** strikethrough text; same a <s> (officially deprecated)

■ **<tt>** teletype or monospace text

■ **<u>** underlined text (officially deprecated)

In the vast majority of HTML pages, phrase elements are not used. Many web page designers prefer to set fonts and styles for their pages explicitly. On top of the uncertainty of how different browsers will render these tags, using such predefined document structure elements limits designers' design choices.

Hundreds of millions of web pages exist that use only HTML elements like the ones listed here to style the text on their pages. For example, the following HTML code creates a web page that uses many of the style tags discussed so far in this chapter.

```
<html>
    <head><title>Sample document</title></head>
    <body>
    <h1>Traveling to the Caribbean</h1>

    <p><b>Barbados</b> - Barbados is a lovely island, with
    <i>wonderful weather</i> and a <i>constant cool breeze</i>. The
    locals are friendly, and one can clearly see that a British
    influence still exists, even today.</p>

    <p><b>St. Lucia</b> - St. Lucia is a lush, tropical paradise.
    Fewer tourists tend to visit St. Lucia than some of the other
    islands, which means it is easier to explore the local way
    of life.</p>

    <p><b>Bahamas</b> - Bahamas is <strike>frequently visited
by</strike> <u>a popular spot for</u> Americans. The islands have a
number of casinos, the most spectacular of which is the <i>Atlantis
Hotel on Paradise Island</i>. The rumor is that one of their hotel rooms
goes for <big>$40,000 a night</big>, which is about $39,800 more than
most people can afford to spend on a place to sleep.</p>
    </body>
</html>
```

6

As you can see from the following screen capture, HTML elements style text to make the output easier to read. Text that should be boldface, italic, or crossed out is presented exactly as one would expect.

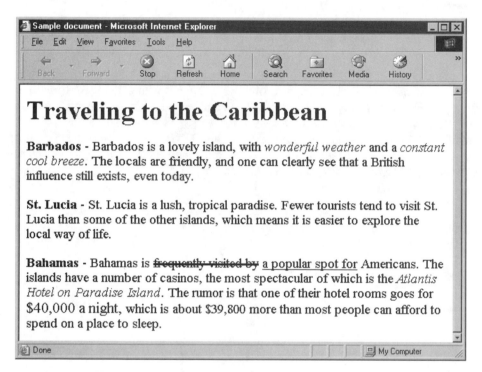

Format Text with Style Sheets

For years, web designers have wanted a more precise way to style and lay out web pages, similar to the tools desktop publishing software has provided for a long time. Finally, along came style sheets, which have alleviated most of the designer's concerns about styling web pages.

 The W3C homepage for Cascading Style Sheets is http://www.w3.org/Style/CSS. Not surprisingly, that page is itself a great example of how style sheets can be used to format a web page.

Style sheets, also sometimes called Cascading Style Sheets (CSS for short), have a number of benefits for web developers. They provide

- The ability to separate style from content
- The ability to apply a single style to an entire web site
- A more fine-grained ability to control style

- The ability to specify exact layout positioning
- The ability to script and dynamically change styles using JavaScript (also called Dynamic HTML)
- The ability to specify different styles depending on browser environment (e.g., PC versus mobile phone)

In fact, the HTML specification is slowly phasing out the use of the HTML tags listed in the last section to define style in favor of style sheets. Using style sheets to define a document's style is the present and future of the language.

A style sheet is defined inside the HTML <style> element, which is usually defined inside the document head section.

```
<html>
    <head>
        <title>HTML Style Sheets</title>
        <style type="text/css">

        // Style sheet goes in here

        </style>
    </head>
    <body>
    <h1>Traveling to the Caribbean</h1>

    <p><b>Barbados</b> - Barbados is a lovely island, with
    <i>wonderful weather</i> and a <i>constant cool breeze</i>. The
    <!-- Etc. -->
    </body>
</html>
```

In the case of our HTML document, we can define a custom style sheet that replaces some of the formatting we were using.

```
<style type="text/css">
    .island {font-weight: bold}
    .highlight {font-style: italic}
    .underlinethis {text-decoration: underline}
    .bigmoney {font-size: larger}
</style>
```

In fact, you could add some really interesting text effects to our boring document, as shown in the following example. And once the style sheet has been defined, you simply alter the HTML to use those styles.

```html
<html>
    <head>
        <title>Sample document</title>
        <style type="text/css">
        .island {
            color: white;
            background-color: black;
            font-weight: bold
        }
        .highlight {
            font-style: italic;
            background-color: yellow
        }
        .underlinethis {
            text-decoration: underline overline
        }
        .bigmoney {
            color: green;
            font-size: xx-large
        }
        </style>
    </head>
    <body>
    <h1>Traveling to the Caribbean</h1>

    <p><span class="island">Barbados</span> - Barbados is a lovely
    island, with <span class="highlight">wonderful weather</span>
    and a <span class="highlight">constant cool breeze</span>. The
    locals are friendly, and one can clearly see that a British
    influence still exists, even today.</p>

    <p><span class="island">St. Lucia</span> - St. Lucia is a lush,
    tropical paradise. Fewer tourists tend to visit St. Lucia than
    some of the other islands, which means it is easier to explore the
    local way of life.</p>

    <p><span class="island">Bahamas</span> - Bahamas is
    <strike>frequently visited by</strike> <span class="underlinethis">a
    popular spot for</span> Americans. The islands have a number of
    casinos, the most spectacular of which is the <span
    class="highlight">Atlantis Hotel on Paradise Island</span>.
    The rumor is that one of their hotel rooms goes for <span
    class="bigmoney">$40,000 a night</span>, which is about $39,800 more
```

```
    than most people can afford to spend on a place to sleep.</p>
    </body>
</html>
```

The resulting web page would not win any design awards, but you can see that style sheets allow you to do things regular HTML does not.

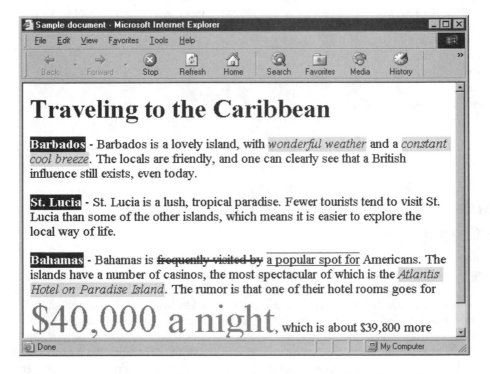

Clearly, style sheets involve much more than the small glimpse I have been able to give you in this short section. I have listed a few web sites you can visit to learn more about style sheets at the end of this chapter. We will also revisit this subject in Chapter 12.

Use <script> to Add JavaScript to a Web Page

Now that you have been introduced to some basic HTML formatting elements, it's time to tie that in to the use of JavaScript. The HTML <script> tag allows web developers to embed JavaScript commands in their web pages. There is no restriction as to the number of <script> sections a web document can contain, although for the sake of programming efficiency it is best to keep the number of scripts on a single page to a minimum.

The HTML <script> element generally accepts only two attributes when you are working with embedded script content: language and type. The language attribute exists for backward compatibility. JavaScript is the only scripting language supported by all major web browsers, so if this attribute is omitted, "JavaScript" is the default.

The type attribute specifies the MIME type for the embedded script, which is "text/javascript" for our purposes. MIME is a standard way to describe the contents of a file over the Internet, such as "text/plain: and "image/gif". This gets around the problem of three-letter filename extensions (.htm or .txt) left over from MS-DOS, 20 years ago.

The MIME standard, which originated with e-mail systems, allows a web server to tell a browser how to interpret the stream of bits being sent. For instance, the only way for a web browser to know that the file http://www.example.com/ is an HTML document is through its MIME type.

```
<script language="JavaScript" type="text/javascript">
    var a = 1;
    var b = 2;
    var c = a + b;
    document.write (c);
</script>
```

Later in this chapter, we will look at another use for the <script> tag that deals with external JavaScript content.

Use <noscript> for Browsers That Don't Support Scripting

Even today, with all the technical advances made in web browsers and web programming languages, not every browser supports JavaScript. For instance, many mobile phones provide Internet access, but they are severely limited in screen size, color, audio, and scripting capabilities. There are also web browsers for PCs (like the one embedded in Microsoft Word) that do not support advanced capabilities such as JavaScript. And some pre-JavaScript browsers are still in use, such as Netscape Navigator 1.0.

It is true, however, that supporting non-JavaScript-compatible devices is less important now than in 1995, when JavaScript first came out. But as the variety of computer operating systems and hardware devices increases over time, it may again become important to provide alternate content for some users.

The HTML <noscript> tag is used to provide content to users whose browsers do not support JavaScript. It works because JavaScript-enabled browsers ignore any content between the <noscript> tag, for instance:

```
<html>
    <head>
        <title>JavaScript Test</title>
    </head>
    <body>
        <h1>for Loop</h1>
        <script language="JavaScript" type="text/javascript">
        <!-- // Begin
```

```
var Fahrenheit;
for (var Celsius = 10; Celsius <= 60; Celsius = Celsius + 5) {
    document.write (Celsius + "&deg;C = ");
    Fahrenheit = (Celsius * 9/5) + 32;
    document.write (Fahrenheit + "&deg;F<BR>");
    if (Fahrenheit > 100) {
        // It's getting hot in here
        break;
    }
}

        // End -->
        </script>
        <noscript>
        You must have a JavaScript-enabled browser
        to visit this web page.
        </noscript>
    </body>
</html>
```

This code will show users with JavaScript-enabled browsers the following output.

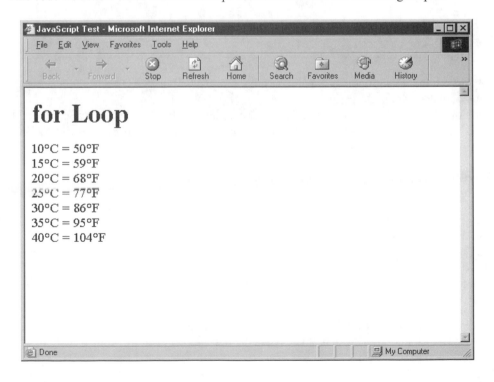

However, users whose browsers do not support JavaScript will see this message instead.

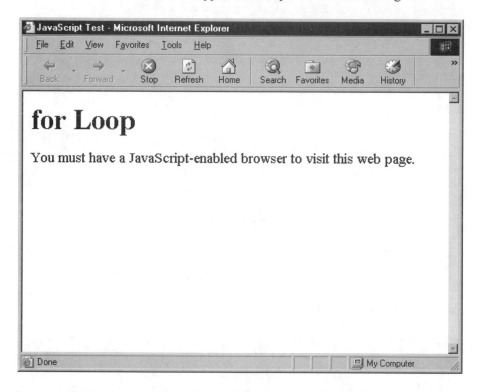

The only reason the JavaScript is not output to the screen as well is the HTML comment tags, <!-- and -->, that surround the script.

Inside the <noscript> tag, you can choose to simply inform the user that a JavaScript-enabled browser is required. But you could also provide replacement content for the JavaScript, as in this example:

```
<noscript>
    10°C = 50°F <BR>
    15°C = 59°F <BR>
    20°C = 68°F <BR>
    25°C = 77°F <BR>
    30°C = 86°F <BR>
    35°C = 95°F <BR>
    40°C = 104°F <BR>
</noscript>
```

This would allow users with a wide variety of browsers and hardware devices to view your web site properly. Of course, it is not always possible to replace JavaScript content with plain HTML text.

Load an External JavaScript File

JavaScript does not always have to be embedded inside the HTML file. Often it is convenient to have one file that contains the JavaScript and have multiple HTML files import it for their use. Using this technique, it would be easier to make changes to the JavaScript, since you do not have to change each of the HTML files.

First, you must have a text file that contains nothing but JavaScript. Let us assume the following file exists on the web server, and is named sample.js.

```
// SAMPLE.JS
//
// isFloat() function:
//     Checks a string to see if it contains a
//     floating-point number; returns true or false
//
function isFloat (s)
{
    // Format accepts "9", "9.", "9.9", and ".9"
    var reFloat = /^(((\d+(\.\d*)?)|((\d*\.)?\d+))$/;

    return reFloat.test(s)
}
```

NOTE   *The .js file extension is commonly used in Windows systems to indicate that the file contains JavaScript, although any extension (such as .txt) can be used.*

We use the src attribute of the HTML <script> tag to import the external JavaScript file.

```
<html>
    <head>
        <title>JavaScript Test</title>
        <script language="javascript" src="sample.js"></script>
    </head>
    <body>
        <h1>Check for a Floating Point Number</h1>

        <script language="JavaScript" type="text/javascript">
            document.write("Is \"12.345\" a float?  " +
                isFloat("12.345") + "<br><br>");
            document.write("Is \"Twelve\" a float?  " +
                isFloat("Twelve") + "<br><br>");
        </script>
    </body>
</html>
```

6

We can then call the isFloat() function defined in our external JavaScript file in another <script> section elsewhere in the web page. In this manner, the isFloat() function can easily be shared among multiple web pages.

HTML <script> tags that import an external JavaScript file cannot also contain JavaScript. They must be empty.

The result of importing an external JavaScript file is shown in Figure 6.1.

Call JavaScript Using Hyperlinks

Not all JavaScript executes immediately after a web page is loaded. We will examine *web browser events,* which allow JavaScript to run in response to user actions, in Chapter 9. Another way to invoke JavaScript in response to a user event is as the destination of a hyperlink.

```
<A HREF="javascript:alert('Hello')">Click me</A>
```

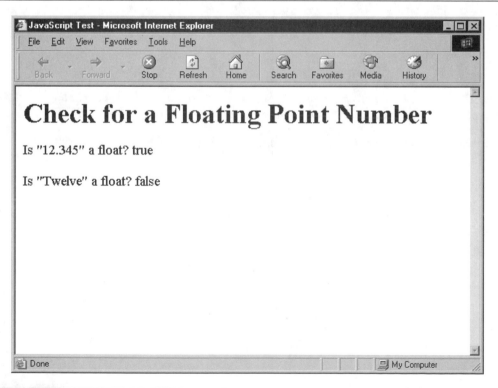

FIGURE 6-1   Functions defined in external JavaScript files can be called elsewhere in the HTML page.

Loading this HTML into a web browser causes a clickable hyperlink to be displayed along with the caption "Click me." When the user clicks the link, a JavaScript alert() message box pops up, saying "Hello." The secret is the special "javascript:" prefix inside the HREF URL. This informs the browser that what we really intend to do is invoke a JavaScript command instead.

Several JavaScript commands can be appended in one string, if separated with a semicolon.

```
<A HREF="javascript:alert('Hello');alert('Goodbye')">Click me</A>
```

More commonly, JavaScript hyperlinks are used to call predefined functions, instead of embedding one or more JavaScript statements inside the HREF attribute value itself.

```
<A HREF="javascript:submitform()">Click here to submit the form</A>
```

In this example, when the user clicks the hyperlink labeled "Click here to submit the form," JavaScript will call a function named submitform(), which we assume is defined elsewhere on the web page.

In the next chapter, we will examine the issues web developers face when creating cross-platform-compatible JavaScript. JavaScript programs that work in one web browser will not necessarily work in another, as there are dozens of combinations of browsers, hardware platforms, and operating systems. Knowing how to work around these differences is important in real-world web development.

Learn More about the Topics in this Chapter

The following are a few web sites where you can learn more about HTML and Cascading Style Sheets:

- Webmonkey HTML Basics: http://hotwired.lycos.com/webmonkey/teachingtool
- SitePoint: http://www.webmasterbase.com
- Web Design Group CSS Reference: http://www.htmlhelp.com/reference/css
- Dave Raggett's Introduction to CSS: http://www.w3.org/MarkUp/Guide/Style

Chapter 7

Create Scripts That Work in Every Browser

How to...

- Understand browser differences
- Detect what type of browser the user is running
- Query the document model
- Stick to web standards
- Write cross-browser code

In the early days of JavaScript development, handling irregularities between the different browser makers and versions was a difficult task. After all, some browsers did not support JavaScript at all (like Netscape 1.0). Even if you had a browser that supported JavaScript, the underlying document model (DOM) was different between different browsers, which meant JavaScript errors were a common sight.

This difficulty of developing JavaScript code that worked correctly in every browser was caused primarily by several factors:

- New browser releases every few months
- An ongoing contest between browser companies to add new features
- Lack of an HTML or JavaScript standard

It took some time, but eventually the problems started to go away as JavaScript stabilized. And as users began to gradually upgrade to version 4.0 browsers and beyond, JavaScript developers had an easier time developing cross-platform-compatible code.

Unfortunately, some of the impending changes to JavaScript will force web developers to have to start coding for browser differences again. The reasons for this new period of instability are likely to include:

- Inconsistent support for JavaScript 2.0
- New browser releases every few months (particularly from Mozilla)
- Inconsistent JavaScript support for new technologies, such as XML and CSS

Only time will tell how much heartache these factors will cause web developers.

Understand Browser Differences

According to a recent survey, Microsoft Internet Explorer (IE) is used by approximately 94 percent of web surfers. Netscape and Mozilla have a combined usage of approximately 2 percent. The remaining 4 percent is divided among other companies such as Opera or is lost due to rounding.

These numbers are likely to change over the coming months and years. The largest Internet service provider (ISP) in the United States recently announced it would start using Netscape as its default browser, and that could potentially have a large impact on these numbers.

Looking at recent browser popularity statistics a little closer, as in Table 7-1, we can see that half of surfers have not yet upgraded to the most recent versions of their preferred web browsers.

Fully 54 percent of all web surfers are using browsers that are not the latest release from either Microsoft or Netscape. So be careful when creating JavaScript programs that rely too much on proprietary or recently added features. Using those features without taking proper precautions can cause errors for a significant portion of your audience, even if the application works fine in the browser installed on your PC.

What Kind of Errors Can Occur?

When designing any computer program, it is important to keep in mind that errors are likely to occur despite the programmer's best efforts to avoid them. This is especially true of JavaScript programs that are used across a wide variety of browsers and operating systems. When developing JavaScript code, you are likely to find the following sources of errors:

- Differences in the Document Object Model of each browser version
- Client computers running old browsers (such as Netscape 3.0) that do not support certain JavaScript functionality
- Client computers with certain technologies turned off, such as cookies or Java
- New web-enabled technologies, such as hand-held devices, mobile phones, and even appliances, such as refrigerators

In this chapter, we will take a look at some of the common techniques for avoiding these types of errors.

Browser	Usage
IE 6	46%
IE 5	44%
IE 4	2%
Netscape 4	2%
Netscape 6, Netscape 7, Mozilla (collectively)	1%
Older IE	less than 1%
Older Netscape	less than 1%

Source: TheCounter.com (http://www.thecounter.com)

TABLE 7-1   Recent Web Browser Usage Statistics

Detect What Type of Browser the User Is Running

Running a modern or complex JavaScript program in an older browser is likely to cause numerous problems. Perhaps the easiest way to avoid these types of errors is to detect what type of browser the user is running and then either disable some of the program features or provide alternative code that performs the same task in a slightly different manner.

Detecting the browser name and version information is often called browser sniffing. *Much as a bloodhound can detect the unique scent of an individual, a browser sniffer attempts to detect and return the unique details of the browser software.*

To detect the browser manufacturer and version number, we will rely on the navigator DOM object. The navigator object has several methods and properties, but the three that we are interested in at the present time are appName, appVersion, and userAgent.

```
var browserString = navigator.appName;
var browserVersion = navigator.appVersion;
var browserAgent = navigator.userAgent;

alert (browserString);
alert (browserVersion);
alert (browserAgent);
```

Did you know?

Specifying JavaScript Version Numbers

The browser makers started off with the best of intentions. Both Netscape and IE allow developers to specify a JavaScript version number within the language attribute of the <script> tag. This prevents scripts from running in browsers that do not support the specified JavaScript version number. To create a script that will only run in browsers that support JavaScript 1.2, you would use the following code:

```
<script language="JavaScript1.2">
```

The same can be done for all versions of JavaScript up to version 1.5. (A listing of JavaScript version numbers and how they relate to browsers can be found in Chapter 1.)

Unfortunately, very few web developers knew that this could be done, and fewer still actually used this technique when creating cross-browser scripts. On top of that, this method does not help developers solve the DOM-related differences between the various browsers.

So, although this technique is still available, it cannot be relied on to solve cross-browser scripting problems.

For Netscape web browsers (including the open-source Mozilla web browser), the navigator.appName property always returns the same value regardless of the version or operating system.

For Microsoft Internet Explorer, the navigator.appName property also returns a predictable value, regardless of the version.

Therefore, if your web page needed to display different text depending on the browser a visitor was running, you could simply query the navigator.appName property, like so:

```
var browserString = navigator.appName;

if (browserString == "Netscape") {
    // Do something for Netscape/Mozilla here
    document.write ("Long live the lizard.");

} else if (browserString == "Microsoft Internet Explorer") {
    // Do something for Microsoft here
    document.write ("You will be assimilated.");

} else {
    // The browser is not one of the major two
    document.write ("Why must you always be so different?");
}
```

However, navigator.appName is extremely limited in the amount of information it provides. Other navigator properties provide more useful information. For instance, the navigator.appVersion property provides more specific browser version information. For Netscape browsers, the string returned from that property is quite straightforward.

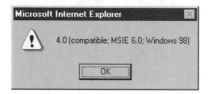

This screenshot was taken from Netscape 7.0 running on Windows 98. Just to make life more confusing for web developers, both Netscape 6 and 7 return their version number as "5.0." However, Netscape did not produce a version 5 (the version number jumped from 4.8 to 6.0), so this version number is inaccurate.

Similarly, Microsoft Internet Explorer returns its version information in the navigator.appVersion string, as we can see from the following snapshot taken from Microsoft Internet Explorer 6.0.

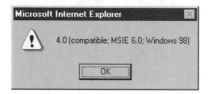

Recent releases of the Microsoft web browser always report the version number as 4.0 compatible. However, the actual version number is embedded later in the same string (in this case, MSIE 6.0).

The Mozilla 1.x, Netscape 6.0, and Netscape 7.0 browsers are all based on the same source code, so their behavior is very similar. If you ever need to get the exact browser name and version number from these browsers, you can query the userAgent property of the navigator object. As you can see from the following illustration, it contains some very specific version number information, right down to the exact date the browser was compiled.

Using these three properties, we can create a JavaScript function that will detect the exact browser type the user is running:

```
function getBrowserInfo() {
    // Define variables to contain the results
    var browserName = navigator.appName;
    var browserVersionNum = parseFloat(navigator.appVersion);
    var browserAgent = navigator.userAgent;

    // Boolean (true or false) variables to detect browser type
    var is_IE = (browserAgent.indexOf("MSIE") != -1);
    var is_NN = (browserName.indexOf("Netscape") != -1);

    // Based on browser type, retrieve version number
    if (is_NN) {
        if (browserVersionNum >= 5.0) {
            var tempStart = browserAgent.indexOf("Netscape/");
            if (tempStart == -1) {
                // "Netscape/" not found; must be Mozilla
                tempStart = browserAgent.indexOf("rv:");
                tempStart += 3;
                browserName = "Mozilla"
                var tempEnd = browserAgent.indexOf(")", tempStart);
            } else {
                // "Netscape/" found; must be Netscape Gecko
                tempStart += 9;
                var tempEnd = browserAgent.length;
            }
            var browserVersion =
                browserAgent.substring(tempStart, tempEnd);
        } else {
            // version < 5.0; must be old Netscape
            var browserVersion = browserVersionNum;
        }

    } else if (is_IE) {
        var tempStart = browserAgent.indexOf("MSIE");
        tempStart += 5;
        var tempEnd = browserAgent.indexOf(";", tempStart);
        var browserVersion =
            browserAgent.substring(tempStart, tempEnd);
    }

    // Create new property of navigator object based on real
```

7

```
    //      version number
    navigator.appRealVersion = browserVersion;

    return;
}


getBrowserInfo();

document.write ("<h1>You appear to be running:<br><br>");
document.write ("<b>" + navigator.appName + "</b> <i>version</i> ");
document.write ("<b>" + navigator.appRealVersion + "</b></h1>");
```

As you can see, we have to do a fair amount of coding gymnastics to figure out the actual version number of the various flavors of Netscape browser. For Netscape 4 and earlier, the navigator.appVersion property returns the correct value. Since Netscape 6 and 7 and Mozilla all return 5.0 as the navigator.appVersion, we have to start searching the navigator.userAgent property for the appropriate value.

NOTE *The preceding code has been simplified for the purposes of this example and thus does not cover all the possible browser types or versions. For an excellent example of a browser-detecting script, I recommend checking out Bob Clary's* Practical Browser Sniffing Script *at http://bclary.com/xbProjects-docs/ua, which uses the properties of the navigator object to determine the browser type and version. That web site also contains a script (at http://bclary.com/xbProjects-docs/xbDOM) that allows you to use one standard set of DOM objects across all browsers.*

The following illustrations show how our little function runs in Netscape 2.0 and Netscape 7.0.

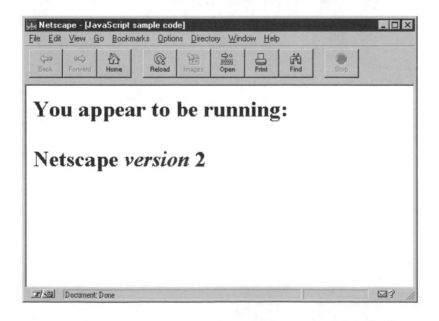

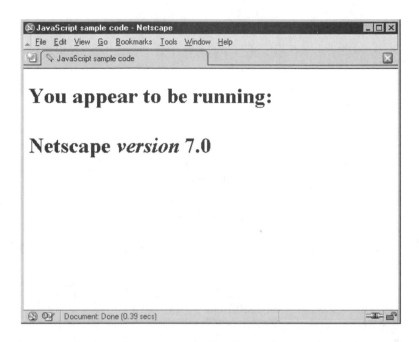

Microsoft Internet Explorer has always provided its version number in the exact same way. It reports itself as Netscape 4.0 compatible in the navigator.appVersion property and leaves the actual software version number embedded elsewhere in the same string. It is relatively easy to search for it using the indexOf() method of the JavaScript String object.

Query the Document Model

The problem with relying on code that checks for browsers by name and version is that it's not foolproof. Currently, about 96 percent of web surfers use one of the two major browsers—Netscape or IE. But what about the other 4 percent—surfers who choose another brand, such as Opera or Konqueror? New browsers are being developed, and web sites will not work reliably if they are only coded to work with the top two brands.

The other problem is that as new versions of IE and Netscape are released, support for different features changes. For instance, Netscape 4 supported a layout method called layers, but support was later dropped when Netscape 6 came out. (We will discuss layers more in the section entitled "Write Cross-Browser Code.")

The easiest way to get around the problem of the wide variety of available browsers (both in the present and in the future) is to write code that checks to see if a DOM method exists before attempting to use it.

The first official version of the Document Object Model (known as DOM 1) defines a method of the document object called getElementById(). Recent browsers (such as IE 5 and Netscape 6) support it, but older browsers do not.

Simply calling the getElementById() method in a browser that does not support it will cause an error:

```
var objptr = document.getElementById("carname");
```

So if you wanted to check to see if the current browser supports the getElementById() method before using it, you would simply query the document object to see if it has a member by that name before calling it:

```
if (document.getElementById) {
    var objptr = document.getElementById("carname");
}
```

The preceding code will work in any browser, since browsers that do not support that method will not execute the code inside the **if** statement. Of course, in those browsers, the variable objptr would not be set, so it is best to have alternate code to handle those situations:

```
if (document.getElementById) {
    var objptr = document.getElementById("carname");
} else {
    alert ("Sorry, this web page will not work in your browser.");
}
```

Of course, if you have to surround each and every call to a DOM method with its own **if** statement, your program will be long and inefficient. So the best approach may be to combine the browser sniffing method with the DOM detection method to get the best of both worlds.

Stick to Web Standards

In the early days of web development, the two largest browser makers were competing aggressively for market share—perhaps too aggressively. One of their favorite tactics was to try to outdo each other in terms of features. Consumers would download and install the newest release of their favorite browser, and within days the next release would be available for download. Large companies, who sometimes require months to test and approve new software for use, found themselves up to two full versions behind the current release.

Of course, this led to two HTML standards instead of one, which made the web developer's job a lot more complicated than it had to be. Luckily for us, both Microsoft and Netscape eventually decided that they would hold off implementing new HTML and JavaScript features until they were approved by a standards committee.

However, as a result of the early "wild West" mentality, there are a number of nonstandard coding practices that should be avoided in order to achieve cross-platform compatibility. Table 7-2 contains a list of elements that are not part of the HTML 4 standard.

These proprietary markup tags should be avoided if you wish to create web pages that work consistently in any browser.

> TIP   *If you want to check your web page to see if it conforms to the official standards, the W3C web site provides an HTML validation service at http://validator.w3.org. This tool is the easiest way to see how far your web page deviates from the official standards. It even identifies any HTML code that contains problems.*

Proprietary Markup	Supporting Browser(s)
<layer>	Netscape 4 (only)
<marquee>	IE
<bgsound>	IE
<embed>	IE, Netscape
<noembed>	IE, Netscape
<multicol>	Netscape
<spacer>	Netscape
<nobr>	IE, Netscape
<wbr>	IE, Netscape
<blink>	Netscape
<xmp>	IE, Netscape
<listing>	IE, Netscape
<plaintext>	IE, Netscape
<keygen>	Netscape
<layer>, <ilayer>	Netscape
<nolayer>	Netscape
<server>	Netscape

TABLE 7-2 Proprietary Markup Tags, Not Part of Official HTML Standard

Write Cross-Browser Code

Earlier in this chapter, we played with some JavaScript code that could be used to detect the exact name and version number of the client browser. In this section, we will put similar code to use with *dynamic HTML*.

Dynamic HTML (or DHTML for short) is an extension of the HTML standard that allows JavaScript programs to change and modify a web page after it has been loaded in the browser, without having to go back to the web server for a new page. For the most part, JavaScript accomplishes this through the manipulation of methods and properties in the browser's DOM.

Dynamic HTML is used regularly by Internet sites to provide fancy drop-down menus, images, and text that change when you move the mouse cursor over them and e-commerce shopping carts that recalculate the total cost of an order every time a check box is selected or cleared. In recent months, advertisers have caught the DHTML bug and are creating dynamic advertising that travels across the web page (and can't be turned off or avoided).

Cross-browser DHTML is difficult to code, however, since the JavaScript code required for Netscape and Microsoft browsers is quite different. While standardization has made programming HTML and basic JavaScript much easier, compared with only a few years ago, the implementation of vastly different DOMs among the browsers is one of the last remaining wilderness areas.

Figure 7-1 shows an example of a web page that uses DHTML. The hierarchical tree on the left side of the screen can be expanded and contracted with a simple mouse click. Menu items are displayed and hidden dynamically, without having to request new HTML from the web server. This type of DHTML menu gives a nice effect for visitors to your web page.

One of the first difficulties you are likely to encounter is that Netscape 4 uses a method called layers to define areas of a web document that can have a style applied to them.

```
<html>
    <head><title>Layers sample</title></head>
    <body>

        <h1>Netscape Layers Example</h1>

        <layer id="mylayer">
        <font color="white"><b>A black square</b></font>
        </layer>

        <layer id="mylayer2">
        <b>A gray square</b>
        </layer>

        <script language="JavaScript" type="text/javascript">
            document.layers["mylayer"].bgColor = "black";
            document.layers["mylayer2"].bgColor = "#CCCCCC";
            document.layers["mylayer2"].moveBy (60, 10);
        </script>
    </body>
</html>
```

This HTML code is designed to work in Netscape 4.x web browsers only. Our code defines a Netscape layer named mylayer using the HTML <layer> tag. We define a second layer named mylayer2. Using JavaScript, we are able to change the background colors of the two layers, and move one of them so that they don't completely overlap. The effect can be seen in Figure 7-2.

Unfortunately, the preceding code does not work in any version of IE or in the newer Netscape 6 browsers. We will have to modify our code a little to detect the type of browser running, and perform different tasks based on that.

First, we need to change the layers to work in all browsers. The following code does not properly conform to HTML standards (since the <layer> tag is not part of the standard), but it will work in both IE and Netscape.

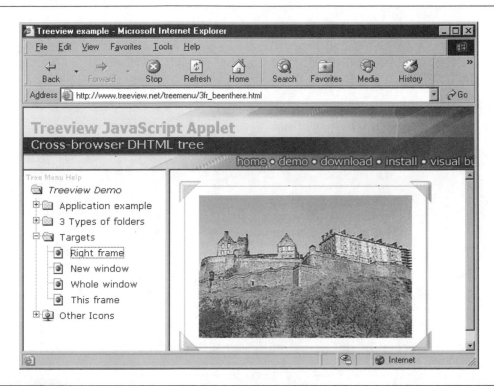

FIGURE 7-1   An expandable tree menu using DHTML

```
<layer id='mylayer'>
    <div id='mydiv' style='position:absolute'>
        <font color="white"><b>A black square</b></font>
    </div>
</layer>

<layer id='mylayer2'>
    <div id='mydiv2' style='position:absolute'>
        <b>A gray square</b>
    </div>
</layer>
```

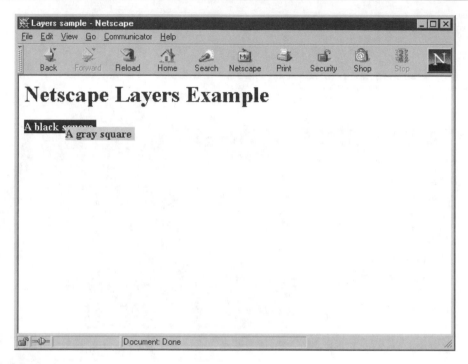

FIGURE 7-2   Creating layers in Netscape 4

Notice how we use the HTML standard <div> tag nested inside the nonstandard <layer> tag. Browsers that do not support <layer> will ignore it, as browsers that do not support <div> will ignore that tag.

Next we need to modify the script to detect the type of browser running. We could use the getBrowserInfo() script from earlier in the chapter, but our needs are much simpler than that. All we need to do is detect the difference between Netscape 4, Netscape 6, and IE. To do that, we can use the following JavaScript code.

```
<script language="JavaScript" type="text/javascript">
    var ua = navigator.userAgent.toLowerCase();
    var ie4 = ua.indexOf("msie") != -1;

    if (document.layers) {
        // Netscape 4 code goes here
    } else if (document.getElementById && ie4) {
        // IE code goes here
    } else if (document.getElementById) {
        // Netscape 6 code goes here
```

```
    }
</script>
```

This code works in a fairly simple fashion. Netscape 4 is the only browser whose document object has a layers property, so checking for that property's existence confirms that the browser type is Netscape 4. We can do the same trick using the getElementById method of the document object, except we still need to differentiate between IE 4 and Netscape 6. The navigator.userAgent property allows us to do that.

Finally, we add in the browser-specific DHTML code to manipulate the two <layer> or <div> tags on the screen to create a visual effect.

```
<html>
    <head><title>Layers sample</title></head>
    <body>

        <h1>Cross-Browser Style Sheets Example</h1>

        <layer id='mylayer'>
            <div id='mydiv' style='position:absolute'>
                <font color="white"><b>A black square</b></font>
            </div>
        </layer>

        <layer id='mylayer2'>
            <div id='mydiv2' style='position:absolute'>
                <b>A gray square</b>
            </div>
        </layer>

        <script language="JavaScript" type="text/javascript">
        var ua = navigator.userAgent.toLowerCase();
        var ie4 = ua.indexOf("msie") != -1;

        if (document.layers) {
            // Netscape 4 code goes here
            document.layers["mylayer"].bgColor = "black";
            document.layers["mylayer2"].bgColor = "#CCCCCC";
            document.layers["mylayer2"].moveBy (60, 10);

        } else if (document.getElementById && ie4) {
            // IE code goes here
            var div1 = document.getElementById("mydiv");
            var div2 = document.getElementById("mydiv2");
            div1.style.backgroundColor = "black";
            div2.style.backgroundColor = "#CCCCCC";
```

```
                div2.style.pixelLeft = div1.offsetLeft + 60;
                div2.style.pixelTop = div1.offsetTop + 10;

        } else if (document.getElementById) {
            // Netscape 6 code goes here
            var div1 = document.getElementById("mydiv");
            var div2 = document.getElementById("mydiv2");
            div1.style.backgroundColor = "black";
            div2.style.backgroundColor = "#CCCCCC";
            div2.style.left = (div1.offsetLeft + 60) + "px";
            div2.style.top = (div1.offsetTop + 10) + "px";

        }
        </script>
    </body>
</html>
```

The resulting cross-browser compatible code can be seen in IE 6 in Figure 7-3 and Netscape 7.0 in Figure 7-4. The results are completely identical to those in Netscape 4.

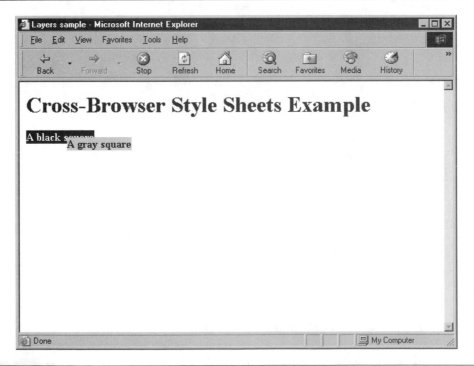

FIGURE 7-3   Microsoft IE 6 interprets the <div> tag and the DHTML JavaScript code correctly.

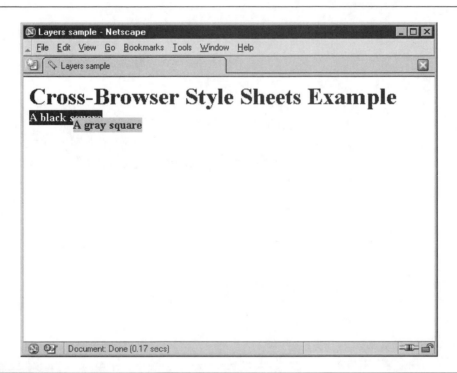

FIGURE 7-4   Even though Netscape 7.0 requires slightly different JavaScript, the same effect is created.

This is a good example of the difficulties JavaScript programmers sometimes face when developing code that works in any browser.

In the next chapter, we will take a look at one of JavaScript's primary duties on the Internet—helping users fill out forms. You will learn how to build a form in HTML, learn about all the controls that can go into a form, and see how JavaScript can be used to validate the data entered before it is sent to the server for processing.

Chapter 8

Manipulate Web Forms

How to...

- Request user input using an HTML form
- Retrieve and set form control values
- Prepare form data for server submission
- Handle multiple forms

In previous chapters, we have seen how JavaScript can be used to provide dynamic web pages that contain animated menus or are slightly different depending on the web browser being used or the time of day. As time goes on, developers will find it easier than ever to include these special JavaScript tricks on their own personal home pages.

What has made JavaScript indispensable as a development tool for most professional web developers is its ability to handle user input. JavaScript makes the gathering and processing of user information easier—for both the user and the web developer. JavaScript can assist in many ways:

- Store and retrieve bits of information on the user's computer (called *cookies*)
- Verify that all mandatory form fields were provided
- Validate the proper formatting of user-entered data
- Provide instant feedback to the user without having to go to the web server

And best of all, it is often very easy to do all these things—only a few lines of code are needed. By solving many more problems than it created, JavaScript quickly became an indispensable tool for serious web developers.

Understand HTML Forms

The best and most flexible way to ask for user input is with HTML forms. A *form,* in web programming, is a series of one or more user controls that are designed to capture user input. A user control is typically a text box, a list box, or a button of some sort that allows the user to provide information to the web browser. In fact, web forms are modeled after paper forms, like those you fill out for a job application or a survey.

There are 13 user controls in HTML:

- **Text box**   Allows a single line of text input
- **Password box**   Allows a single line of text input, protected by asterisks
- **Text area**   Allows one or more lines of text input
- **Hidden**   Can contain a single line of text, hidden from the user
- **List box**   User can choose from one or more predefined choices
- **Radio button**   User can choose one of many predefined choices
- **Check box**   User can choose any number of many predefined choices

- ■ **File**   User can upload a file from the local machine to the web server
- ■ **Push button**   Causes a program-defined action to occur
- ■ **Submit button**   Causes the form to be submitted
- ■ **Image button**   Creates a graphical submit button
- ■ **Reset button**   Causes the form to be cleared
- ■ **Object**   Creates a special (user-defined) input control

Each of these controls performs a special function in requesting user input. Which control you use depends a lot on the individual circumstances. For instance, when you need the user to select one of 50 choices (like selecting which state they live in), you would normally go with a list box control, which allows you to provide dozens of options in very little space. Choosing to display 50 radio buttons instead takes up a lot more space and may cause the rest of the form to scroll off the bottom of the screen.

Request User Input Using an HTML Form

To see what a typical HTML form looks like, let's examine the web page in Figure 8-1. The United States Postal Service (www.usps.gov) provides this online form to register address changes of families or businesses that move and would like their mail forwarded to their new location.

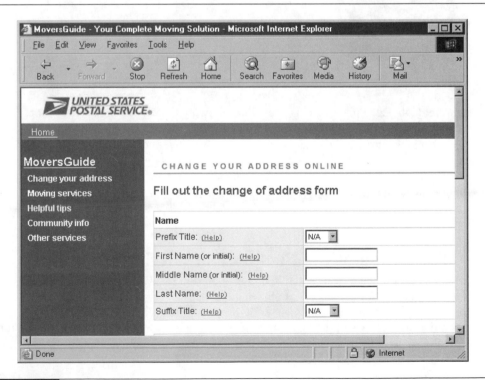

FIGURE 8-1   The change of address form on the U.S. Postal Service web site

The first form field on the screen, labeled "Prefix Title," allows the user to select from a number of name prefixes (such as "Dr.," "Mr.," and "Mrs."). If they do not use a prefix before their name, they can select "N/A" for not applicable. This control is called a list box, since by pressing the down arrow button, the user will see several options from which they can choose.

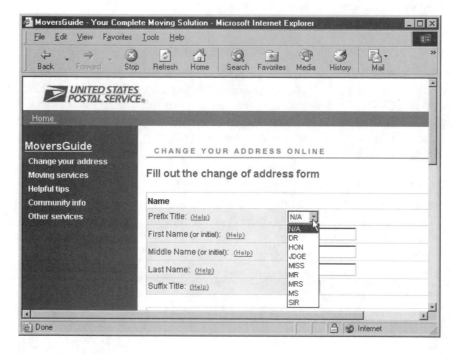

The form field labeled "First Name" is a text box, allowing the user to enter one or more characters using the keyboard. Sometimes, programmers place restrictions on this field using JavaScript, but often the user can enter any combination of letters, numbers, or special symbols. Programmers can use HTML to specify a maximum length for this field.

When the user has finished entering his or her personal data, they are asked to click on an HTML submit button. The submit button causes the data from the web form to be sent to a program waiting on a web server for processing. Using JavaScript, web developers can have the data validated before allowing the web server submission to proceed.

Process Form Input with Client-Side JavaScript

Once the form has been filled out and submitted, it is often sent to a web server for processing. It is important to note that it does not *have* to be sent to a web server—oftentimes web forms can be processed entirely on the client using JavaScript. You will often see these *client-side forms* in the form of online calculators and similar tools, where JavaScript is smart enough to calculate the desired result and perform the requested action without needing help from a web server.

Figure 8-2 shows an example of such a client-side form. The web page displayed in the figure (http://javascript.internet.com/calculators/amortization.html) can calculate the monthly mortgage payments if you provide the amount of the loan, the interest rate, and the amortization term. This is calculated using a JavaScript function embedded in the web page.

We will examine how to create JavaScript code that can respond to web forms later in this chapter, in the "Catch Web Form Submissions with onsubmit" section.

Process Form Input on a Web Server

Web forms that require complex processing—those that access a database, for instance—must be submitted to an application waiting on the server. There are many prominent technologies available to create these form-handling programs:

- Server-side JavaScript
- Application Server Pages (ASP)
- Java Servlets

8

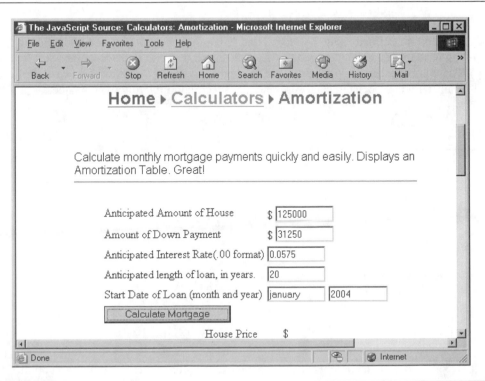

FIGURE 8-2   Calculating monthly mortgage payments using an HTML form

- Java Server Pages (JSP)
- Perl
- PHP
- A compiled binary written in almost any language (such as C)

Once these programs accept the data submitted by the web form, they usually perform any processing required and then respond to the browser with another HTML page. The communication process between client and server is depicted in Figure 8-3. It shows an example of a user performing a search at one of the major search engine web sites. The web server accepts the keywords using an HTML form, checks its database for related web pages, and returns a new HTML web page with the results.

Insert an HTML Form into a Web Page

Forms are added to web pages in the same way that images, text, and other elements of the page are, with HTML markup. Developers can define all the parts of a form, including the controls it contains and how they are arranged, using standard HTML tags.

Use the <form> Tag

In HTML, forms are defined using the <form> tag. The <form> tag allows you to define the type of form you wish to create, including the URL of the program waiting to accept the user's input (if any). These are specified using the <form> element's *attributes*. An attribute is an element's named parameter and associated data. Attributes are specified in the following manner:

```
<element attribute1="value1" attribute2="value2" ... attribute3="value3">
```

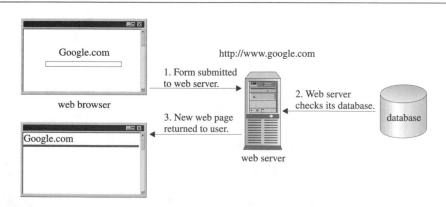

FIGURE 8-3   Communication between client and server when an HTML form is submitted

The <form> element has the following attributes:

- **id**   String that must be unique across the entire web page
- **class**   List of associated CSS classes
- **style**   Inline CSS style commands
- **title**   Advisory title
- **lang**   ISO language code
- **dir**   Direction of text (right to left or left to right)
- **action**   URI of program that will handle form data
- **method**   The way data will be transmitted to the server (either GET or POST)
- **enctype**   MIME encoding type
- **accept**   List of MIME types accepted for file upload
- **accept-charset**   List of supported charsets

In addition to all those attributes, the <form> element can also contain a number of event handlers. *Events* are actions usually initiated by the user, such as a mouse movement or certain keypresses. *Event handlers* are JavaScript code and functions that are designed to act when certain events happen. We will examine all the predefined HTML event handlers in more detail in Chapter 9.

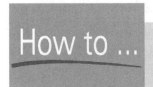

Have a Form's Contents Mailed to You

The <form> tag's **action** attribute allows you to specify the web server URI for the program that will process the form. Typically, this program is an ASP page, Java servlet, or a Perl script running on the target web server.

You can also direct the browser to e-mail you the contents of the form instead. This is done by providing an e-mail address using the mailto: protocol to the **action** attribute. To construct a URI using the mailto: protocol, you simply append the actual e-mail address to the mailto: string, like so:

```
mailto:president@whitehouse.gov
```

If you used the preceding string as the URI for the **action** attribute, the contents of the web form would be mailed to the President of the United States.

This technique is not guaranteed, however, since it uses the mail program installed on the user's computer. The program might not be set up correctly for sending e-mail, or the user might cancel the e-mail from being sent.

8

For now, we are only concerned with two possible events that can happen to a web form:

- **onsubmit**   JavaScript code that will be run before the form is submitted
- **onreset**   JavaScript code that will be run before the form's data is erased

Some HTML elements have mandatory attributes, that is, attributes that must always be present. The <form> element is one of those, as the **action** attribute must always be specified in order for the HTML to be valid.

The most basic type of form is the following:

```
<form action="#">
</form>
```

This HTML code creates an empty form that does not contain any controls. Forms such as this are quite useless, of course, because they have no purpose. HTML <form> elements by themselves are invisible, in that they do not have a visual component. Form controls (buttons and text boxes, for instance) are the visual components of forms. Forms can also contain text, tables, and other HTML elements.

*It is common to use the pound sign (#) as the value of the **action** attribute of the <form> tag when none is needed, since the **action** attribute is mandatory and cannot be omitted. You might use this for forms designed to only exist on the client, which will never need to be submitted to a server. The pound sign (#) is one of the shortest valid URLs.*

Add Form Controls

As we have seen, forms are pretty useless without controls. Form controls allow a web page to accept user input. Some controls allow users to enter text themselves, and some provide users several predefined options to choose from. Form controls are added to <form> elements with HTML of their own. Table 8-1 lists the common input controls along with the HTML required to add them to a web page.

Accept Text Input with a Text Box

Perhaps the most common type of form control is the text box. In fact, the text box control is the default type of the <input> element. The following HTML code will create a web form with a single text box inside.

```
<form action="#">
    <input>
</form>
```

Control Name	HTML Code
Text box	<input type="text"...>
Password box	<input type="password"...>
Text area	<textarea...> </textarea>
Hidden text	<input type="hidden"...>
List box	<select...> </select>
Radio button	<input type="radio"...>
Check box	<input type="checkbox"...>
File upload	<input type="file"...>
Push button	<input type="button"...>
Push button	<button...>
Submit button	<input type="submit"...>
Image button	<input type="image"...>
Reset button	<input type="reset"...>
Object control	<object...> </object>

TABLE 8-1   A List of HTML Form Controls

Of course, creating a form like that has several drawbacks. First, anyone who encountered that form in their web browser would not know what to do with it—the control is unlabeled. It's just a text box sitting on a page by itself. Second, web developers looking at that code might find it a bit confusing, since the <input> control has so many forms. It might be better to explicitly set the control type.

A better example of a web form would be the following:

```
<form action="#">
    Please enter your age: <br>
    <input type="text" name="age">
</form>
```

This type of web form is easier to use for both the web developer and the web page visitor.

The text box control has several attributes that give developers more control over the look and behavior of the control:

- **id**   String that must be unique across the entire web page
- **class**   List of associated CSS classes

- **style**   Inline CSS style commands
- **title**   Advisory title
- **lang**   ISO language code
- **dir**   Direction of text (right to left or left to right)
- **name**   The name of the control
- **value**   The default value
- **size**   The size of the control on the screen, in characters
- **maxlength**   The maximum number of characters that can be entered
- **readonly**   Locks the control so its value cannot be modified by the user
- **accesskey**   Sets the keyboard shortcut key
- **tabindex**   Sets the order in which controls receive focus on a form
- **disabled**   Locks the control so that it cannot receive focus or be modified by the user

NOTE   *In web programming, we say a control has focus when it is the currently active control. The browser often lets us know which control has focus by using a flashing vertical line for text boxes or some other highlight for buttons and other controls. Most browsers draw a temporary dotted box around nontext controls that have focus.*

Besides the preceding attributes, our input control can also capture a number of events as well. We will examine all the predefined HTML event handlers in more detail in Chapter 9. For now, we will only concern ourselves with the following HTML events:

- **onfocus**   JavaScript code that will be run when a control receives focus
- **onblur**   JavaScript code that will be run when a control loses focus
- **onchange**   JavaScript code that will be run when a control loses focus and the value of its contents has been altered

By using some of these attributes on our text box, we can improve the look and behavior of our control:

```
<form action="#">
    Please enter your <u>a</u>ge: <br>
    <input type="text" name="age" size="5" maxlength="3"
        value="" accesskey="A">
</form>
```

We have reduced the horizontal length of the control to five characters wide by using the **size="5"** attribute on the <input> control. By specifying **maxlength="3"** we are restricting input to a maximum of three characters in length. Since we are asking for an age, it is reasonable to assume three digits will be enough.

The **value=""** attribute sets the default contents of the field to an empty string. The **accesskey** parameter, which is set to "A" in our example, allows users to jump to the control by using the ALT-A key combination in most versions of Windows, or the CONTROL-A key combination for most Mac systems.

NOTE *The key combination required to activate an access key is dependent on both the browser type and operating system, so check your browser documentation if you cannot get it to work.*

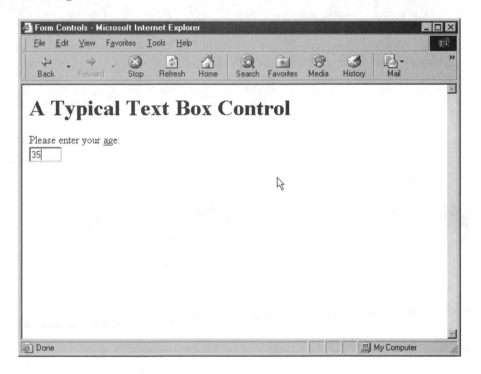

Provide a List Box Control

A list box is a convenient control to use when you need the user to select one of multiple choices. In HTML, list boxes are created using the <select> element, and items in the list are defined using the <option> element. There are two types of list boxes you can use inside your web-based forms: the *drop-down list box* and the *scrolled list box*.

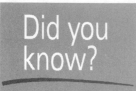

Privacy and the Internet

HTML forms are commonly used to allow visitors to log in to a web site. Users must normally supply a valid user ID and password to the server before being allowed into the restricted areas of the site.

From a developer's point of view, a text box should be used to request the user ID from the user. As an added level of security, a password box control should be used to request a user's password. The password box replaces the characters typed in with asterisks, so that *password* becomes ********. This is done so that other individuals looking at the same computer monitor (from over the user's shoulder, for instance) will not be able to read the password.

You should know, however, that this is a very weak type of security. Unless the form data is encrypted using Secure Sockets Layer (SSL), typically using HTTPS protocol, the password will be sent over the Internet as plain text, which can be easily read by anyone along the path or by anyone with access to the web server's activity logs.

The drop-down list box appears as a text box with a small arrow button next to it. Clicking the arrow causes the control to create a scrollable pop-up window in which the user can select one of multiple choices, as you can see here.

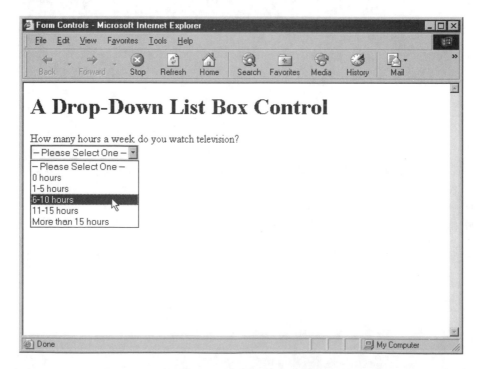

Users cannot type their own text into the text box—they must select one of the predefined items. This type of control is best used when there are at least three options to choose from, such as when asking the user to select their home state or country. Other controls, such as radio buttons and check boxes, are better for having the user select from only two or three options.

The scrolled list box appears as a combination of a multiline text box attached to a vertical scroll bar, as you can see here.

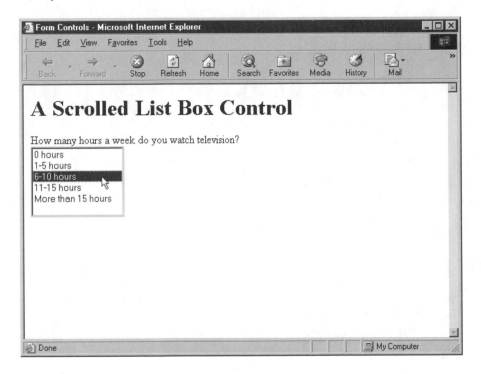

A scrolled list box is created by specifying the number of items to be displayed at once using the **size** attribute of the HTML <select> element. Users may select more than one option from a scrolled list box if the developer has specified the **multiple** attribute. A user can select multiple options by holding down the CTRL (PC) or COMMAND (Mac) key on the keyboard when selecting items from the list.

The following HTML will create a form with a single drop-down list box inside it.

```
<form action="#">
What would you like for dinner?<br>
    <select name="dinner">
        <option selected value="1">Chicken</option>
        <option value="2">Beef</option>
        <option value="3">Pork</option>
        <option value="4">Fish</option>
        <option value="5">Vegetables</option>
```

```
    </select>
</form>
```

By specifying the **size** attribute, we can modify the drop-down list box to become a scrolling list box. Since our **size** attribute only allows three items to display at once, the user will be able to see the remaining two items by using the scroll bar.

```
<form action="#">
What would you like for dinner?<br>
    <select name="dinner" size="3">
        <option value="1" selected>Chicken</option>
        <option value="2">Beef</option>
        <option value="3">Pork</option>
        <option value="4">Fish</option>
        <option value="5">Vegetables</option>
    </select>
</form>
```

The HTML <select> element has several attributes that give web developers more control over the look and behavior of the list box control:

- **id** String that must be unique across the entire web page
- **class** List of associated CSS classes
- **style** Inline CSS style commands
- **title** Advisory title
- **lang** ISO language code
- **dir** Direction of text (right to left or left to right)
- **name** Name of the control
- **size** Number of rows to display at once
- **multiple** Allows the control to accept multiple selections
- **tabindex** Sets the order in which controls receive focus on a form
- **disabled** Locks the control so that it cannot receive focus or be modified by the user

Beside the preceding attributes, our list box control can also capture a number of events as well. We will examine the predefined HTML event handlers in more detail in Chapter 9. The list box can capture the following three events:

- **onfocus** JavaScript code that will be run when a control receives focus
- **onblur** JavaScript code that will be run when a control loses focus
- **onchange** JavaScript code that will be run when a control loses focus and the value of its contents has been altered

The HTML <option> element has several attributes of its own:

- **id**   String that must be unique across the entire web page
- **class**   List of associated CSS classes
- **style**   Inline CSS style commands
- **title**   Advisory title
- **lang**   ISO language code
- **dir**   Direction of text (right to left or left to right)
- **selected**   Defines this list item as the default
- **disabled**   Locks the control so that it cannot receive focus or be modified by the user
- **label**   Defines a label for the list item
- **value**   The string returned to the server when a user selects the item

The <option> element can also receive a number of events. We will examine all the predefined HTML event handlers in more detail in Chapter 9.

Accept Text Input with a Text Area

One variation of the text box is the *text area*. The text area control accepts multiple lines of input and is defined using the HTML <textarea> element. One drawback of the text area control is that you cannot easily restrict the amount of data a user adds to that control.

The most common attributes for the <textarea> element are **rows, cols** (columns), and **name**. As you would expect, you specify the height of the control using the **rows** attribute, and the width of the control using the **cols** attribute. For example, the following text area will hold 5 rows that are 60 characters wide.

```
<form action="#">
    <textarea rows="5" cols="60">
    This is my example text area.
    </textarea>
</form>
```

Default text is inserted between the <textarea> and </textarea> tags.

Add a Push Button Control to a Form

Unlike other controls, *push buttons* (or just *buttons*) are generally not used to provide user input. Their purpose is to cause the browser to execute some JavaScript code through the button's onclick event handler. There is a special type of push button control called a *submit button* that can be used to provide user input. We will examine submit buttons in the next section.

In HTML, there are two ways to create a simple push button: with the <input> element and with the <button> element. The <input> element is used to create the most basic type of push button, as follows:

```
<form action="#">
    <input type="button" value="Push me" onclick="dothis()">
</form>
```

The push button defined in this form will call a JavaScript function named dothis() when pressed. The **value** attribute defines the button's *caption*, or the text label on the button.

The <button> element allows developers to create a more complex type of push button. The <button> element accepts complex HTML input (including text and images) as its caption. For example, the following push button displays a check mark image next to the word OK, which is in bold print. It too will call the JavaScript dothis() function when clicked.

```
<form action="#">
    <button onclick="dothis()">
        <img src="checkmark.gif">
        <font size="6"><b><i>OK</i></b></font>
    </button>
</form>
```

Here is how this special type of push button looks in a browser window.

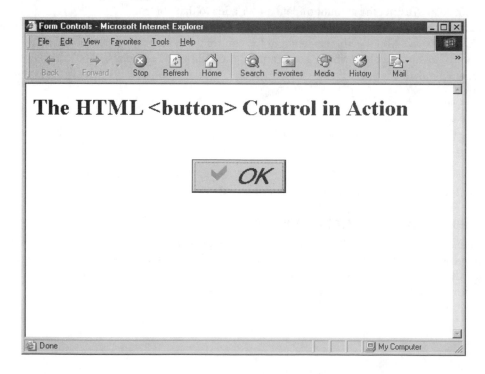

Add a Submit Button

Submit buttons are a special type of form control, in that they cause a form to submit itself to the server. The variables and data defined in the form are sent to the web server application defined in the **action** attribute of the <form> element, using the method defined in the **method** attribute.

For instance, the following code defines a form that submits itself to an ASP web page. The ASP web page is responsible for processing the data and sending a new web page for the browser to display.

```
<form
    action="http://www.example.com/scripts/myscript.asp"
    method="GET">
    Full Name: <input type="text" name="fullname"><br>
    Age: <input type="text" name="age" size="5"><br>
    Date of Birth: <input type="text" name="DOB" size="10"><br>
    <input type="submit" value="Submit Form">
</form>
```

When the user clicks the Submit Form button, the three other form controls on the form (fullname, age, and DOB) will be sent to the ASP web page, along with whatever text the user entered in those fields.

> **NOTE** *Only named form fields will be submitted to the server for processing. Fields without an assigned **name** attribute, even text fields, will not be submitted to the server. It is common to omit the name of submit buttons. The only time it would be useful to name them would be if there were more than one submit button on a form and the server needed to know which button was used to submit the form.*

Catch Web Form Submissions with onsubmit

Previously in this chapter, in the section entitled "Use the <form> Tag," we saw that the HTML <form> element has a number of predefined event handlers. Handling an event is known as *catching* it, and in this section we will take a brief look at one of the <form> element's events and how to catch it.

The **onsubmit** attribute allows us to specify some JavaScript code that will be executed before the web form is submitted to the web server. This JavaScript code is usually stored inside a function, and so the event handler only refers to that function. But sometimes the JavaScript code will appear directly in the event handler attribute.

```
<script language="JavaScript" type="text/javascript">
function checkname() {
    alert("Your name is " + document.forms[0].fullname.value);
}
</script>

<form action="http://www.myserver.com/formhandler"
```

8

```
     method="GET"
     onsubmit="return checkname()">
     What is your name? <br>
     <input type="text" name="fullname"> <br>
     <input type="submit" value="Submit Form">
</form>
```

In the preceding HTML code, we have specified a JavaScript function that will be called at the time the form is submitted to the web server using the **onsubmit** event handler attribute of the <form> element. The function that will be called is checkname(), which we have defined just above the form. Once the checkname() function finishes, the form data will be sent to the URL http://www.myserver.com/formhandler for processing.

Here you can see the HTML form that is created. I have already typed in the five letters of my first name as an example.

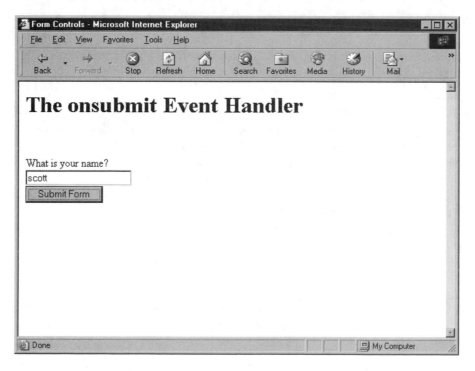

The button labeled "Submit Form" is actually a submit button, which will cause the form to be sent to the web server. Before it is submitted, however, the checkname() function is called. That function simply retrieves the contents of the text box and displays it in a JavaScript alert box. Once the alert box is accepted by the user, the form sends its data to the web server for processing.

Our onsubmit event handler actually has the ability to stop the web form from being submitted. Returning the Boolean value false from the function causes processing to stop without the form being submitted to the server.

```
<script language="JavaScript" type="text/javascript">
function checkname() {
    var username = document.forms[0].fullname.value;
    if (username != "Scott") {
        alert("Sorry, " + username + ". I cannot let you proceed.");
        return false;
    } else {
        return true;
    }
}
</script>
```

The preceding JavaScript function, when called by the same HTML form, will not submit to the web server if the user does not type Scott into the name field.

Catch Events on Form Controls

Like the HTML <form> tag, form controls can also have programmable events. A program can define a JavaScript function or code that will be executed when a certain event occurs. For instance, JavaScript can detect when the mouse cursor passes over a control, when it has gained or lost focus, or when its value has changed.

For example, the following code demonstrates how some of the text box control's events can be captured.

```
<html>
    <head>
        <title>Capture Form Control Events</title>
        <script language="JavaScript" type="text/javascript">
        <!-- // Begin

        function modifylayer(changetext) {
            var lefield = document.getElementById("lastevent");
            lefield.innerHTML = changetext + "<br><br> ";
```

```
        }

        // End -->
        </script>
    </head>
    <body>
        <h1>Capture Form Control Events</h1>

        <form action="#" method="get">
        Move the mouse in and out of this field,
        or change its contents.<br>
        <textarea name="samplefield" rows="10" cols="30"
            onmouseover="modifylayer('mouseover')"
            onmouseout="modifylayer('mouseout')"
            onchange="modifylayer('change')"
            onkeypress="modifylayer('keypress')"
            >Sample text</textarea><br><br>

        Last event captured:
        <div id="lastevent"
            style="background-color:#CCCCCC; font-weight:bold">
        <br><br> 
        </div>
        </form>

    </body>
</html>
```

The body of the HTML document has an HTML <form> that contains a single control—a multiline text box called a <textarea>. We have also defined an HTML <div> area, which contains text that we can change using JavaScript.

The <textarea> also defines a number of event handlers. The web browser will call a JavaScript function named modifylayer() if any of the following events occurs for this control:

- **onmouseover**   When the mouse cursor enters the control
- **onmouseout**   When the mouse cursor leaves the control
- **onchange**   When the contents of the control have changed and the control has lost focus
- **onkeypress**   When a keyboard key has been pressed

We define the modifylayer() function using the <script> tag inside the document header section. That function will write the name of the event out to the <div> area we have defined.

NOTE *You can see a list of all the browser events supported by Internet Explorer on Microsoft's web site at http://msdn.microsoft.com/workshop/author/dhtml/reference/ events.asp. We also discuss web browser events more thoroughly in Chapter 9.*

Of course, there is also a way to capture the name of the event without having to pass it to the function explicitly using the **window.event** DOM object. We could modify our JavaScript code to the following to take advantage of this technique.

```
function modifylayer() {
    var lefield = document.getElementById("lastevent");
    var ename = window.event.type;
    lefield.innerHTML = ename + "<br><br> ";
}
```

With this type of function, we would no longer need to pass the name of the event inside each event handler. The modifylayer() function can handle all four events on its own.

```
<textarea name="samplefield" rows="10" cols="30"
    onmouseover="modifylayer()"
    onmouseout="modifylayer()"
    onchange="modifylayer()"
    onkeypress="modifylayer()"
    >Sample text</textarea><br><br>
```

We can see from the following screen capture what this web page will look and act like in a web browser.

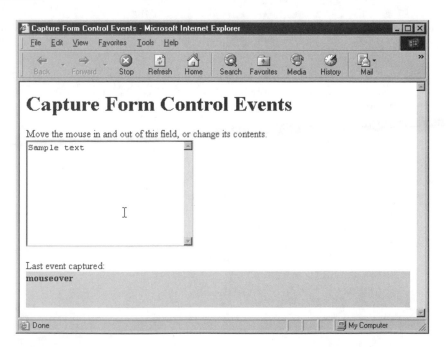

Retrieve and Set Form Control Values in JavaScript

One of the code samples from the preceding section demonstrated one of the many possible ways of retrieving values from a web form. The DOM provides JavaScript programs several ways to access the controls on a form and their values, including:

- As a property of the forms array
- As key values in the elements array
- Using one of three different methods of the document object

NOTE *Not all of these techniques work in older versions of the major browsers, so you may have to employ some of the cross-browser scripting techniques discussed in Chapter 7.*

Access Form Values Using the forms Array

One technique that will work in all JavaScript-enabled browsers is accessing form controls using the *forms array*. The forms array is a property of the DOM document object; it contains an indexed list of all the forms on a web page. Indexes in JavaScript start at zero.

We start by creating a variable that refers to the form itself.

```
var myform = document.forms[0];
```

We can then access any control on the form by name. For instance, the following code allows you to access the contents of a text box called fullname:

```
var fullname = myform.fullname.value;
```

As in "Accept Text Input with a Text Box," earlier in this chapter, value is a property of the text box control. The preceding code placed the contents of that text box in a variable we called fullname.

Using this technique allows us to access any control on the form, as long as it is named. The following code demonstrates a form that contains a text boxes, a list box, and a group of radio buttons. Before the form is submitted, a function named checkform() verifies that the user entered text or made a selection in each of the fields.

```
<html>
  <head>
    <title>JavaScript Test</title>
    <script language="JavaScript" type="text/javascript">
    <!-- // Begin

    function checkform() {
        var myform = document.forms[0];

        // Accessing text boxes is easy
```

```
      var fullname = myform.fullname.value;
      var emailaddr = myform.email.value;

      // Which drop down item is selected?
      var ageIdx = myform.age.selectedIndex;
      var age = myform.age.options[ageIdx].value;

      // Which radio button is selected?
      var hearObj = myform.hear;
      var hear = "";

      for (var i = 0; i < hearObj.length; i++) {
         if (hearObj[i].checked) {
            hear = hearObj[i].value;
         }
      }

      // Check if any fields are blank
      if ((fullname == "") || (emailaddr == "") ||
         (age == "None") || (hear == "")) {
         alert("Some information appears to be missing.");
         return false;
      } else {
         return true;
      }
   }

   // End -->
   </script>
</head>
<body>
   <h1>JavaScript forms Array</h1>

   <form action="#" onsubmit="return checkform()">
   <center>
   <table width="400" cellspacing="12">
   <tr>
      <td align="right"><b>Name:</b></td>
      <td><input type="text" name="fullname"></td>
   </tr>
   <tr>
      <td align="right"><b>Email:</b></td>
```

8

```
        <td><input type="text" name="email"></td>
    </tr>
    <tr>
        <td align="right"><b>Age:</b></td>
        <td><select name="age">
        <option value="None">-- Please select --</option>
        <option value="16-32">16-32</option>
        <option value="33-49">33-49</option>
        <option value="Over 50">50+</option>
        </select></td>
    </tr>
    <tr>
        <td align="right"><b>How did you<br>
           hear about us?</b></td>
        <td valign="top">
        <input type="radio" name="hear" value="t"> TV<br>
        <input type="radio" name="hear" value="r"> Radio<br>
        <input type="radio" name="hear" value="n"> Newspaper<br>
        <input type="radio" name="hear" value="o"> Other</td>
    </tr>
    <tr>
        <td align="middle" colspan="2">
        <input type="submit" value="Send to server"></td>
    </tr>
    </table>

    </center>
    </form>
  </body>
</html>
```

Figure 8-4 shows how this form would look in a typical web browser.

If we were to try to submit this form without filling out one of the fields, the checkform() function would catch it, and report this error:

Access Form Values Using the elements Array

Another way to access the controls on forms is through the *elements array*. The elements array is a sequential list of all the form controls that appear on a web page. To access the value of

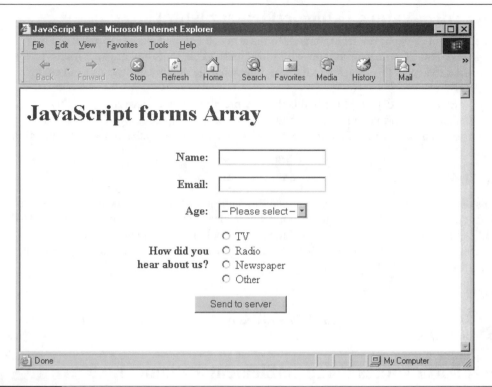

FIGURE 8-4   A web page that contains various form controls

a specific control, you need to know its position in the array beforehand. This array is convenient if you need to access all the controls in an array or search the array for a specific control.

```
var earray = document.forms[0].elements;
for (var count = 0; count < earray.length; count++) {
    alert(earray[count].name);
}
```

The preceding code demonstrates how the elements array can be queried. It successfully finds the first control on the form.

Access Form Values Using getElementById()

Both the techniques we have just examined (forms array and elements array) are the old way of using the DOM. The main problem with those methods is that they are specific to forms. If you wanted to access the contents of the <h1> element (the document heading) and change it, you could not.

The getElementById() DOM method is the new preferred way to access any object on a web page—whether it is a form control, a <div> tag, or even a Java applet embedded in the page.

To retrieve the value of the fullname text box, we would use the getElementById() function as follows:

```
var fullname = document.getElementById("fullname").value;
```

This code looks for an element with an ID of fullname anywhere inside the current document. JavaScript does not know (or care) at this point what type of object it is—it could be any HTML element. As its name implies, this function attempts to look up an element by its ID. Most HTML elements have an ID attribute (**id=""**), and in order to use this function on an element, you should set the ID attribute accordingly.

```
<input type="text" id="fullname" name="fullname">
```

NOTE   *Most browsers will also search for elements by their name attributes if they cannot find an ID that matches.*

Access Form Values Using getElementsByName()

Just as the getElementById() function will search for elements by ID attribute, the getElementsByName() function will search for elements by their name. The one difference between the two functions is that getElementsByName returns an array of elements. Thus, it can return more than one element.

```
var hearObj = document.getElementsByName("hear");
```

This code will return an array of all the elements named hear on the web page. Earlier we created some HTML that included a set of radio buttons named hear—there were four elements named hear on the page (see "Access Form Values Using the forms Array"). Using this code on that form would return an array of four elements. The JavaScript code we used would then correctly determine which of the four radio buttons were selected.

```
for (var i = 0; i < hearObj.length; i++) {
    if (hearObj[i].checked) {
        hear = hearObj[i].value;
    }
}
```

Access Form Values Using getElementsByTagName()

The final method provided by the new JavaScript DOM is getElementsByTagName(). This method is very helpful in retrieving elements that are not named, such as the submit button on our previous form example. This function allows us to look up objects on a web page by their HTML element name.

```
var mybutton = document.getElementsByTagName("input");
mybutton[6].value = "Please wait...";
mybutton[6].disabled = true;
```

By adding this code to the beginning of our checkform() function, we can disable the submit button to stop the user from submitting the form more than once. The getElementsByTagName("input") function returns an array of all the <input> elements on a web page. We know the submit button is the seventh element on the web page created using the HTML <input> tag—the other six are two text boxes and four radio buttons. Since the array starts at index zero, the submit button is located in the sixth index in the array.

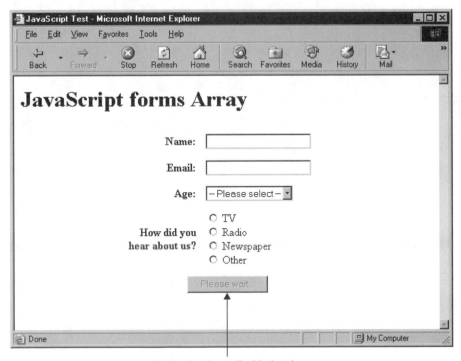

Button has been disabled and
caption set to "Please wait."

8

So as you can see, the DOM provides a number of different methods for accessing the contents of a form. In the next chapter, we will examine the ins and outs of browser events. We will start off by looking at the different types of events in HTML and how to write event handlers to deal with them. And we will look at some of the special cross-browser compatibility issues that arise when dealing with events.

Chapter 9

Handle Browser Events

How to...

- Write JavaScript event handlers
- Handle events using the event property
- Trigger events in JavaScript
- Overcome browser incompatibility

The dictionary defines an *event* as "something that takes place" and that is exactly what it means in web programming as well. An *event handler* is JavaScript code that is designed to run each time a particular event occurs. Of course, this means that your JavaScript code may execute dozens of times, or not at all, depending on the circumstances.

There are 18 events officially defined in the HTML 4.01 specification. In addition, browsers that support the official DOM Level 2 Events specification need to provide several more events for programmers to work with. However, Microsoft and Netscape have gone beyond the events listed in the official specifications and provide many more: IE supports more than 75 events, and Netscape supports at least 50.

> **NOTE**   *The DOM Level 2 Events specification can be found on the official W3C web site at http://www.w3.org/TR/DOM-Level-2-Events.*

The key to knowing how to write appropriate event handlers is understanding what the events are and when they occur. For instance, the following events are just three of the official 18 HTML 4.01 events:

- **load event**   Occurs when the HTML document has finished loading in the browser window
- **click event**   Occurs when the left mouse button has been clicked
- **keypress event**   Occurs when a keyboard key has been pressed

JavaScript can be used to intercept these events when they occur and take certain actions (sometimes it is allowed to cancel the event). Intercepting an event is called *capturing* the event, and it is done by writing event handler code. If no event handling code is written, the browser will continue to process the event as normal using default behavior.

In this chapter, we will examine the various events provided by most HTML elements and how event handlers should be written for each. We will also see how a JavaScript program can cause these events to occur manually, and we'll look into the differences in event handling between the various browsers.

Write JavaScript Event Handlers

You saw some examples of event handlers in the previous chapter, in the "Catch Web Form Submissions with onsubmit" section. Writing an onsubmit event handler enabled our JavaScript program to check that all the fields on a form were filled out before the form submission was allowed to continue.

Events fall into four major categories:

- User interface events
- Mouse events
- Key events
- HTML events

User interface events happen as controls or other objects on a web page gain and lose focus. These events are often caused by other user actions (such as a tab key press or a mouse click), but they can happen programmatically as well.

Mouse events occur when the user moves the mouse or presses one of the mouse buttons. These events allow a web page to respond to mouse movements by, for example, highlighting an image when the mouse moves over it.

Key events occur when the user presses and/or releases one of the keyboard keys. Only certain HTML elements can capture keyboard events, as we will see later in this chapter.

Finally, there are several events specific to certain HTML elements. They often relate to the browser window itself or to form controls and other objects embedded in a web page. The onsubmit event handler discussed in the last chapter falls into this category.

Handle User Interface Events

User interface events deal exclusively with the transfer of focus from one object inside the web page to another. There are three user interface events defined in most web browsers.

Event Name	Event Handler Name	Defined In
focus	onfocus	HTML 4.01
blur	onblur	HTML 4.01
activate	onactivate	DOM Level 2

For example, let's assume we have a web page with two text boxes.

```
<form action="#">
    <input type="text" name="box1"><br>
    <input type="text" name="box2">
</form>
```

Say the active cursor is presently inside the text box named box1. When we hit the keyboard TAB key, we expect focus to transfer to the second text box, box2. Ignoring for a moment the keyboard events, the three user interface events *fire* (occur) in a predictable order.

First, the activate event fires on box2. Next, the blur event fires on box1. Finally, the focus event fires on box2. We can modify the web page slightly to see that the events always fire in a predictable order.

```
<script type="text/javascript" language="javascript">
 function upd(instr) {
    document.forms[0].statusbox.value += instr + "; ";
}
</script>
<form action="#">
    <input type="text" name="box1"
        onblur="upd('blur box1')"><br>
    <input type="text" name="box2"
        onfocus="upd('focus box2')"
        onactivate="upd('activate box2')"><br><br>
    Event firing order:
    <input type="text" name="statusbox" size="40">
</form>
```

In the preceding code, we have added a third text box called statusbox to the screen, to display the results of our event firing test. We have provided JavaScript to the three event handlers (onblur, onfocus, and onactivate) that will append the event and control names to the end of the statusbox text box.

The results of the test are shown in Figure 9-1. As you can see, the events listed in the status box match the order we expected.

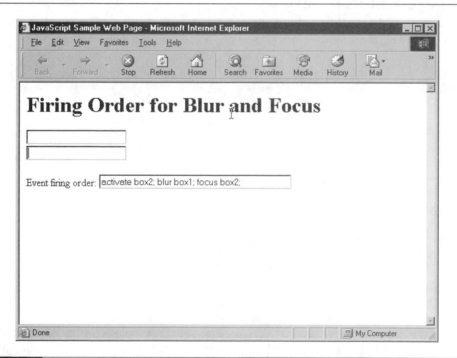

FIGURE 9-1   User interface events are fired in a predictable order.

Handle Mouse Events

The seven mouse events listed in the following table all relate to actions taken by the user using the mouse. JavaScript programs have the ability to track mouse movement and button clicks as they relate to the web page and controls inside.

Event Name	Event Handler Name	Defined In
mousedown	onmousedown	HTML 4.01
mouseup	onmouseup	HTML 4.01
mouseover	onmouseover	HTML 4.01
mousemove	onmousemove	HTML 4.01
mouseout	onmouseout	HTML 4.01
click	onclick	HTML 4.01
dblclick	ondblclick	HTML 4.01

Tracking these mouse events is often done to enhance the user's experience by highlighting menu items as the mouse pointer rolls over them or by updating screen text to provide more information about the element beneath the pointer.

For example, the following HTML code inserts an image into an web page using the <img> element. By capturing the mouseover and mouseout events, we can cause the image to change when the mouse pointer is over the image and change back to the original image once it leaves.

```
<script type="text/javascript" language="javascript">
function changeimage(num) {
    var img = document.getElementById("SampleImage");
    if (num == 1) {
        img.src = "NewImg.gif";
    } else {
        img.src = "OriginalImg.gif";
    }
}
</script>

<img src="OriginalImg.gif"
    id="SampleImage"
    alt="Sample image"
    onmouseover="changeimage(1)"
    onmouseout="changeimage(2)" >
```

The mouseover event fires the moment the mouse pointer enters the boundaries of the image. The onmouseover event handler calls the changeimage() function with a parameter of 1. The changeimage() function starts off by assigning a reference to the image to a variable based on its id, SampleImage. The **src** attribute of the image allows us to dynamically modify the image displayed in the browser.

9

The mouseout event fires once the mouse pointer leaves the boundaries of the image. The changeimage() function handles this event as well, causing the image to go back to its original source.

We can see the effects of this image rollover in Figure 9-2.

Handle Key Events

JavaScript programmers rarely use key event handlers to catch key events. While there are a few situations where you might want to use them, this type of event handling is more commonly found in Windows applications (such as Visual Basic programs) than in web-based programming.

Like the user interface events, key events fire in a predictable sequence. There are three main key events in HTML.

Event Name	Event Handler Name	Defined In
keypress	onkeypress	HTML 4.01
keydown	onkeydown	HTML 4.01
keyup	onkeyup	HTML 4.01

By slightly modifying the code found in the "Handle User Interface Events" section, we can see the predictable order the events fire in.

```
<script type="text/javascript" language="javascript">
 function upd(instr) {
    document.forms[0].statusbox.value += instr + "; ";
}
</script>
<form action="#">
    <input type="text" name="box1"
        onkeypress="upd('keypress')"
        onkeydown="upd('keydown')"
        onkeyup="upd('keyup')"><br><br>
    Event firing order:
    <input type="text" name="statusbox" size="40">
</form>
```

Before

After

FIGURE 9-2   The mouseover and mouseout events power image rollover effects.

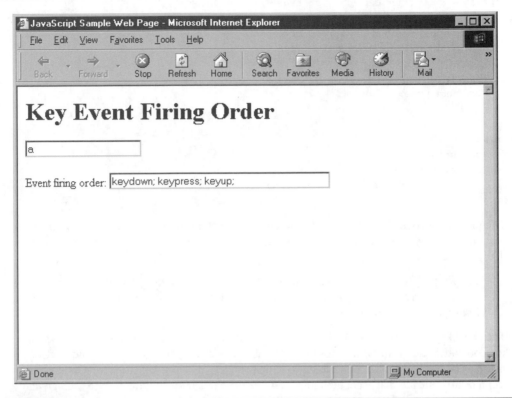

FIGURE 9-3   The order of the key events is keydown, keypress, and keyup.

As you can see from the screenshot in Figure 9-3, the order of events is

1. keydown

2. keypress

3. keyup

The keydown event occurs when almost any keyboard key has been pressed down, including nonalphanumeric keys such as HOME, ESCAPE, INSERT, and DELETE. The keypress event, on the other hand, only fires when certain alphanumeric keys are pressed, including punctuation, SPACEBAR, and ENTER. The keyup event is the complement to keydown, since it fires when almost any key has been released.

Both the keydown and keypress events can be canceled. To cancel an event, you just need to make its event handler return false. Canceling a keydown or keypress event will cause the browser to ignore those keys. For example, if you wanted to restrict the types of characters entered into a form field, you could capture its keydown event and return false anytime a key is not in an acceptable range.

```
<script type="text/javascript" language="javascript">
 function checkkey() {
    var keycode = window.event.keyCode;
    if (keycode < 48 || keycode > 57) {
        return false;
    } else {
        return true;
    }
}
</script>
<form action="#">
    <input type="text" name="box1"
        onkeydown="return checkkey()"><br>
</form>
```

The preceding code shows how the keydown event can be captured. Since we want to be able to cancel the event, we include a return statement inside the event handler along with a call to the checkkey() function.

NOTE *The first 127 characters of the Unicode character set match the corresponding ASCII codes character for character. More information on the Unicode character set can be found at http://www.unicode.org.*

The checkkey() function gets the Unicode character code associated with the key by checking the keyCode attribute of the window.event DOM object. We compare the value of the keyCode against the range of values for numeric keys, which happen to be 48–57. If the keyCode we intercepted falls outside that acceptable range, we return false from the function to indicate that the key is to be ignored. Of course, we return true if the key falls inside the acceptable range.

NOTE *The keyCode property of the window.event object is only available in Netscape version 6 and later and Internet Explorer.*

This results in a text box that only accepts numeric input and ignores all other characters. The following table lists several common characters along with their keyCode values.

keyCode Values	Correspond To
48 through 57	0 through 9
65 through 90	*A* through *Z* (capital letters)
97 through 122	*a* through *z* (lowercase letters)
46	. (period)
44	, (comma)
40 and 41	(and) (parentheses)
36	$ (dollar sign)
35	% (percent sign)
34	" (quotation mark)

Handle HTML Events

In this context, *HTML events* means any events that do not belong in the user interface, mouse, or key event categories. Some HTML events are triggered directly by a user action, while others are fired only as an indirect result of a user action.

The following table lists the HTML events, the event handler name, and the official specification that defined them.

Event Name	Event Handler Name	Fires When (Event)	Defined In
load	onload	Browser finishes loading document	HTML 4.01
unload	onunload	Browser about to unload document	HTML 4.01
submit	onsubmit	Form about to be submitted	HTML 4.01
reset	onreset	Form about to be reset	HTML 4.01
select	onselect	Text box contents selected	HTML 4.01
change	onchange	Form control contents changed	HTML 4.01
abort	onabort	User aborts download of image	DOM Level 2
error	onerror	Error occurs on object loading	DOM Level 2
resize	onresize	Size of object about to change	DOM Level 2
scroll	onscroll	User uses the scroll bar	DOM Level 2

Let's take a quick look at what these events do.

- **load event**   The onload event handler is called when the HTML document finishes loading into the browser window. This event is commonly relied on to do any initialization required in the document. For instance, if form fields need to be preloaded with text, and that was not covered by the HTML code itself, it is best to wait until the document is fully loaded before initializing those fields.

- **unload event**   The unload event fires when a browser is leaving the current document. This happens when the browser window is being closed or the user has moved on to another document. The main purpose of this event is to perform cleanup tasks before the document closes.

CAUTION   *The unload event is commonly used in some of the seedier web locations to provide final pop-up advertising before a user leaves a web site. This is generally considered bad etiquette. The unload event should be avoided unless absolutely necessary.*

- **submit event**   The submit event occurs just before a form is submitted to a web server. It is common to capture this event to perform edit checking before allowing a form submission to continue. Since this event can be canceled, JavaScript can stop the form from being processed if everything is not in order.

- **reset event**   The reset event occurs when the reset button on a form is clicked. The reset button clears a form by resetting all the values back to their defaults.

- **select event**   The select event occurs when the user selects text inside a text box or text area. Text can be selected by holding the left mouse button down while dragging across the text or by holding the SHIFT key down while using the arrow keys to move the cursor across the text.

- **change event**   The change event occurs when a control loses focus (the user tabs out of it) and its value has been altered. This way, in text boxes the change event does not fire for each and every keystroke when a user is entering a value but only when the user leaves the field. This same event fires on radio buttons, check boxes, and select lists in the same manner.

- **abort event**   The abort event occurs when the browser stops trying to load an image on the web page. This can occur when the user hits the browser's Stop button or clicks a link to go to another page. In my experience, this event is rarely used.

- **error event**   The error event occurs when an error happens while the web page is being loaded. This could be an error specific to a particular object (such as a Java applet's failing to load) or a run-time error caused by poorly written JavaScript code. This is another event that is rarely captured in most web pages.

- **resize event**   The resize event fires when an object is being resized—for instance, if a browser window has been resized by the user, or a frame. There may be times when you would like to be able to resize the individual controls inside the window based on the available space, although capturing this event is still rare.

- **scroll event**   For web objects that scroll, such as the browser window or a text area form control, the scroll event is fired anytime the object's scroll bar is changed. This can be done using the mouse to move the scroll bar manually, by using arrow keys, or by other means.

The following code demonstrates how the load event can be captured using the onload event handler. Our web page contains a form, and the onload event handler code populates a list box on that form with some predefined values.

```
<html>
    <head>
        <title>JavaScript Sample Web Page</title>
        <script language="JavaScript" type="text/javascript">
        <!-- // Begin

        function initialize() {
            var lst = document.getElementById("samplelist");
            var opn = new Array(20);
            var temp;
            var counter;

            for (counter = 1; counter <= 10; counter++) {
                opn[counter] = document.createElement("option");
                lst.options.add(opn[counter]);
                temp = counter * 10;
                opn[counter].innerText = temp.toString();
```

```
        }
    }

    // End -->
    </script>
</head>
<body onload="initialize()">
    <h1>Initialize a Form with onload</h1>

    <form action="#">
        <select id="samplelist"></select>
    </form>

</body>
</html>
```

In the preceding HTML code, the browser calls the JavaScript initialize() function as soon as it finishes loading into the browser window. This is done by programming the onload event handler in the <body> tag.

Inside the initialize() function, the program adds 10 items to the empty <select> list box defined in the body of the web page. We can see the results of this function in Figure 9-4.

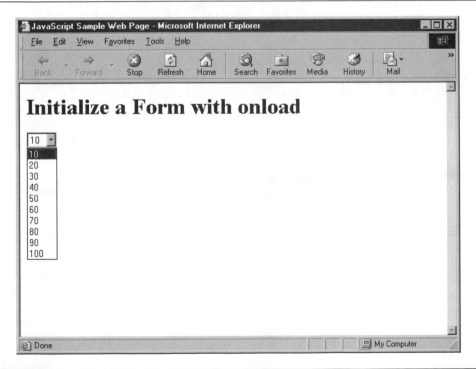

FIGURE 9-4   Ten items have been added to the drop-down list box.

Handle Events Using the Event Property

There are two ways to set the JavaScript event handler for an HTML tag:

- Set the event handler property inside HTML
- Set the event handler property inside JavaScript

We have already seen how to set the event property in HTML:

```
<img src="OriginalImg.gif"
   id="SampleImage"
   alt="Sample image"
   onmouseover="changeimage(1)"
   onmouseout="changeimage(2)" >
```

In this code, we have set the JavaScript functions that will handle the mouseover and mouseout events using the corresponding event handlers.

We could rewrite the code using JavaScript to set the event handlers:

```
<img src="OriginalImg.gif"
   id="SampleImage"
   alt="Sample image">


<script type="text/javascript" language="javascript">
   var img = document.getElementById("SampleImage");
   img.onmouseover = changeimageover;
   img.onmouseout = changeimageout;
   function changeimageover() {
       img.src = "NewImg.gif";
   }
   function changeimageout() {
       img.src = "OriginalImg.gif";
   }
</script>
```

The HTML <img> tag has two attributes called **onmouseover** and **onmouseout** that can be set using HTML and JavaScript. Setting event attributes using JavaScript adds some flexibility, in that the JavaScript function used to handle the event can be changed dynamically, after the page has been displayed. But as you can see from the sample JavaScript code, you cannot pass parameters using this technique, so it is also less flexible in some respects.

How Event Bubbling Works

Let's assume you have a web form that contains a push button. You have created JavaScript onclick event handlers for both the <form> tag and the <input type="button"> tag. When you click the push button control using the mouse, which onclick event handler do you think will be called—the one for the button or the one for the form? In fact, the browser will execute both event handlers.

The onclick event handler for the button will be called first, since it is the innermost element. Next, the onclick event handler for the form will be called. If there are any other onclick event handlers eligible to handle this event (for instance, on the <body> tag), they will be called in turn as well. This process, where an event is first handled by the innermost element, followed by the next innermost element, and so on, is called *event bubbling*.

Trigger Events in JavaScript

There will be times when you would like to have your JavaScript program cause an event to occur. This is called *triggering* the event, and many objects inside the web page provide methods you can call to trigger the event.

There are two ways to cause an event to be triggered in JavaScript:

- Call the method associated with the event
- Call the fireEvent method to fire the event manually

Call the Method Associated with an Event

The first technique is to call the method associated with an event. Most events have a method that will simulate the activity that causes the event to fire. For instance, the HTML <form> object has a method called submit() that will attempt to submit the form, causing the submit event to fire.

We can demonstrate this with the following HTML code. The code shows how to use a hyperlink to simulate a submit button.

```
<script type="text/javascript" language="javascript">
function clickme() {
    document.forms[0].submit();
}
</script>
<form action="http://www.example.com/cgi-bin/entry.pl"
```

9

```
    method="get">
    Please enter your full name: <br>
    <input type="text" name="fullname"><br>
    <a href="javascript:clickme()">Click here to
        <b>submit</b> the form</a>
</form>
```

When the user clicks the hyperlink inside the form, JavaScript calls the clickme() function. The clickme() function calls the submit() method on the form object, which causes the form to submit itself. The submit() method acts exactly as if the user clicked a submit button on the form, causing the submit event to fire.

*In IE, calling the submit() method will cause the form to submit, but will not call any submit event handlers attached to the form. If your <form> has an **onsubmit** attribute, you will have to call those JavaScript functions manually before calling the submit() method.*

Other events also have associated methods that cause the event to occur. For instance, the focus() method will cause a control to gain focus, while the blur() method will cause a control to lose focus. Similarly, there is a click() method that allows HTML objects to simulate being clicked with the mouse.

Use the fireEvent Method

The second technique is to call the fireEvent() method to trigger the event manually. In IE, fireEvent() is a method of most objects in the DOM, and it can be used to trigger events. For example, you can trigger the onclick event of a push button control in the following manner:

```
    var btn1 = document.forms[0].helpButton;
    btn1.fireEvent("onclick");
```

Unfortunately, this method is not very reliable. Although this technique is supposed to be able to trigger events on any object, I have found that it does not work for certain events or objects, such as the onsubmit event on a form object, or the onclick event on a submit button object.

Given that it is not part of the official DOM standard and does not work in any browser other than IE, developers should be very careful when using this technique.

Overcome Browser Incompatibility

Browser events are a weak spot when it comes to cross-browser compatibility. Sure, HTML defined a small number of standard events, and the various DOM specifications (Levels 1 and 2) have taken events a step further. But browser manufacturers have added many more programmable events for JavaScript developers to use, as evidenced by the more than 50 events supported by both Netscape and IE.

Some of the additional events are slight modifications of existing events. For instance, IE provides onbeforeactivate and onbeforeunload event handlers to allow programmers to capture the onactivate and onunload events before they fire. These additional events are cancelable, which means you can stop the activate or unload events from occurring, while the existing onactivate and onunload events fire after the event occurs, and therefore cannot be canceled.

Other event handlers allow programmers access to events that are not specified by the standards:

- onbeforeprint and onafterprint allow access to browser print events.

- ondrag, ondragstart, and ondragend allow access to drag-and-drop events.

- onmousewheel allows access to the mouse wheel movements.

- oncut, oncopy, and onpaste allow access to copy-and-paste events.

The problem is, of course, that these events are generally supported by only one browser and not another. They are also often supported only by newer versions and not by older browsers. Although having access to some of these interesting events might be tempting from a programmer's point of view, you will have to take some of the precautions listed in Chapter 7 and use browser sniffing code before relying on these methods.

Of course, one good thing about these proprietary events is that they will generally not cause the browser to crash if they are coded properly. For instance, the following code tries to capture the onpaste event on a text box control.

```
<form action="#">
    <input type="text" name="myctl" onpaste="pasteevent()">
</form>
```

Of course, since the onpaste event handler is being set inside the HTML element, the browser will simply ignore that code if it does not support the paste event on that control. The only consequence is that the paste event will not be captured in incompatible browsers.

However, if you are absolutely relying on this event handler to perform some critical code, such as submitting the form, you will have to use browser sniffing code to provide alternate code for browsers that do not support it.

In the next chapter, we will discuss browser frames. JavaScript programs face special challenges when dealing with a multiple-frame environment, and we will examine some of the issues and how best to work around them.

9

Chapter 10

Communicate Between Browser Frames

How to...

- ■ Create a frameset
- ■ Define and name frames in a frameset
- ■ Call JavaScript functions from other frames
- ■ Handle synchronization between frames

In web programming, a *frameset* is used to divide a single web page into two or more smaller pieces. Each of these pieces, or *frames*, is a separate HTML web page. Web developers can define several important properties for these frames, including the overall dimensions, location, and visibility of the borders.

In this chapter, we will examine the use of framesets on the Internet today. In particular, we will see some the challenges faced by JavaScript programmers when using frames and look at some suggestions for overcoming them.

Learn the Basics of HTML Frames

Frames are extremely useful for displaying the static sections of a web site, such as menus, banners, and site-navigation tools. Since all the frames in a frameset are independent of each other, they provide several important benefits to web site developers and visitors. When used properly, frames can

- ■ Decrease the length of time required to navigate a web site
- ■ Make a web site easier and more intuitive for visitors to use
- ■ Make a web site easier for developers to maintain

Figure 10-1 shows an example of a web page that uses frames. The figure contains three frames: a top frame with links to other areas of the site, a left frame that contains a menu, and a center frame (known as the *main frame*) that contains the key contents of the web site.

As convenient as frames are for both web programmers and visitors, there are quite a few people who do not like them. A number of problems can be introduced when frames aren't used properly:

- ■ Browser bookmarks can't be properly set.
- ■ Web sites look awful at very small or very large monitor resolutions.
- ■ Search engines can't accurately index the contents of a frameset.

Adding to these problems is the increasing use of and browser support for Cascading Style Sheets (CSS). Style sheets can provide many of the same benefits as frames, including user-friendly navigation and even static banners and menus. Many popular web sites that once contained framesets now use DHTML menus and other more modern dynamic elements.

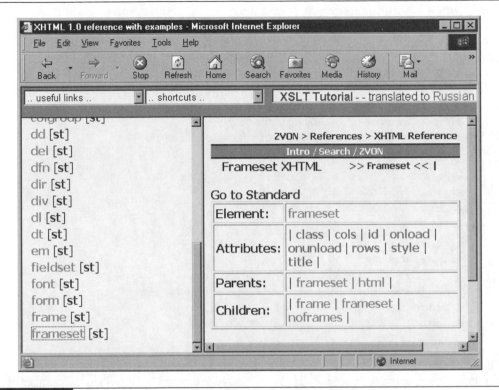

FIGURE 10-1   Example of a web site (ZVON.org) that contains frames

Create a Frameset in HTML

In HTML, frames are created using a combination of two tags: <frameset> and <frame>.
The <frameset> tag is used to define the dimensions and positioning of the frames inside the
frameset. The <frame> tag is used to define the properties of the individual frames, such as
the source HTML document, and the visibility of the frames borders.

The <frameset> element has the following attributes:

- **id**   String that must be unique across the entire web page
- **class**   List of associated CSS classes
- **style**   Inline CSS style commands
- **title**   Advisory title
- **lang**   ISO language code
- **dir**   Direction of text (right to left or left to right)
- **rows**   A comma-separated list of row heights
- **cols**   A comma-separated list of column widths

The <frameset> tag also supports the onload and onunload event handlers.

The web page shown in Figure 10-1 consists of four separate HTML files. One HTML file contains the frameset layout—typically only a <head> section and the <frameset> and <frame> tags. The other three HTML files contain the individual contents of each of the three frames— each HTML file in this example relates to exactly one frame.

Of course, this is not always true. More than one frame can relate to the same HTML file, and some frames can be dynamically generated using JavaScript, and so will have no file associated with them. The only way to tell is by looking at the code.

The following code is a complete example of a frameset document.

```html
<html>
    <head>
        <title>Framesets</title>
    </head>
    <frameset rows="100, *">
        <frame src="banner.html" name="banner">
        <frameset cols="150, *">
            <frame src="menu.html" name="menu">
            <frame src="mainbody.html" name="bodyframe">
        </frameset>
    </frameset>
</html>
```

The preceding HTML code defines a frameset with three frames. It uses a technique discussed later in this chapter, in the section entitled "Create Nested Framesets." We can tell the number of frames in a document by counting the number of <frame> tags.

Notice that the frameset document contains the usual <html>, <head>, and <title> tags, but it does not contain a <body> tag. This is because a frameset document cannot contain a <body> of its own—that is not allowed. We can, however, use all the valid contents of the <head> section, including JavaScript code, meta data, and style sheet definitions using the appropriate HTML tags.

Handle Browsers That Do Not Support Frames

Providing a site using frames may be convenient to many visitors to your site. The vast majority of web surfers today (more than 99 percent, by the latest estimates) have browsers capable of displaying frames. But there is still a small minority of web browsers that do not support them. Many early browsers, such as IE 2 for Windows or Netscape 2 for OS/2, do not. And other web-enabled devices, such as PDAs and mobile phones, often have difficulty rendering frames correctly.

HTML provides the <noframes> tag to allow web developers to display content for users whose browsers do not support the <frameset> tag. Browsers that do support the tag will ignore the contents of any <noframes> sections.

For instance, we can revise the HTML code we saw earlier to include a <noframes> tag;

```html
<html>
    <head>
        <title>Framesets</title>
    </head>
    <frameset rows="100, *">
        <frame src="banner.html" name="banner">
        <frameset cols="150, *">
            <frame src="menu.html" name="menu">
            <frame src="mainbody.html" name="bodyframe">
        </frameset>
        <noframes>
        It appears you are using a browser that does not support
        frames. If you would like to view this site, you will
        need to upgrade your browser. I suggest either Netscape
        or IE.
        </noframes>
    </frameset>
</html>
```

According to the HTML 4.01 specification, the <noframes> tag must be contained inside a <frameset> tag.

Set Frame Size Values with the rows and cols Attributes

As we saw earlier in the chapter, the size and positioning of frames inside the frameset are handled with the HTML <frameset> tag. The two main attributes of the <frameset> tag are **rows** and **cols**. The **rows** attribute is used to define the row heights of the horizontal frames of a frameset, and the **cols** attribute is used to define the column widths of the vertical frames. Each attribute accepts a list of one or more values, separated by commas.

There are three ways to specify a size value in the **rows** and **cols** attributes:

■ Absolute size, in pixels

■ Relative size, as a percentage

■ A combination of absolute and relative sizes, using the asterisk symbol

Both **rows** and **cols** are optional attributes. The default value for each is "100%"; this defines one frame that takes up all the available space in a browser window.

Examples of the three types of size value and what they represent are shown in Table 10-1.

10

Value	Frame Size
250	250 screen or print pixels
25%	25 percent (1/4) of the total available screen or print pixels
*	An equal share of the available space, after the sizes of the other frames have been taken into account
3*	An unequal share of the available space, after the sizes of the other frames have been taken into account

TABLE 10-1   Examples of Size Values and How They Affect the Frameset

> *The special asterisk value is explained in more detail later in this chapter, in the section entitled "Set Frame Size Values Using Both Absolute and Relative Values."*

Both the **rows** and **cols** attributes accept one or more values, separated by commas. Each value you provide creates one frame inside the frameset.

Set Frame Size Values Using Absolute Pixel Values

HTML allows you to define the exact size of a frame, called its *absolute size*. The absolute size of a frame is set by specifying a positive integer value for the **rows** and/or **cols** attributes.

For example, a frameset with two horizontal frames, one 200 pixels high and the other 280 pixels high, would be created with the following HTML code:

```
<frameset rows="200, 280">
    <!-- <frame> tags go here -->
</frameset>
```

> *Even absolute sizes are not always absolute. If the actual size of the browser window does not match the sum of the sizes of the frames, the browser will automatically resize the frames to fit into the available space.*

Of course, you're not restricted to only two frames. You can set any number of frames in a frameset. The following code sample defines four horizontal frames:

```
<frameset rows="200, 200, 400, 400">
    <!-- <frame> tags go here -->
</frameset>
```

> *Although there is theoretically no maximum number of frames you can define in one frameset, for aesthetic reasons you might want to limit the number to three or four.*

Set Frame Size Values Using Relative Values

There is another way to define the size of frames beside specifying their exact pixel measurements. Developers can specify the size as a percentage of total available space. This is called a *relative size,* because the size of the frame is based purely on the size of the browser window, which can vary between one computer and another.

```
<frameset rows="50%, 50%">
    <!-- <frame> tags go here -->
</frameset>
```

The preceding code will create two frames, each taking up 50 percent of the available vertical space in the browser window. In a window that is 480 pixels high, this would create two horizontal frames, each 240 pixels high. If the user's browser window were taller than 480 pixels, the actual height of each frame in pixels would be adjusted to the proper relative size.

Set Frame Size Values Using Both Absolute and Relative Values

The third alternative is to combine the two approaches—to create some frames that are absolute in size and others with sizes relative to the available space. To create this useful effect, specify the absolute number of pixels for the fixed frames and use an asterisk (*) in place of the relative sizes.

For example, if you wanted to make the first frame 200 pixels high and to let the second frame automatically resize to fit the rest of the window, you could use the asterisk (*) when setting the height:

```
<frameset rows="200, *">
    <!-- <frame> tags go here -->
</frameset>
```

This results in a frameset that contains two frames, one 200 pixels high and the other which takes up all of the remaining vertical space.

If you were to use the asterisk more than once, the web browser would automatically resize those frames equally to fill the available space after the fixed-height frames were taken into consideration.

```
<frameset rows="200, 200, *, *">
    <!-- <frame> tags go here -->
</frameset>
```

The <frameset> tag in the preceding code will create a frameset that contains four frames. The first two frames will each be 200 pixels high, for a total of 400 pixels. If the viewable area of the browser window is 480 pixels in height, the last two will split the remaining 80 pixels evenly, so they will each be 40 pixels high. And if the browser window's height expands to 600 pixels, those two frames will have heights of 100 pixels each, since they will evenly split the 200 pixels left after the fixed-height frames are accounted for.

There is also a way to instruct the browser to distribute available space unevenly when using asterisks, by providing an *asterisk multiplier*. An asterisk multiplier is a number that can optionally precede an asterisk, causing it to get more than an equal distribution of space.

For instance, the following frameset defines four frames, two of which are automatically sized by the browser. But the remaining space will be allocated unequally.

```
<frameset rows="200, 200, *, 3*">
    <!-- <frame> tags go here -->
</frameset>
```

Prefixing the asterisk that defines the final frame with the number 3 will cause that frame to have a height that is three times that of the third frame. This means that the fourth frame will get three-quarters of the available space, while the third frame will only get one-quarter of the available space. So, if the browser window had a height of 800 pixels, the browser would split the remaining 400 pixels by assigning 100 pixels to the third frame and 300 pixels to the fourth frame.

Define Horizontal Frames with Rows

So far throughout this chapter, you have seen code like the following, which will create three horizontal frames.

```
<frameset rows="80, 45, *">
    <!-- <frame> tags go here -->
    <frame src="frame1.html">
    <frame src="frame2.html">
    <frame src="frame3.html">
</frameset>
```

These are called horizontal frames because each frame spans the entire width of the browser window. Since we have used the **rows** attribute, horizontal lines separate the three frames in the preceding example. In Figure 10-2 you can see how these horizontal frames would look in a browser.

Define Vertical Frames with Columns

Defining a set of vertical frames is not much different than defining horizontal ones. The **cols** attribute of the <frameset> tag allows you to create frames that have a vertical border instead of a horizontal one.

```
<frameset cols="165, *">
    <!-- <frame> tags go here -->
    <frame src="frame1.html">
    <frame src="frame2.html">
</frameset>
```

The preceding HTML code will create a frameset that contains two frames. The first will have a width of 165 pixels, while the second will take up the remaining horizontal space in the browser window. Figure 10-3 shows how vertical frames look.

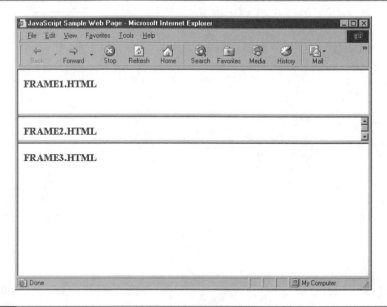

FIGURE 10-2 An example of horizontal frames created using the **rows** attribute

10

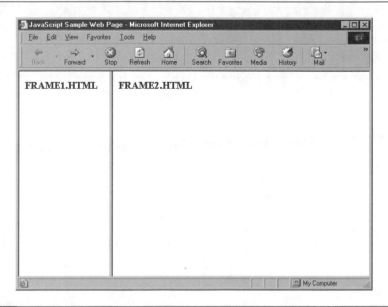

FIGURE 10-3 Creating vertical frames using the **cols** attribute

Define Frames with Rows and Columns

Framesets need not be only horizontal or only vertical. Web developers can create framesets that contain both rows and columns, like a grid. This is done by specifying values for both the **rows** and **cols** attributes.

For instance, to create a frameset that has three rows and two columns, you would use the following HTML code:

```
<frameset rows="50, 100, *" cols="50%, 50%">
    <!-- <frame> tags go here -->
    <frame src="frame1.html">
    <frame src="frame2.html">
    <frame src="frame3.html">
    <frame src="frame4.html">
    <frame src="frame5.html">
    <frame src="frame6.html">
</frameset>
```

The preceding code creates a frameset that contains six frames, arranged into three rows and two columns. Notice that the number of rows and columns does not have to be equal. Figure 10-4 shows how this complex frameset will look in a browser.

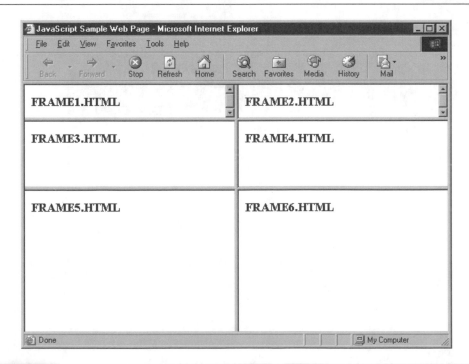

FIGURE 10-4   A frameset with both rows and columns

Create Nested Framesets

Creating complex framesets using both the **rows** and **cols** attributes has its limitations. Specifically, the rows and columns are created in a grid pattern—all the columns in one row will be the same width, and all the rows will be the same height, as shown in Figure 10-4. It will always be a perfectly aligned grid, although the size of the cells in the grid can differ.

What could you do if you wanted to create unequal rows and columns? How could you create a row that has only one column, but define several columns for the next row? The answer is nested framesets.

A *nested frameset* is achieved by placing one or more framesets inside another, thus subdividing a single frame into smaller pieces. All nested framesets must begin with a single, outer frameset.

```
<frameset rows="80, *">
    <!-- <frame> tags go here -->
    <frame src="frame1.html">
    <frame src="frame2.html">
</frameset>
```

For instance, the preceding HTML code creates a simple frameset that contains two horizontal frames.

Now let's say we want to further subdivide the second frame into two columns. This can be done with a second frameset:

```
<frameset rows="80, *">
    <!-- <frame> tags go here -->
    <frame src="frame1.html">
    <frameset cols="150, *">
        <frame src="frame2.html">
        <frame src="frame3.html">
    </frameset>
</frameset>
```

I have replaced the second frame in the original code with a second frameset. This nested frameset divides the second frame into two columns. You can see the effect of this type of frameset in Figure 10-5.

Define and Name Frames in a Frameset

Now that you understand how simple and complex framesets are created using the <frameset> tag, we should take a brief look at how the frames themselves are defined. Individual frames are defined using the <frame> tag. The <frame> tag has the following attributes:

- ■ **id**   Documentwide unique ID
- ■ **class**   List of associated CSS classes
- ■ **style**   Inline CSS style commands

- ■ **title**   Advisory title
- ■ **longdesc**   Link to a longer description of the frame
- ■ **name**   Internal name of the frame
- ■ **src**   URI to the HTML document
- ■ **frameborder**   Visibility of the frame borders
- ■ **marginwidth**   Amount of space, in pixels, between the vertical border (or window frame) and the HTML contents
- ■ **marginheight**   Amount of space, in pixels, between the horizontal border (or window frame) and the HTML contents
- ■ **noresize**   Controls whether the user can resize the frame
- ■ **scrolling**   Visibility of the scroll bar

All of the preceding attributes are optional. However, the <frame> tag is rarely defined without an explicit **src** attribute. This is the attribute that allows you to specify the source HTML file for the frame.

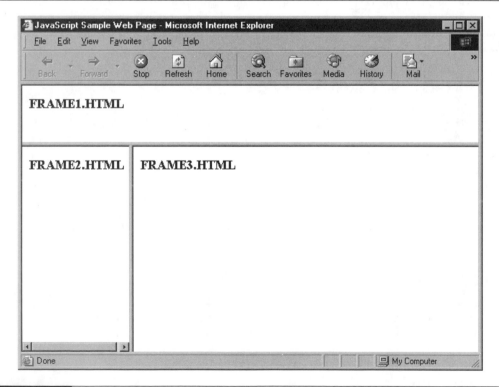

FIGURE 10-5   Using a nested frameset to subdivide frames into unequal pieces

When using JavaScript in conjunction with frames, it is often handy to use the **name** attribute to assign a unique name to the frame.

```
<frame src="/dir/subdir/myframe.html" name="frame1">
```

The frame's source can be any valid URI—it does not even have to exist on the same web server as the other frames.

```
<frame src="http://www.cnn.com/" name="frame1">
```

Using the contents of another web site inside your own site is known as web site framing, *and that practice has some potential legal ramifications involving trademark and copyright law. There is a very good article on the topic at http://www.gigalaw.com/ articles/2000-all/kubiszyn-2000-04-all.html that you should read if you are interested in framing another web site without the owner's permission.*

The default frame is created with resizable borders. You can easily create borders that cannot be resized by specifying the **noresize** attribute.

```
<frame src="myframe.html" name="frame1" noresize>
```

The **noresize** attribute does not need to have a value assigned to it—its presence inside a <frame> tag signifies a fixed border.

10

NOTE *In XHTML, the XML-compliant version of HTML, every attribute must be assigned a value. In XHTML, you would assign **noresize** the value of its own name, such as noresize="noresize".*

By default, frames have visible borders separating one frame from the next. However, this is not always desirable, since these borders do not always match the style of a site. Fortunately, it is fairly easy to make the borders invisible, making the individual frames less noticeable.

```
<frame src="myframe.html" name="frame1" noresize
    frameborder="0">
```

Of course, you will need to add this **frameborder** attribute to each of the frame tags in a frameset to remove all borders.

Call JavaScript Functions from Other Frames

As discussed in the first section of this chapter, a web page made up of three frames actually consists of four separate HTML files—one file for each of the frames and one master file for the frameset.

These frames are independent of each other, but they are not ignorant of each other. It is possible for each frame to access the contents of any other frame, including any JavaScript variables and functions defined there.

Access Another Frame Using JavaScript

As discussed in Chapter 8, we can use the following JavaScript code to access the contents of a form:

```
var myform = document.forms[0];
var fullname = myform.fullname.value;
```

This code will create a variable named myform, which directly refers to the first form on a web page. It will then use the myform variable to access a control named fullname and its contents.

But how would we access the contents of that form if it were in another frame? Let's assume for a minute that we have a frameset that is defined with the following HTML code.

```
<html>
    <head>
        <title>Framesets</title>
    </head>
    <frameset rows="100, *">
        <frame src="banner.html" name="banner">
        <frameset cols="150, *">
            <frame src="menu.html" name="menu">
            <frame src="mainbody.html" name="bodyframe">
        </frameset>
    </frameset>
</html>
```

If we were in the second frame of that frameset (menu), how would we access the contents of a form contained in the third frame (bodyframe)?

We do this by accessing the window object for the frameset. JavaScript provides several types of window objects for use in programs. The various JavaScript window objects, and their descriptions, are listed in Table 10-2.

> **NOTE** *The window object and the Document Object Model in general are discussed in greater detail in Chapter 11.*

Object Name	Description
window	The current frame or window
top	The topmost window
parent	The frameset that contains the current frame (not always the topmost window)
self	The current frame or window; same as the window object

TABLE 10-2   The JavaScript Window Objects

Each of the window objects listed in Table 10-2 contains an array named frames. When a window object refers to an entire frameset, that object's frames array contains one element for each of the frames contained in the document. When a window object refers to a single frame, this array will normally be empty. Of course, if the individual frames are also framesets, the frames array will not be empty.

To access the contents of the bodyframe frame from JavaScript code inside the menu frame, we start with the topmost window, using the top object. We then access the third element (index 2, since arrays start at index 0) in that array.

```
var bodyframe = top.frames[2];
```

The bodyframe variable represents a reference to the third frame defined in our frameset. We can then access the document contained by that window using the document object from that frame.

```
var bodyframe = top.frames[2];
var bodydocument = bodyframe.document;
```

Finally, we can access the form, and the elements on that form, in the usual manner from the document object represented by bodydocument.

```
var bodyframe = top.frames[2];
var bodydocument = bodyframe.document;
var myform = bodydocument.forms[0];
var fullname = myform.fullname.value;
```

This code is broken into four lines for manageability and easy reading. If a program needed to reference more than a few elements on that form, or other objects on the bodyframe frame, having a local variable that refers to that frame would be handy. To save some unnecessary keystrokes, the preceding code can be written all on one line, like this.

```
var fullname = top.frames[2].document.forms[0].fullname.value;
```

This code is harder for the average programmer to read, however, and is slightly more confusing. Code that is difficult to understand can often be a source of errors.

Instead of using the frames array, a frame can also be accessed by name.

```
var fullname = top.bodyframe.document.forms[0].fullname.value;
```

Accessing the frame by name makes the code a bit easier to read and allows frames to be resorted without large code changes.

Call a JavaScript Function Located in Another Frame

You've already seen how the contents of a frame (its forms and other HTML components) can be accessed from external frames, so it should be no surprise that JavaScript variables and functions can be accessed externally as well.

To demonstrate, let's assume we have a JavaScript function named sayhello() defined in the menu frame.

```
function sayhello() {
    // This function says "hello" to the user
    alert("Hello!");
}
```

We could define a button in the bodyframe frame that will call the sayhello() function from the menu frame when clicked.

```
<form action="#">
    <input type="button" value="Say Hello"
        onclick="top.menu.sayhello()">
</form>
```

Figure 10-6 shows the result of clicking the Say Hello button in the browser window.

As long as JavaScript variables are defined outside of any function, they too can be accessed from another frame.

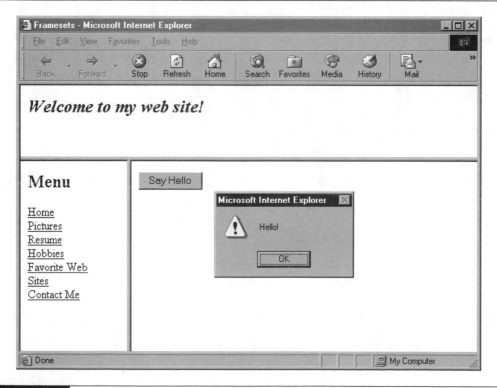

FIGURE 10-6 Calling a JavaScript function defined in another frame

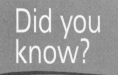

Cross-Frame Scripting Can Be Risky

Cross-frame scripting occurs when a frame that originates in one domain (like www.myserver.com) attempts to access a frame that originates in a different domain (like www.example.com) using JavaScript.

The problem with cross-frame scripting is that a web site could define a frame that points to a secure web site, such as Microsoft's Hotmail. The originating web site could then access any cookies or other sensitive user information from the frame, allowing them to use that information in a malicious manner. Because this a security risk, all IE browsers from version 4 on do not allow cross-frame scripting.

Handle Synchronization Between Frames

In the last section, we saw some JavaScript code that relied on the existence of a JavaScript function in another frame.

```
<form action="#">
    <input type="button" value="Say Hello"
        onclick="top.menu.sayhello()">
</form>
```

But what happens if the user clicks the button before the menu frame has even finished loading? Most web browsers load frames in no particular order, and it is quite possible (actually, quite probable) that some frames will load slower than others. In this case, a JavaScript error will occur, since the sayhello() function could not be found.

This problem can be described as one of synchronization. When dealing with frames that communicate with each other, we need a way to determine if all the frames are fully loaded before proceeding. There are several techniques a JavaScript programmer can employ to handle synchronization between frames.

The first technique is to create a cascading effect between the frames, where each frame is responsible for loading the frames that depend on it. Using this method, we would have the menu frame load the contents of the bodyframe frame.

```
top.bodyframe.document.location = "mainbody.html";
```

We could then be guaranteed that the menu frame has already loaded in the browser window by the time the bodyframe document has finished loading as well.

The second technique is to create one or more Boolean JavaScript variables in the frameset document. Each of the frames can set its respective Boolean variable to true when

10

it has completely loaded. For example, we can modify our frameset document to the following HTML and JavaScript code:

```html
<html>
    <head>
        <title>Framesets</title>
        <script type="text/javascript" language="JavaScript">
        var banner_loaded = false;
        var menu_loaded = false;
        var body_loaded = false;
        </script>
    </head>
    <frameset rows="100, *">
        <frame src="banner.html" name="banner">
        <frameset cols="150, *">
            <frame src="menu.html" name="menu">
            <frame src="mainbody.html" name="bodyframe">
        </frameset>
    </frameset>
</html>
```

We can then add the following JavaScript code to the end of the menu frame in order to set the appropriate variable to true.

```html
<script type="text/javascript" language="JavaScript">
    var menu_loaded = true;
</script>
```

Inside the code for the bodyframe, we should move the call to the sayhello() function into a separate function, and add an **if** statement around it for safety.

```html
<script type="text/javascript" language="JavaScript">
    function callhello() {
        // Check the variable named menu_loaded first
        if (top.menu_loaded == true) {
            top.menu.sayhello();
        }
    }
</script>
<form action="#">
    <input type="button" value="Say Hello" onclick="callhello()">
</form>
```

In this example, the Say Hello button will not work until the menu frame has completely loaded.

Lastly, we could use a technique similar to the DOM-based browser sniffing code from Chapter 7. We could simply test for the existence of the frame and the sayhello() function before accessing them.

```
<script type="text/javascript" language="JavaScript">
    function callhello() {
        // Check if the frame and function exist first
        if (top.menu) {
            if (top.menu.sayhello) {
                top.menu.sayhello();
            }
        }
    }
</script>
<form action="#">
    <input type="button" value="Say Hello" onclick="callhello()">
</form>
```

This same technique can be used to test for the existence of JavaScript variables or web form controls.

In the next chapter, we will investigate the various objects that make up the DOM. It is through the methods and properties of these objects that we are able to interact with the web browser.

10

Chapter 11

Interact with the Web Browser

How to...

- ■ Manipulate the contents of a web page
- ■ Examine the entire browser window
- ■ Retrieve properties from the web browser software
- ■ Examine the operating system's display settings
- ■ Access the web browser history list
- ■ Send the browser to a new location

Although JavaScript has a powerful yet flexible core language syntax, it doesn't have any built-in functions for reading data from file, database, or keyboard input, nor for writing data to a screen or printer. In each of its environments, JavaScript relies on an external object model to provide it basic input-output functionality.

Table 11-1 lists some of the environments that provide support for JavaScript (or some version of it), and the object model that provides additional functionality beyond the core JavaScript functions.

The object model used by web browsers is called the Document Object Model, or DOM for short. The DOM is a standard API (application programming interface) to the structure of documents. It allows JavaScript developers easy access to the document contents (such as forms, text, and style) as well as to browser-specific features (such as menus, scroll bars, and events). The DOM has evolved since the first browser was introduced many years ago, but the basic objects in a browser have not changed.

The DOM specification is managed by the W3C, along with the HTML and XML specifications. Recent releases of the DOM standard now include methods and properties related to browser events, manipulation of style sheets, document validation, and XPath expressions.

Many of the extensions to the DOM standard will not be covered in this chapter, as they either do not relate directly to HTML or are too advanced for our purposes. If you are interested in learning more about the new DOM, I encourage you to check out the specifications and other documents located on the W3C DOM web site: http://www.w3.org/DOM.

JavaScript Environment	Object Model
Web browsers	DOM
.NET (JScript)	.NET Framework
ASP (JScript)	ASP object model
Server-side JavaScript	Server-side extensions

TABLE 11-1   JavaScript Environments and Their Respective Object Models

Learn the Basics of the Document Object Model

To understand the DOM, you must first understand how the specification has evolved. There were six basic objects in the original DOM, sometimes called *DOM Level 0*:

- document
- window
- history
- location
- screen
- navigator

DOM 0 defines some other objects as well, such as forms, frames, and images. But to get to these objects, programs have to go through the top-level objects listed here. Objects could not be dynamically created, modified, or removed, since DOM 0 was static and the document could not be altered once rendered by the browser.

Figure 11-1 is a good representation of the objects in the original DOM and how they related to each other.

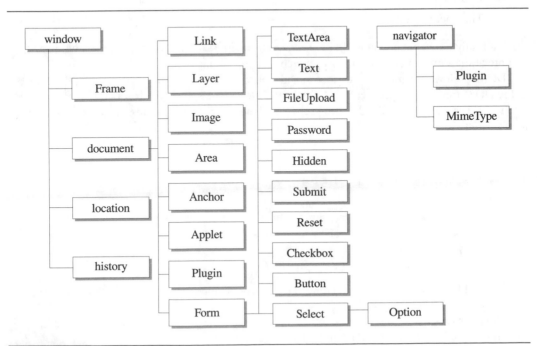

FIGURE 11-1   The original Netscape DOM

When the W3C adopted the DOM as a new web standard in 1998, it was called *DOM Level 1,* which is sometimes abbreviated to *DOM 1*. DOM 1 was the first attempt to adapt the object model for the emerging XML standard, which was set to revolutionize structured document formatting.

NOTE   *Unlike subsequent versions of the DOM, DOM Level 0 was never an official standard.*

The DOM standard treats HTML (and XML) documents as hierarchies of data (called *nodes*). In DOM, the following parts of the document are all considered nodes:

- Markup tags (elements)
- Attributes
- Text
- XML character data (CDATA) sections
- Entity references
- Entities
- Processing instructions
- Comments
- The document itself

Nodes that are contained in other nodes are considered children of those nodes, while nodes that are at the same level as other nodes are considered siblings.

DOM 1 allows programmers to access, add, delete, move, or modify almost any of the objects in the DOM tree. More specifically, DOM 1 separates a core set of API from an HTML-specific set. The HTML-specific API adds browser-related methods and properties to the objects defined in the core set.

For example, let's consider the following simple HTML code:

```
<html>
    <head><title>My title</title></head>
    <body>
        This is <b>a test</b> of the <i>emergency broadcast system</i>.
        I repeat, this is only a test.
    </body>
</html>
```

Figure 11-2 shows how the preceding HTML code would look in a DOM 1 hierarchy. This hierarchy is also called the *DOM tree*.

The next version of the DOM, known as *Level 2*, became an official W3C standard in November 2000. The core standard did not change much from the previous release, as DOM 2 only added a few new properties and methods to the interfaces already defined in DOM 1. Its

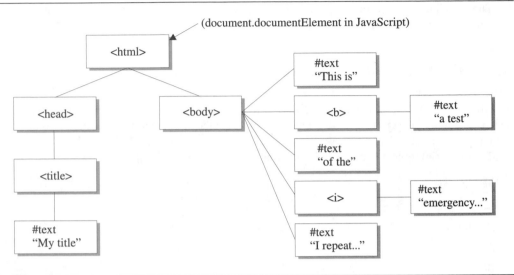

FIGURE 11-2 How a simple HTML document would look in a DOM tree

main purpose was to add support for views, events, and style sheets to the DOM API. It also defined a specification for DOM traversal, the ability to move forward and backward through a DOM hierarchy.

DOM Level 3 was still in the W3C Working Draft stage at the time this book was published. DOM 3 proposes to add two new interfaces to the core specification and will also add support for XPath.

11

The Uses of XPath

XPath is a simple yet powerful language for addressing parts of an XML document. For instance, you would use the following XPath expression to access the first <form> element on an XHTML web page.

/html/body//form[1]

This expression will match the first <form> element that is a descendant (but not necessarily a direct child) of a <body> element, which is itself the direct child of the root <html> element.

The remainder of this chapter focuses on JavaScript programming for DOM 1, since the vast majority of browsers in use today support that version.

Manipulate the Contents of a Web Page

Perhaps the most useful of all the DOM objects is the document object. The document object provides access to the entire contents of a web page, as it is the root of all other objects in the HTML hierarchy. In Figure 11-2, the document object stands in place of the <html> element, at the top of the tree.

The document object contains the following five arrays in JavaScript:

- images
- applets
- links
- forms
- anchors

Each of the document object's arrays contains an enumerated list of the related elements on a web page. The images array contains a list of images, the applets array contains a list of Java applets, and so on. We have already seen how the forms array is a convenient way of accessing all the HTML <form> elements on a web page.

In addition to the five arrays, the document object also provides JavaScript read and write access to any cookies associated with a web site (through the document.cookie property). A *cookie* is a piece of text a browser will store locally on behalf of a web site. Cookies are frequently used to store user ID and session information, so that a web site will be able to recognize known users when they return.

The document object also contains the following six methods:

- open()
- close()
- write()
- writeln()
- getElementById()
- getElementsByName()

The open(), close(), write(), and writeln() methods are used for printing raw HTML text to a web page. I have often used document.write() in this book's sample code as a simple way of outputting results.

The getElementById() and getElementsByName() methods allow us to quickly search a DOM for specific elements. This is a better approach than manually searching up and down the DOM tree for what we need, since these functions are optimized to return quickly.

Should we wish to navigate the contents of the HTML document without the convenience of the various arrays (like the forms array) or the built-in search functionality (like getElementById), we can access the body property of the document object directly. The body property allows us to access all the HTML objects below the document object, starting from the HTML <body> element. This property is not typically used in JavaScript programming, as searching the DOM using the document arrays or using the built-in search functions is generally quicker and easier.

Dynamically Modify the Contents of a Web Page

One of the more interesting ways to use JavaScript and the DOM together is for creating web pages that can change themselves according to the user's behavior. This can be done without having to get the web server itself involved.

Let's start by looking at a very basic web page.

```html
<html>
    <head><title>Basic Web Page</title></head>
    <body>

        <h2>The time now is: <span id="time">00:00:00</span></h2>

    </body>
</html>
```

As you can see in Figure 11-3, this HTML code creates a static web page. No matter what time of day, it will always report the time as 00:00:00 (midnight).

11

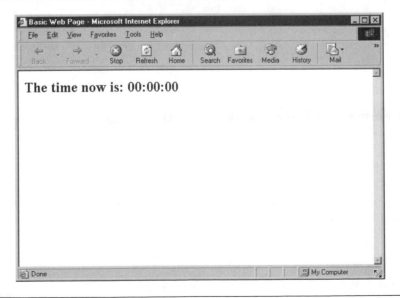

FIGURE 11-3   A simple web page, before adding JavaScript

But what if we wanted to add a small JavaScript script to the page that will constantly keep the time updated to the correct time? We can use the DOM document object to modify the contents of the web page.

```
<script language="JavaScript" type="text/javascript">
    function update_time() {
        // The current date and time
        var rightnow = new Date();

        // Capture the hours as a string, "00" thru "23"
        var hours = rightnow.getHours();
        if (hours < 10)
            var hourstring = "0" + hours.toString();
        else
            var hourstring = hours.toString();

        // Capture the minutes as a string, "00" thru "59"
        var minutes = rightnow.getMinutes();
        if (minutes < 10)
            var minutestring = "0" + minutes.toString();
        else
            var minutestring = minutes.toString();

        // Capture the seconds as a string, "00" thru "59"
        var seconds = rightnow.getSeconds();
        if (seconds < 10)
            var secondstring = "0" + seconds.toString();
        else
            var secondstring = seconds.toString();

        // Put it all together, "00:00:00"
        var timestring = hourstring + ":" +
                         minutestring + ":" +
                         secondstring;

        // Manipulate the DOM, display it to the screen!
        var timeplace = document.getElementById("time");
        timeplace.childNodes[0].nodeValue = timestring;
    }
</script>
```

By calling the update_time() function when the document first loads, we can get the browser to update the string "00:00:00" with the current time.

```
<body onload="update_time()">
```

The screenshot in Figure 11-4 shows how the browser has replaced the original HTML string with the correct time.

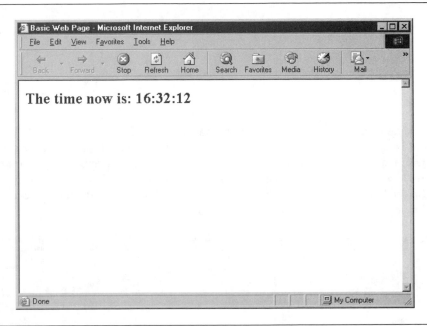

Using the document object to update the web page with the correct time

Using browser timers, we can even get our web page to update with the correct time every second. All we need to do is add the following code to the end of our update_time() function.

```
setTimeout('update_time()', 1000);
```

The setTimeout() function tells JavaScript that we would like to execute certain JavaScript code at a certain time in the future. In the preceding code, we are saying that we would like to call the function update_time() 1,000 milliseconds (1 second) from now. This will cause the update_time() function to be called once per second until the user leaves the web page.

Change the Items in a Drop-Down List Box

Not only can developers modify the contents of an HTML web page, even the items in a drop-down list box can change after the web page has loaded.

```
How many calories does a cheeseburger contain?<br>
<select id="listbox1">
<option>-- Please Select One --</option>
</select>

<script language="JavaScript" type="text/javascript">
```

```
var counter;
var listbox = document.getElementById("listbox1");
for (counter = 100; counter < 500; counter += 50) {
    listbox.options[listbox.length] =
        new Option(counter + " - " + (counter+49));
}
</script>
```

The preceding code creates an HTML drop-down list box with one item in it—"Please Select One." Using JavaScript, it then adds eight more items to the list. Our JavaScript code starts by getting a reference to the list box and storing it in the variable named listbox. Using a **for** loop, we then create several new Option objects and add them to the end of the options array.

You can see how the browser displays our dynamic list box here. (I do not, however, care to know how many calories a cheeseburger actually does contain.)

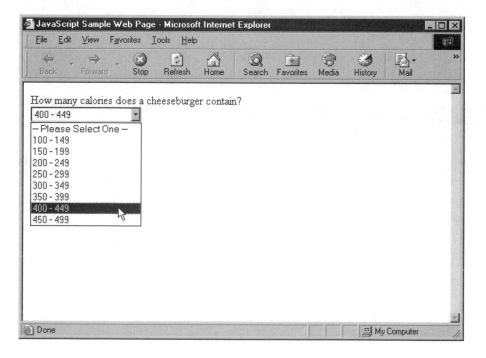

Examine the Entire Browser Window

The window object is not technically an official DOM Level 1 object. It provides access to other frames or open browser windows.

In the last chapter, we discovered that there are four types of window objects in JavaScript. Table 11-2 summarizes those objects.

Object Name	Description
window	Current frame or window
top	Topmost window
parent	Frameset that contains the current frame (not always the topmost window)
self	Current frame or window; same as the window object

TABLE 11-2   JavaScript Window Objects

The four window objects may (or may not) point to different windows in the browser. Typically, for a web page that does not contain framesets, all four objects refer to the same underlying window.

The window object provides access to three underlying DOM objects:

- document
- history
- location

We discussed document in the last section, and we will have a chance to look at history and location in the sections that follow this one.

The window object also provides access to the browser status bar, using the status property. The status bar is the thin area below the main browser window that usually reports on the progress of a page load and shows the URL of a hypertext link when the mouse pointer moves over it. The following JavaScript code modifies the browser status bar to a custom value:

```
window.status = "Welcome to my web site!";
```

The following screenshot shows how this affects the status bar after our web page has loaded.

In the last chapter you also learned that the window object contains an array named frames that enumerates all the frames in a frameset. It is through the frames array that we can access the HTML and JavaScript code located in another frame.

The window object also provides several methods that can be used to communicate with the user or to open and close new browser windows. Table 11-3 lists some of the more interesting window methods.

11

Method	Description
alert()	Creates an alert dialog box
blur()	Causes the window to lose focus
close()	Attempts to close the browser window
focus()	Causes the window to gain focus
moveBy(), moveTo()	Repositions the browser window
navigate()	Loads a specific URL into the browser
open()	Opens a new browser window
print()	Attempts to print the browser contents to a printer
resizeBy(), resizeTo()	Resizes the browser window
scroll(), scrollBy(), scrollTo()	Causes the window to scroll
setTimeout(), clearTimeout()	Causes JavaScript code to be executed after a specified delay

TABLE 11-3   Useful window Methods

One interesting window method is open(). This method is used to create a new browser window when you do not wish to interrupt the current web page. Sadly, this is the technique used for most pop-up web advertisements. It is still quite useful, however, when you want to direct the user at their request to some online help, such as a user manual or online glossary.

```
window.open("userhelp.htm", "_blank",
    "height=300,width=200,toolbar=no," +
    "status=no,menubar=no,location=no");
```

The preceding code will open a new browser window and direct it to the HTML file userhelp.htm. The code specifies a specific height and width for the window (300 by 200) and removes all toolbars, menu bars, and the status bar, leaving a sparse window.

Figure 11-5 shows how this new HTML window will look in a typical web browser.

Retrieve Properties of the Web Browser Software

The programmers at Netscape probably still get some joy over the fact that the standard object for retrieving browser information is called navigator, named after what used to be the most widely used browser in the early days of the Web. You might recall that we talked about some of the properties of the navigator object in Chapter 7, when it was used to retrieve the name and version information from the user's browser.

The navigator object contains one array, called plugins. This array contains a list of browser plug-ins (although the contents of the list vary by browser maker). A browser *plug-in* is an application that runs inside the browser, usually to provide support for embedded multimedia. Shockwave Flash and RealNetworks RealPlayer are two popular plug-ins.

In Netscape and Mozilla web browsers, the plugins array can be used to determine which browser plug-ins have been installed on the client PC. In Internet Explorer, the only plug-ins listed in the plugins array are the ones currently in use on the web page.

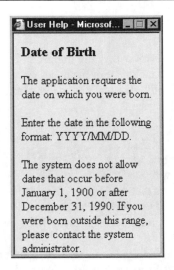

Date of Birth

The application requires the date on which you were born.

Enter the date in the following format: YYYY/MM/DD.

The system does not allow dates that occur before January 1, 1900 or after December 31, 1990. If you were born outside this range, please contact the system administrator.

FIGURE 11-5   A pop-up window can be used to provide quick online help.

For example, the following code, for Netscape web browsers, checks to see if the Macromedia Flash plug-in is installed on the user's computer.

```
var flashinstalled = false;
for (var i=0; i < navigator.plugins.length; i++) {
    if (navigator.plugins[i].name == "Shockwave Flash") {
        flashinstalled = true;
        break;
    }
}

if (flashinstalled) {
    document.write ("I see you have Macromedia Flash installed!");
} else {
    document.write ("If you want to see the multimedia installed ");
    document.write ("on this web site, you will need to install ");
    document.write ("Macromedia Flash.");
}
```

The navigator object also supports several properties, such as the following.

- appCodeName
- appName
- appVersion

11

- userAgent
- userLanguage

These properties provide JavaScript with some important information about the exact browser type running on the client machine. For instance, you may wish to provide content formatted in a simpler manner for older browsers (version 4) and content that relies on style sheets for visitors using a newer browser.

Examine the Operating System's Display Settings

Web programmers often develop web pages with a specific screen size in mind. For instance, some sites are developed for screens that are 800 pixels wide by 600 pixels high (often called *800 by 600 resolution*). If a user's resolution is smaller, say 640 by 480, they will be unable to see parts of the page. If a user's resolution is bigger, say 1024 by 768, the web page will have a lot of blank space.

The best-designed sites are frequently developed to expand or contract based on available space. We have seen this with frames using relative sizing, and it can also be done with HTML tables. Both these solutions allow the browser to automatically resize components based on the amount of available screen space. (You may sometimes hear available screen space referred to as *real estate*.)

But when dealing with Dynamic HTML, where elements are frequently placed in specific X and Y coordinates on the screen, it is helpful to have some information about the screen resolution. The DOM provides the screen object to give JavaScript a little more information about the technical properties of the user's display.

The screen object was not part of the original release of JavaScript. It was added in version 4 of the IE and Netscape browsers. The following table lists some of the properties of this object.

Property Name	Purpose
availHeight	Returns the height of the working area of the system screen, excluding the Windows taskbar
availWidth	Returns the width of the working area of the system screen, excluding the Windows taskbar
colorDepth	Returns the number of bits per pixel used for colors
height	Returns the vertical resolution of the screen
width	Returns the horizontal resolution of the screen

For example, the following JavaScript code will allow you to resize and then center the browser window on the user's monitor.

```
var newTopLeftX = (screen.availWidth - 640) / 2.0;
var newTopLeftY = (screen.availHeight - 480) / 2.0;
window.resizeTo (640, 480);
window.moveTo (newTopLeftX, newTopLeftY);
```

The code uses the window.resize() function to resize the browser to 640 pixels wide by 480 pixels tall. It then uses a common centering technique to place the window perfectly in the center of the screen, regardless of the resolution setting of the user's monitor.

Access the Web Browser History List

JavaScript has limited access to the browser history list through the history object. The browser history list is an ordered list of web pages you recently visited, and it is stored internally by your web browser. You access the browser history list every time you use the back and forward buttons of your web browser.

Through the history object, JavaScript has the ability to send a browser back to the previous web page—or back by an arbitrary number of web pages. For example, the following JavaScript code will send the browser to the web page most recently visited before the current one.

```
history.back();
```

Programmers can also tell the browser to go back by any number of pages, by specifying an integer to the history object's go() method. The following code will send the browser back five pages.

```
history.go(-5);
```

The history object only has one property, length. The length property will return the number of items in the history list.

The history object has three methods.

Method Name	Purpose
back()	Go back one item in the history list; simulates the Back browser button.
forward()	Go forward one item in the history list; simulates the Forward browser button.
go()	Go back or forward the specified number of items in the history list; a positive number goes forward and a negative one goes back.

The history object is often used as an easy way to direct the user back to the previous page.

```
<html>
    <head><tile>User Login Script</title></head>
    <body>

    <h1>Error: Unable to Log In</h1>

    I'm sorry, the password you supplied was incorrect.
    Please use the Back button on your browser to try again,
    or <a href="javascript:history.back()">click here</a> to
```

```
be automatically sent there.

    </body>
</html>
```

 For security reasons, the history object does not provide JavaScript access to the names or URLs of the web pages you have visited.

Send the Browser to a New Location

The location object gives JavaScript access to the browser address bar. Specifically, programmers can determine the URL of the current page, reload the current page, or send the browser to a new URL.

The location object has eight properties.

Property Name	Purpose
href	Gets or sets the entire URL as a string
hash	Gets or sets the portion of the URL after the hash sign (#)
host	Gets or sets the hostname and port number portion of the URL
hostname	Gets or sets the hostname portion of the URL
pathname	Gets or sets the filename or path of the web page
port	Gets or sets the port number portion of the URL
protocol	Gets or sets the web protocol name of the URL (e.g., HTTP)
search	Gets or sets the portion of the URL after the question mark (?)

The location object also has three methods.

Method Name	Purpose
assign	Loads a new web page
reload	Reloads the existing web page
replace	Replaces the existing web page by loading a new web page

The location object is commonly used to redirect the browser to a new web page.

```
location.href = "http://www.example.com/another/page.html";
```

But it can also be used just to reload the current page, similar to a browser refresh action.

```
location.reload();
```

In the next chapter, we will examine how to perform some simple animation using JavaScript, CSS, and Dynamic HTML. Using a technique known as *absolute positioning*, we will be able to place text and images anywhere we wish inside a web page.

Chapter 12

Perform Simple Animation

How to...

- ▪ Format a web page using style sheets
- ▪ Control text and image positioning
- ▪ Modify styles using JavaScript
- ▪ Perform basic animation using JavaScript

In Chapter 11, you saw how the browser DOM can be manipulated using JavaScript to modify the HTML in a web page after it has already been loaded into the browser. This technique is often used for allowing JavaScript to respond to user events or input without having to go back to the web server to re-create the page.

As you'll see in this chapter, Cascading Style Sheets (CSS) allow developers to specify the exact layout and positioning of elements on the web page. Style sheets can be dynamically modified in JavaScript as well, allowing elements to be given a different appearance or even moved to a different position on the screen.

Animation is often nothing more than the repeated manipulation of the DOM and/or style sheets using JavaScript. An animated butterfly can appear to flutter across the screen with nothing more than the repeated swapping of a small number of images combined with the slow repositioning of those images across the page. In this chapter, we will examine how style sheets can be dynamically modified using JavaScript and how that technique can be used to create some simple animation effects.

Learn the Basics of Cascading Style Sheets

We have touched briefly on the topic of style sheets before, but in this section we will examine it in more detail to gain a better understanding of what style sheets can do for web developers and how JavaScript can be used to dynamically affect style.

The *style* of a web page is the manner in which the contents of the web page, such as the text and graphics, are formatted and arranged. Style encompasses everything from how fonts and colors are used to the sizes and positioning of objects inside the browser window.

When the Web was first developed in 1991, very little consideration was given to style—the emphasis was on content. The Web was used for the presentation and linking of related text documents. In fact, one of the overriding philosophies of its design was that web clients (generally browsers) should be responsible for rendering the web page in the manner they best saw fit.

For instance, the <h1> tag simply defined a first level heading, and it was up to the browser to define the exact font type and size used for displaying the heading text. The content of <h1> tags could theoretically look completely different depending on the brand of browser you were using or the operating system you were running.

Of course, many developers needed more precise methods to format the contents of a web page, so some pretty elaborate schemes were sometimes used to provide a complex page layout, such as the use of invisible images to help solve spacing problems.

Did you
know?

Why CSS Are "Cascading"

We say that style sheets *cascade* because, aside from a few exceptions, HTML elements inherit the style attributes of the elements they're contained in. For example, assume you have an HTML <b> element that is inside a <u> element:

   <u>This is <b>some</b> text.</u>

If you were to set the CSS **font** attribute of the <u> element, the <b> element would inherit that font setting as well. You can, however, override the cascading effect by assigning a different font setting to the <b> element.

The W3C introduced the CSS Level 1 standard in late 1996. IE 3 was the first browser to include partial support for this new standard, and Netscape 4 soon followed with some partial (albeit extremely buggy) support for CSS as well.

A *style sheet* is a group of definitions that describe the style for a set of HTML elements. Using style sheets, you can completely redefine the way a certain element is rendered inside the web browser, as each element exposes a number of attributes whose value can be changed.

NOTE   *The W3C has a very good web site for learning more about style sheets; go to http://www.w3.org/Style.*

Assign Style to Web Pages Using HTML Elements

12

The original method of formatting the contents of a web page was by using HTML style-related elements and attributes. For instance, the <font> tag could be used to set the typeface, size, or color for text inside a document. The <b> tag could be used to make text bold, <i> would create italics, and so on.

However, this was a very inefficient method for styling a web page, for a number of reasons:

- The style and layout of a web page could not be easily reused between two or more HTML files, which created extra development work for web page authors.

- Frames, nested tables, invisible images, and other complex and messy techniques needed to be used to place text or graphics in a particular spot.

- Duplicate HTML style tags, such as the <font> tag, needed to be repeated many times on the same web page.

- It was a lot of work to change the style of a web page or of an entire site.

- Web pages were larger, which meant it took longer for them to download to browsers.

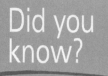

How to Specify Colors in HTML

There are several places in HTML, CSS, and JavaScript that require a programmer to specify a color. For instance, the HTML <font> tag has a **color** attribute with which you can specify the font's color.

Colors can be specified by name or by RGB (red-green-blue) value. Several colors have predefined names in HTML, such as black, white, yellow, and blue. There are dozens of predefined colors.

If you would like to use a color that does not already have a name, you can specify an exact RGB value. RGB values start with the pound symbol (#) followed by three pairs of hexadecimal digits, such as #FF33C0.

The first pair of hexadecimal digits represents the amount of red in a color, ranging from a value of 00 (darkest) to FF (brightest)— that's 256 unique settings for red. The second pair represents the amount of green, while the third pair represents the amount of blue.

So the color #FF33C0 represents a combination of bright red, dark green, and medium blue, which comes out looking a lot like fuchsia (a bright purplish-pink color). #FFFFFF represents pure white, and #000000 represents pure black.

For example, the following HTML code defines a page with a moderately complex style. The HTML code is messy and difficult to read due to all the extra HTML tags and attributes that are required.

```
<html>
    <head><title>Style sheets example</title></head>
    <body bgcolor="white" link="purple" vlink="green">

    <center>
       <h1>
          <font color="#333399" face="Arial">
             Introduction to XML
          </font>
       </h1>
    </center>

    <p><font color="#993333" face="Arial" size="3">
        <b>XML is one of the most
    important new standards to come out of the W3C<br>
        since HTML.</b> All developers
```

```
should be aware of what XML is and how it<br>
    should be used. In this article,
we introduce the basics of XML, including a<br>
    discussion on DTDs.</font></p>

    </body>
</html>
```

The preceding code includes a number of formatting tags such as <center>, <font>, and <b>. There are also a number of nonbreaking spaces ( ) to help indent the paragraph, and the <body> tag contains three style-related attributes. I also had to add manual line breaks (<br>) to artificially set the spot where the text wraps to the next line.

Figure 12-1 shows how the browser is able to render a well-styled page from our sample HTML code.

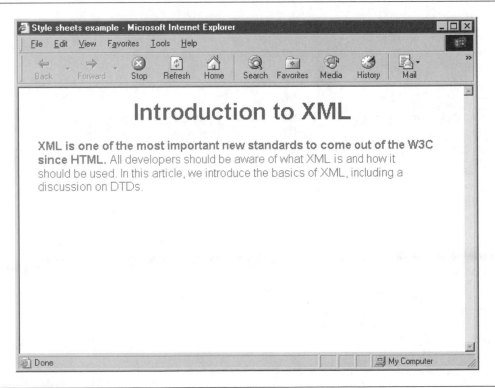

FIGURE 12-1   The traditional method of formatting a page using HTML style tags

Assign Style to Web Pages Using Style Sheets

Of course, we can create the same effect shown in Figure 12-1 using style sheets. The style sheet solution, however, will be neater, easier to develop, and simpler to maintain in the future. We can even share this style definition with any number of other web pages, saving us valuable development time. We can also do some pretty cool things this way that HTML style tags just cannot do.

First, we will take our web page example and remove the HTML style tags and attributes from it. We will use HTML <div> tags instead to mark the text that needs to be styled.

```
<html>
    <head><title>Style sheets example</title></head>
    <body>

    <div id="heading">
        Introduction to XML
    </div>

    <div id="summary">
    <span id="boldintro">
    XML is one of the most important new standards to come
    out of the W3C since HTML.
    </span>

    All developers should be aware of what XML is and how it
    should be used. In this article, we introduce the basics
    of XML, including a discussion on DTDs.
    </div>

    </body>
</html>
```

We can create a simple style sheet for this document, and insert it into the web page using the HTML <style> element. The <style> element belongs inside the <head> section of the document.

```
<style type="text/css">
#heading {
    font: 24pt Arial;
    color: #333399;
    text-align: center;
    margin-bottom: 20pt;
}

#summary {
    font: 12pt Arial;
    color: #993333;
```

```
        margin-left: 20pt;
}

#boldintro {
        font-weight: bold;
}
</style>
```

We will examine the syntax of the style sheet itself later in the chapter. But even without knowing exactly what the style sheet means, you can see what it does. The resulting web page is almost identical to the one displayed in Figure 12-1, which was styled with traditional HTML, but the style sheet method is many times more flexible and powerful.

Use <div> and <span> to Mark Dynamic Text

HTML 4.01 provides two special elements to support the integration of CSS and HTML: <div> and <span>.

The <div> element is a marker for text blocks. A *text block* is one or more complete paragraphs that must start and end on a new line. The <div> element makes it easier for a document to be styled using style sheets.

```
<div id="FirstError">Error! You have entered an incorrect user ID
and/or password. Please try again, and if you continue to have
difficulty, please contact a system administrator for help.</div>
```

The <span> element is very similar, except it deals with inline text. *Inline text* does not have to start or end on a new line, so <span> can be used for applying style to single characters, words, or sentences.

```
<span style="font-size:14pt">H</span>is main goal in life was
<span style="font-weight:bold">world domination</span>, although
tonight he was willing to settle for a nice steak and a cold beer.
```

The primary attributes of <div> and <span> are **id**, **style**, and **class**. **id** allows you to specify a name for the enclosed text. This makes it easy to access the text using JavaScript or CSS. The **style** attribute allows you to specify CSS directly inside the HTML. The **class** attribute is similar to the **id** attribute, except several tags can have the same **class** attribute while the **id** attribute is unique to a single tag.

Define Inline Styles

The HTML standard allows CSS style syntax to be defined inside the body of the document using a technique called *inline styles*. Most HTML elements have an attribute called **style** that can accept CSS definitions, like so:

```
<p style="font:Arial;font-weight:bold">
    This is some text
</p>
```

12

Using this technique is quick and convenient, but you lose some of the benefits of using style sheets. Specifically, the body of the document remains complex, messy, and hard to maintain. The style sheet code is impossible to easily reuse. In fact, since the style is not separated from the content at all, this technique is equivalent to using HTML style tags and attributes.

The one benefit you do get is the ability to use complex styles not available using the HTML style tag method. For small web pages or those with unique style requirements this might be an acceptable method.

Define Embedded Style Sheets

The next step up from inline styles is the use of embedded style sheets. An *embedded style sheet* is one defined using the HTML <style> tag inside the header section of the document. Styles defined in this manner are available to the entire web page, so it is entirely possible to define only one or two style definitions for a large and complex document.

A style sheet is made up of one or more rules. A *rule* is a single definition for a style, in the following format:

```
selector {
    attribute1 : value;
    attribute2 : value;
    ...
    attributeN : value;
}
```

For example, in the previous section we had a style sheet with three rules. One of the rules was defined with the following code:

```
#summary {
    font: 12pt Arial;
    color: #993333;
    margin-left: 20pt;
}
```

The rule has a selector (#summary) and defines values for three attributes (font, color, and margin-left). The *selector* determines which HTML tags have their attributes set to the specified values. By the way, the rule does not have to be spaced over several lines as I have been doing. You can place the rule all on one line, or break it up over several more lines to improve readability, if you wish.

The following table shows how selectors work in CSS.

Selector	HTML Code Affected
h1	Affects all <h1> tags in the document.
#heading	Affects the tag with an **id** attribute set to heading.
.blue	Affects all tags with a **class** attribute set to blue.

Selector	HTML Code Affected
p#heading	Affects all <p> tags in the document with an **id** attribute set to heading.
p.blue	Affects all <p> tags in the document with a **class** attribute set to blue.
h1, h2, h3	Affects all <h1>, <h2>, and <h3> tags in the document.
p b	Affects all <p> tags that are contained inside <p> tags; <b> tags not inside <p> tags are not affected.
ul ul li	Affects all <li> tags that are inside at least two <ul> tags.
div .red	Affects all tags with a **class** attribute set to red that are also inside a **div** attribute.

As you can see, there are ways to set the style for the entire document all at once and ways to set the style of very specific elements within the document. You can ultimately create some very complex and comprehensive style sheets using sophisticated selectors.

Import External Styles

There are two ways to import a style sheet from an external file into an HTML document:

- The HTML <link> element
- The style sheet @import command

This means that you can create a single style sheet file that can be applied to all the pages on a web site. And with a few simple keystrokes in a text editor, you can radically change the style of all the pages on your site at once.

To use the <link> element, place the following HTML code in the <head> section of your web page:

```
<link rel="STYLESHEET" type="text/css"
      href="http://www.example.com/mystyle.css">
```

The preceding code will cause the style sheet which is located at http://www.example.com/mystyle.css to be imported into the web page. The file extension .css is often used for style sheets.

To import the same style sheet using the @import command, we actually need to add a <style> section to the document header.

```
<style type="text/css">
   @import url(http://www.example.com/mystyle.css);
</style>
```

All three types of style sheets (inline, embedded, and external) can be combined in a single document. If styles conflict, the inline styles have precedence, followed by the embedded styles, and lastly the external styles.

12

Use Basic Style Attributes

As mentioned in the "Define Embedded Style Sheets" section, a style sheet is made up one or more of rules, and rules are made up of a selector plus one or more attributes. In this section, we will look at the different types of attributes that can be used to set styles.

There are literally dozens of attributes defined in the official CSS 1 specification—so many that I won't even attempt to cover them all in this book. For more information on the available CSS attributes, I suggest the following two excellent sources:

- The official W3C CSS 1 specification can be found at http://www.w3.org/TR/REC-CSS1.

- The Microsoft MSDN web site has an excellent reference guide at http://msdn.microsoft.com/workshop/author/css/reference/css_ref_entry.asp.

The MSDN reference guide is particularly well organized; CSS attributes are cross-referenced with their related HTML elements. In fact, I believe this web site to be the most complete web programming reference available on the Internet—not just for CSS, but for all web-related programming topics.

Table 12-1 describes some of the most frequently used CSS attributes.

Several of the attributes listed in Table 12-1 are *compound attributes;* that is, they allow you to set many properties of an element at once. For instance, the **font** attribute allows you to set up to 14 font-related properties in one string:

```
BODY {
    font: italic normal bold 12pt Arial;
}
```

This convenient shortcut is equivalent to the following code:

```
BODY {
    font-style: italic;
    font-variant: normal;
    font-weight: bold;
    font-size: 12pt;
    font-family: Arial;
}
```

So as you can see, compound attributes save time and effort but add additional complexity, in that they are more difficult to construct.

Position Elements on a Web Page

Some CSS attributes have nothing to do with text style and deal instead with layout and positioning. Setting the positioning of an element allows you to specify the exact size (height and width) of the object as well as its exact physical location (x and y coordinates) on the screen.

Attribute Name	Purpose
font	Allows you to set up to a dozen font-related properties, including size and style
color	Allows you to set the foreground color of an element
background	Allows you to set up to five background-related properties, including color and image
text-align	Allows you to set left, center, or right alignment for text
margin	Allows you to set the size of the empty space around an element
border	Allows you to set the size, style, and color of the border around an element

TABLE 12-1   Common CSS Attributes

For example, let's assume we have the following HTML code:

```
<html>
    <head>
        <title>Style sheets example</title>
        <link rel="STYLESHEET" type="text/css"
            href="example.css">
    </head>
    <body>

    <div id="special">This is a great example of separating
    content from layout. From an HTML perspective, this text
    is a pretty simple paragraph, with no formatting requirements.
    Browsers that do not support style sheets will render
    this text to the screen in a plain and simple manner.
    </div>

    </body>
</html>
```

This HTML code contains no formatting instructions. All we have done is provide a paragraph of text surrounded by a <div> tag. The <div> tag does not do anything other than provide a way to name a block of text. (We examined the difference between <div> and <span> earlier in the chapter, in the "Use <div> and <span> to Mark Dynamic Text" section.)

Our HTML code does, however, contain a <link> reference to a style sheet file. The file, example.css, will contain the formatting instructions we wish to use. In our case, it will define CSS positioning attributes.

The example.css file will contain the following code:

```
#special {
    position: absolute;
    top: 50px;
```

```
    left: 100px;
    width: 3in;

    background-color: #CCCCCC;
    padding: 15px;
    font: 12pt Arial;
    border: solid 2pt black;
}
```

The preceding style sheet contains four of the CSS size and positioning attributes:

- **position**   Tells the browser we wish to position the content ourselves
- **top**   Sets the position of the top edge of the element
- **left**   Sets the position of the left edge of the element
- **width**   Sets the width of the element

In our case, the element is the <div> tag that surrounds our text. The <div> tag has an **id** attribute of **special**, which matches the #special selector assigned to the rule.

There are a couple of additional positioning attributes that were not used, most notably **height**, which can be used to set the height of the element. In our case, we are allowing the browser to calculate the proper height for the element based on the size of the text contents. There is also an attribute named **visibility**, which can make an element invisible.

Figure 12-2 shows how the text inside our HTML document has been positioned and sized exactly as specified in our style sheet.

Modify Styles Using JavaScript

Now that we have examined what style sheets are and how they can be used to format a web page, we can take a look at how JavaScript can be used to modify styles dynamically.

The DOM provides JavaScript access to the style-related properties of almost any object on the page. For instance, assume we have a web form defined as follows:

```
<form action="#" method="get">

    <div style="position:absolute;top:50px;left:100px;">

    Full Name:<br>
    <input type="text" name="fullname" id="fullname"><br><br>

    Email Address:<br>
    <input type="text" name="email" id="email">

    </div>

</form>
```

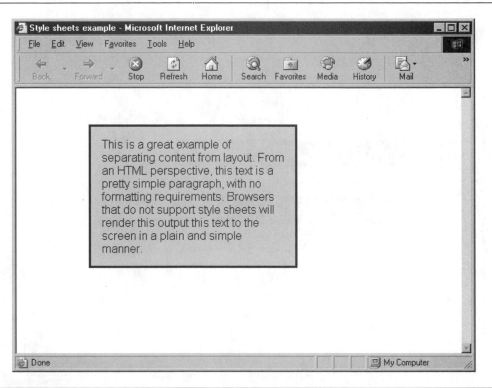

FIGURE 12-2 The browser has successfully interpreted our style sheet.

Our JavaScript program can access the text box control named fullname using the DOM and manipulate its style.

```
var TextBoxes = document.getElementsByTagName("input");

for (var counter=0; counter < TextBoxes.length; counter++) {

    var myTextBox = TextBoxes[counter];
    myTextBox.style.backgroundColor = "black";
    myTextBox.style.color = "white";
    myTextBox.style.font = "22pt Arial";

}
```

The preceding JavaScript code will locate all the <input> elements on the page and alter their style properties. What we will end up with are two text boxes that have black backgrounds, white text, and a large, 22-point Arial font. You can see the results of this code in Figure 12-3.

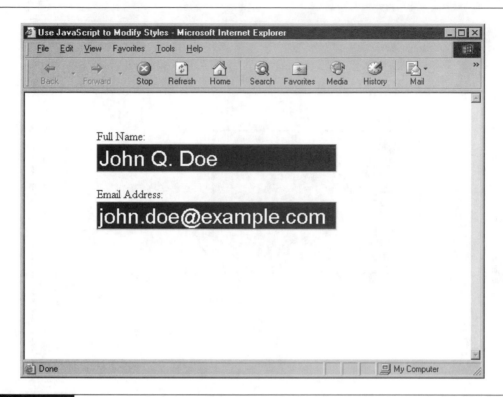

FIGURE 12-3   The styles have been altered dynamically using JavaScript.

The names of the JavaScript properties are often different than the names of the corresponding CSS attributes. For instance, the CSS attribute background-color is set using the JavaScript property backgroundColor.

Table 12-2 lists some of the CSS attribute names we have been using and the corresponding DOM style property names.

As you can see, there is some consistency between the naming of CSS style attributes and the corresponding JavaScript DOM property, but occasionally the two names differ, so it is best to check whenever you are uncertain of the correct name.

Understand Cross-Platform Issues

CSS support used to be extremely inconsistent between the top two or three browser manufacturers. Today, the vast majority of browsers in use fully support CSS 1. Most browsers have at least partial support for the CSS 2 specification, and CSS 3 is currently under development.

CSS Attribute	Corresponding DOM Property
background	background
background-color	backgroundColor
border	border
border-bottom	borderBottom
border-left	borderLeft
border-right	borderRight
border-top	borderTop
color	color
font	font
font-family	fontFamily
font-size	fontSize
font-weight	fontWeight
margin	margin
margin-bottom	marginBottom
margin-left	marginLeft
margin-right	marginRight
margin-top	marginTop
text-align	textAlign

TABLE 12-2   The Relationship Between CSS and JavaScript DOM Styles

12

Internet Explorer was the first browser to contain support for style sheets, and Microsoft added several of their own attributes that were not part of the standard and do not work in other browsers. Obviously, if you want your style sheets to work in all browsers, stick to attributes and commands that are part of the official standard and avoid proprietary extensions.

Netscape 4 contains a buggy, partial implementation of the CSS standard. It is quite difficult to get style sheets to work for that browser beyond a few basic attributes, so understand that a web page that relies heavily on style sheets might not look as intended in the Netscape 4 web browser. Fortunately, the market share for that browser has dipped below 3 percent, so the problem will eventually go away on its own.

TIP

The W3C provides a CSS validator service. The CSS validator, located at http://jigsaw.w3.org/css-validator, will examine any HTML web page (or individual style sheet) you specify to ensure the style sheet is completely valid. The tool provides helpful feedback for finding out where problems lie, and so is very useful when developing CSS-enabled web pages.

Perform Basic Animation Using JavaScript

We have discussed how JavaScript can be used to change elements within the DOM as well as CSS style and positioning attributes. In this section, we will examine two of the most common techniques for creating animation on a web page using JavaScript.

Dynamically Load Images

The simplest type of animation in JavaScript is accomplished by just switching images. You see something similar to this all the time on the Web, where a graphical menu or button changes when your mouse moves over it. In fact, you saw an example of that effect in Chapter 9, in the discussion on mouse events:

```
<script type="text/javascript" language="javascript">
function changeimage(num) {
    var img = document.getElementById("SampleImage");
    if (num == 1) {
        img.src = "NewImg.gif";
    } else {
        img.src = "OriginalImg.gif";
    }
}
</script>

<img src="OriginalImg.gif"
    id="SampleImage"
    alt="Sample image"
    onmouseover="changeimage(1)"
    onmouseout="changeimage(2)" >
```

In the JavaScript function changeimage(), we used the document.getElementById() function to retrieve the image object defined in the body of the HTML document. Depending on the type of event (onmouseover or onmouseout), the src property of the image is pointed to a different file.

Mouseover events are the shortest form of animation—sort of like a half-second movie. In order to create a longer effect, we need to do several rapid image switches in a row. For instance, let's build a fairly simple animation effect that uses timer events:

1. Start with a set of related images that make up the animation.

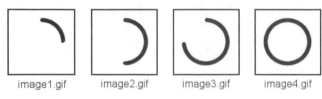

image1.gif   image2.gif   image3.gif   image4.gif

2. Place the first image on a web page using the HTML <img> tag. Be sure to assign the <img> an **id** attribute.

```
<img src="image1.gif" id="anim">
```

3. Then create a JavaScript function called animate() that alternates between each of the three images at regular intervals, say every ¼ second.

```
// The counter variable controls the animation
var counter = 0;

function animate() {
    var img = document.getElementById("anim");

    // Proceed to the next image
    counter ++;
    // There are only four images, so restart when we're done
    if (counter > 3) counter = 0;

    if (counter == 0) {
        // Display the first image
        img.src = "image1.gif";
    } else if (counter == 1) {
        // Display the second image
        img.src = "image2.gif";
    } else if (counter == 2) {
        // Display the third image
        img.src = "image3.gif";
    } else {
        // Display the fourth image
        img.src = "image4.gif";
    }

    // We need to call the animate function again in 0.10 seconds
    // Pause for 1 second between the fourth and first image
    if (counter == 3) {
        setTimeout("animate()", 1000);
    } else {
        setTimeout("animate()", 100);
    }
}
```

12

4. We can start the animation by calling the function from within the <body> element's onload event handler.

```
<body onload = "animate()">
```

5. The net result is that our graphic appears to be animated inside the browser window.

Rapidly switching sequentially through the different graphics creates an animation that draws a circle in the browser window.

Make Content Move Around the Screen

The other way to perform basic animation is by moving an object around on the screen. We have already seen that JavaScript can access the CSS positioning attributes of any object on a page. It would be fairly easy, then, to use that same technique to create JavaScript animation.

Let's start with the image of a ball.

ball.gif

The image is placed on a web page using the HTML <img> tag:

```
<img src="ball.gif"
    id="ball"
    class="ballstyle">
<div class="boxstyle"> </div>
```

We should also create a style sheet for this page, so that the ball and box will start off with the correct style and positioning.

```
<style type="text/css">

.ballstyle {
    position: absolute;
    top: 50px;
    left: 100px;
}

.boxstyle {
    position: absolute;
```

```
    top: 50px;
    left: 100px;
    height: 250px;
    width: 400px;
    border: solid 1pt black;
}
```

```
</style>
```

We will need a function, called moveball(), to animate the image by altering its **top** and **left** style attributes.

```
// Set the starting coordinates
var mytop, myleft;
mytop = 50;
myleft = 100;

function moveball() {
    img = document.getElementById("ball");
    mytop += 10;
    myleft += 2;

    if (mytop > 230) mytop = 50;
    if (myleft > 430) myleft = 100;

    img.style.top = mytop;
    img.style.left = myleft;

    setTimeout("moveball()", 100);
}
```

We must start the ball moving by calling the moveball() function from within the onload event handler of the <body> element.

As you can see in Figure 12-4, we have created a rather interesting effect. The image of the ball continues to move slowly down and to the right of the screen until it reaches the edge of the box. Once there, it switches back to the other side of the box and continues its motion.

Text can also be animated using this same technique. Instead of moving the position of an image, we could surround some text with a <div> tag and move it around. Obviously, more complicated animations, such as animated objects that move in a random manner or change direction when they reach the edge of the window, require a longer and more complicated script.

12

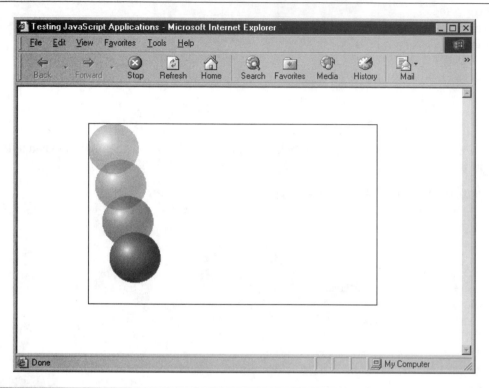

FIGURE 12-4   By modifying the CSS position attributes, we are able to make a ball move.

In the next chapter, we will discuss the fundamentals of debugging JavaScript code. A *bug* is a software flaw, and *debugging* is the process of finding and repairing the bugs in a program. We will take a look at some of the tools available to developers who are looking to discover these errors, as well as some of the programming techniques for making bugs easier to find.

Part III

Take JavaScript to the Next Level

Chapter 13

Debug JavaScript Programs

How to…

- ■ Understand JavaScript error messages

- ■ Add debugging code to your programs

- ■ Use the JavaScript console

- ■ Use a JavaScript debugger

There is nothing more frustrating for a web surfer than to arrive at a web page and immediately be presented with error messages. The visitor will likely be wary of proceeding any further into the site and is less likely to want to return.

Ensuring that the JavaScript scripts on your web page help your visitors rather than annoying them could be as simple as testing your web page using a variety of browser types, operating systems, and version numbers. Yes, it does sound like a lot of work, but there is no substitute for actual testing if you want to make sure your viewers will be happy with what you've done on the site.

But what would you do if a web page you were working on displayed an error message? Or perhaps your code wasn't working the way you had expected—or wasn't working at all. How would you go about finding the source of the problem and fixing it? Several tools are available to help JavaScript developers with this task, and in this chapter we will discuss how to debug JavaScript programs.

Understand the Possible Causes of Errors

Finding an error message while you are testing a web page is like finding a $5 bill on the sidewalk— it's worth the time to stop and pick it up. Not only does the error message tell you that there was a problem, it also shows you the first place you should look for the problem and even gives a brief description of what went wrong.

Of course, the browser is only giving you its *best guess* about what the error might be. When you actually look at the code and figure out the problem, you might find that the error message hadn't pinpointed the problem exactly. That's understandable, since some errors have so many possible causes that it would be impossible for a computer to choose the correct one.

Different browsers have different ways of reporting errors, and it is even possible to turn error reporting off. For instance, in IE, with error reporting turned on, a JavaScript error will cause the following message box to appear:

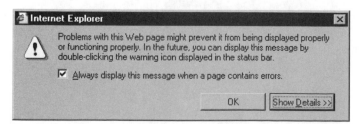

Even with error reporting turned off, IE still gives you a visual hint that the page did not load successfully. An error icon will be placed in the lower left-hand corner of the browser window, like so:

Netscape always hides JavaScript errors from end users—it won't even tell you that one occurred. You'll need to load the JavaScript Console, which is discussed later, in the section "Use the JavaScript Console," to see what if anything went wrong.

There are three basic types of errors in JavaScript:

- **Syntax errors**   Errors in the basic programming syntax of the language, such as mismatched quotes or brackets
- **Run-time errors**   Errors that can be detected only at run time, such as attempting to use variables that do not exist
- **Logic errors**   Errors in your programming logic or algorithms that cause an incorrect result, such as a loop that exits one iteration too early

Any of these types of errors can cause JavaScript to either stop running or return an incorrect result. There are dozens of possible reasons why an error would occur inside a JavaScript 1.5 program, including:

- Calling a function or using a variable that is undefined
- Attempting to modify the value of a constant
- Passing a string to a function or operator that expects a number
- Passing an incorrect number of parameters to a function
- Using an unescaped quotation mark inside a string
- Using statements such as the **for** loop incorrectly

Although JavaScript 2.0 attempts to retain the flexibility of previous versions, some of the new features have the potential to introduce new problems. In addition, JavaScript 2.0 gives programmers the option to enforce a stricter level of error checking (called *strict mode*). Potential errors for JavaScript 2.0 programs include:

- Assigning an incorrect data type to a variable that's expecting another data type
- Trying to access variables or functions defined as private
- Namespace issues
- Running JavaScript 2.0 in a browser that only supports JavaScript 1.5

I have always felt that finding and fixing errors is like unraveling a mystery. You start with only a few clues and, with good detective work and perhaps a little luck, you eventually figure out exactly what went wrong.

13

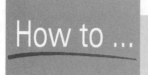

Turn on Error Reporting in IE

Internet Explorer has two advanced options that affect the way JavaScript errors are reported and handled. The Advanced Options menu can be found by selecting Internet Options from the Tools menu and selecting the Advanced tab.

On this tab, the first option setting we are concerned with is called "Display a notification about every script error." This should be enabled in order to see the JavaScript error messages we are talking about in this chapter.

The other option that may affect us is called "Disable script debugging." Depending on the software installed on your computer, IE may give you the option of loading the web page into a tool called a debugger to find out more about the problem.

Generally, this option should be enabled; that is, you do not want to be given the option to view the code in a debugger. (However, if you really do want to go into a debugger for every error and you have some experience in that software, then by all means disable the debugging option.)

Find the Source of an Error Message

When JavaScript encounters an error inside a script and the program does not handle it, then the user is notified of the error by an error message box. In IE, the details of the error are usually hidden, since they can be overly technical to the novice user. Instead, a somewhat friendlier message like the following is displayed.

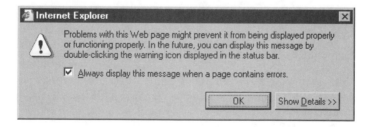

By clicking the Show Details button we can see some of the technical details about the particular error.

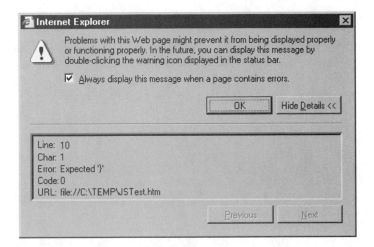

IE gives programmers a number of important details regarding the source of the error:

- **Line**   The line number where JavaScript first noticed the problem. This is not always the line that contains the problem, although it usually is. Having a text editor that shows line numbers will save you from having to manually count them out. Windows Notepad on XP can view line numbers by turning on the status bar (View | Status Bar).

- **Char**   The character number on the line where the problem might lie.

- **Error**   A string that tries to describe what JavaScript believes went wrong.

- **Code**   Some errors have an error code attached to them.

- **URL**   The web address of the HTML file that had the problem, in case there was any doubt.

> **NOTE**   *The line number listed in an error message includes any HTML lines that precede the script, unless the script exists in a file by itself (an external script) in which case it is the actual line number of the script file.*

13

The line number referenced in the details of the error message is usually the best place to start looking for an error. You also want to read the description of the error provided by the message box, since that gives you the second clue needed to solve this mystery.

Interpret Error Messages

Perhaps the best way to see how closely (or not) the JavaScript error message relates to the actual source of the error is to look at an example. In this section, we will examine a piece of JavaScript code that has a serious bug in it and see how the two major browsers (Netscape and IE) report the error.

To start the exercise, let's take a look at the following HTML and JavaScript code.

```
<html>
    <head><title>Interpreting error messages</title></head>
    <body>
    <script language="JavaScript" type="text/javascript">
    function add (input1, input2) {
        return input1 + input2;
    }

    var result = ad (1, 2);
    </script>
    </body>
</html>
```

When we first run this code, we expect that after the add() function is called with the values 1 and 2, the result returned would be 3. Instead, we encounter a JavaScript error. IE gives the rather cryptic message "Object expected."

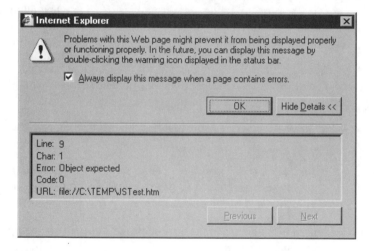

But it does give us a line number. Remember, the line number includes all the HTML code before the script on the web page. The ninth line of code points to a problem with the following line:

```
var result = ad (1, 2);
```

The Netscape JavaScript console does a better job of describing the error—although, as discussed earlier in this chapter, you have to open the console window in order to know that one exists. The console reports, more usefully, "ad is not defined."

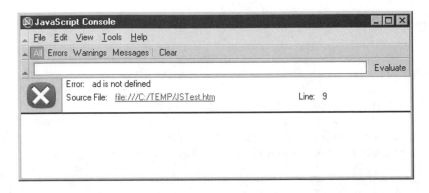

With careful examination, we can see that we have mistyped the name of the function; it should be add(), instead of ad(). Correcting the typo makes the error go away in both browsers.

Use a JavaScript Validator

One way to check your JavaScript code for strange bugs is to run it through a program that checks it to make sure it is *valid*—that it follows the official syntax rules of the language. These programs are called *validating parsers*, or just *validators* for short, and often come with commercial HTML and JavaScript editors.

TIP
One limitation some validating parsers have is that they can only understand JavaScript language components that are part of the official ECMAScript specification. Some of these tools do not understand DOM function calls or some of the extensions to the language added by browser manufacturers that are not part of the ECMAScript specification.

Perhaps the most convenient validator for JavaScript is Douglas Crockford's JavaScript Lint, which is available free online at http://www.crockford.com/javascript/jslint.html. Simply visit that web page, paste your JavaScript code into the text area provided, and click the jslint button. Voilà! The results appear onscreen in seconds.

JavaScript Lint will parse through your JavaScript code, ensuring that any variable and function definitions follow the correct syntax. It will also check JavaScript statements, such as **if** and **while**, to ensure they too follow the correct format. This program will not catch all the errors in your JavaScript programs, but it will catch the obvious ones, such as missing brackets or undefined variables and functions.

Add Debugging Code to Your Programs

Often when a JavaScript script is not producing the desired results it's not obvious why the problem exists. For instance, you may be expecting that after a series of mathematical operations a variable is going to come back with a specific value—but it doesn't. There won't be any JavaScript

13

error messages to help you find the line that is causing the problem, and even a JavaScript validator may not be of any use.

One thing programmers can do to help themselves is to add some *debugging code* to the program. Debugging code is code that exists purely to help the developer figure out what is going on behind the scenes while code is being modified. You would usually remove or comment out the debugging code once regular visitors to your page are using the script.

Programmers commonly use the alert() or document.write() methods when adding debugging code to a program. For instance, the following script has a number of additional alert() message boxes that will give the developer an idea of what is going on inside the program.

```
// Converts a number from "9999999" to "9,999,999"
function convert_number(input) {
    var counter, output;

    alert("input = " + input);
    alert("input length = " + input.length);

    // Not long enough to get commas
    if (input.length < 4) return input;
    alert("length larger than 3");

    // Empty output
    output = "";

    // Loop through input string, three chars at a time
    for (counter = input.length-3; counter > 0; counter -= 3) {
        output = "," + input.substr(counter, counter+2) + output;
        alert("counter = " + counter + ", output = " + output);
    }

    // Final set of numbers
    output = input.substr(0, counter+3) + output;
    alert("counter = " + counter + ", output = " + output);

    return output;
}
```

In the preceding code, all the calls to the alert() message box are used for debugging purposes only. Their sole purpose is to provide the programmer with some clues about what is going on inside the function: what the original value is, what happens after each iteration of the loop, and the final result.

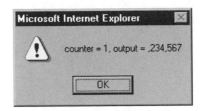

Again, once we are satisfied this function is working properly, we should remove or comment out those alert boxes to save our visitors from a lot of unnecessary mouse clicks.

A similar debugging technique involves the careful and incremental use of comments. Let's say you have a JavaScript function that does not appear to be working correctly. You have looked over the source code, and cannot figure out the source of the problem.

```javascript
// Converts a number from "9999999" to "9,999,999"
function convert_number(input) {
    var counter, output;

    if (input.length < 4) return input;
    output = "";

    for (counter = input.length-3; counter > 0; counter -= 3) {
        output = "," + input.substr(counter, counter+3) + output;
    }
    output = input.substr(0, counter+3) + output;
    return output;
}
```

1. Start by commenting out the contents of the entire function. If the function is supposed to return a value, force it to return a hard-coded value that simulates what you are expecting. Test the script to make sure it is now working correctly with the hard-coded value.

```javascript
// Converts a number from "9999999" to "9,999,999"
function convert_number(input) {
//    var counter, output;
//
//    if (input.length < 4) return input;
//    output = "";
//
//    for (counter = input.length-3; counter > 0; counter -= 3) {
//        output = "," + input.substr(counter, counter+3) + output;
//    }
```

```
//     output = input.substr(0, counter+3) + output;
//     return output;

    // ** Hard-coded return value **
    return "1,234,567";
}
```

2. Next, uncomment a few of those lines. For instance, make the function return its input string instead of the hard-coded value. Again, test that this expected result (the input string) is working correctly.

```
// Converts a number from "9999999" to "9,999,999"
function convert_number(input) {
    var counter, output;

    if (input.length < 4) return input;
    output = "";

//     for (counter = input.length-3; counter > 0; counter -= 3) {
//         output = "," + input.substr(counter, counter+3) + output;
//     }
//     output = input.substr(0, counter+3) + output;
//     return output;

    // ** Return the input value **
    return input;
}
```

3. Carefully uncomment more lines from the script. Know in advance what you expect the return value to be after each set of comments is removed, and then retest.

4. Repeat step 3 as necessary. At some point, you will discover that the return value is not the value you expected. The most recently uncommented lines are the most likely source of the problem!

Adding debugging code and using comments are two of the most useful techniques for manually figuring out the source of errors inside scripts.

Use the JavaScript Console

The Netscape and Mozilla browsers include a useful utility called the JavaScript console. The JavaScript console opens in its own window, and this is the place where Netscape outputs any JavaScript errors it encounters. The console will continue to accumulate error messages from web pages until the browser is closed or the console is cleared manually.

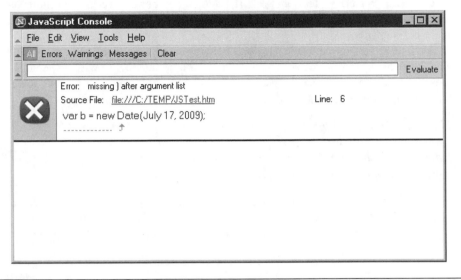

FIGURE 13-1   The Netscape console shows JavaScript errors.

To access the console in Netscape 7, go to Tools | Web Development, and choose JavaScript Console. (In Netscape 6, the JavaScript Console option is located in Tasks | Tools.) The console is empty when the browser is first opened, but will accumulate error messages as they occur for many different pages and sites as you surf.

The console also allows developers to input JavaScript code for the browser to execute. Simply type the variable name into the console, click Evaluate, and the console will tell you the last value for that variable. Or you can have JavaScript manually call a function by typing in the function name along with any parameters.

Figure 13-1 shows what the console looks like in the Netscape 7 web browser.

Use a JavaScript Debugger

The final weapon in the programmer's arsenal against bugs is to use debugging software. A debugger is a program that gives you complete access to the internal workings of the application. A JavaScript debugger will typically include a user-friendly interface and will allow a developer to step through the script one line at a time. The developer can see the current value of any variables and get more detailed feedback in order to help them find the true source of a bug.

Debuggers are typically shipped inside HTML and JavaScript editors. For example, Microsoft FrontPage 2002 contains a JavaScript editor and debugger called Microsoft Script Editor. Macromedia Dreamweaver also contains a JavaScript debugger in its Dreamweaver MX product. There are also a number of third-party editors that contain debuggers, such as C Point's JavaScript Editor (http://www.c-point.com).

13

For those who don't use a professional HTML editor, a number of free JavaScript debuggers are also available. Most prominent among them is the JavaScript Debugger available from the open-source Mozilla project.

As you may know, the Netscape and Mozilla web browsers are based on the same core set of source code. Netscape, however, does not include the JavaScript Debugger with its version, while Mozilla does. So developers who use the Netscape 7 (and later) browsers will need to download and install the debugger as a separate tool.

The latest Netscape web browser is available for download from http://www.netscape.com. The latest version of the Mozilla JavaScript Debugger (code-named Venkman) for both Mozilla and Netscape browsers can be downloaded at http://www.hacksrus.com/~ginda/venkman.

The Mozilla JavaScript Debugger is available on multiple operating systems (specifically Windows, Mac OS, and Unix), and does a great job helping developers step through their JavaScript programs. We can see a screenshot of this debugger in Figure 13-2.

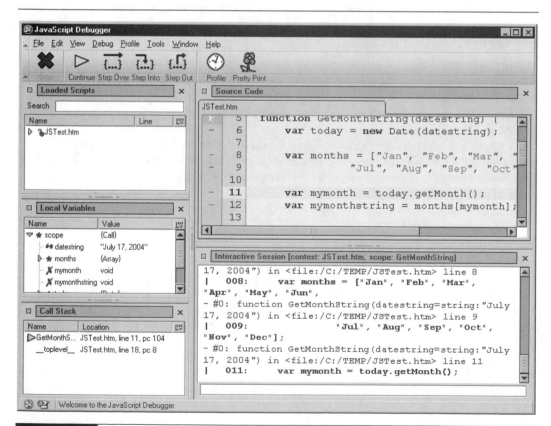

FIGURE 13-2   Stepping through a JavaScript program using the Mozilla debugger

TIP *To access the JavaScript Debugger in Mozilla 1 or Netscape 7, go to the Tools | Web Development menu, and choose JavaScript Debugger.*

Microsoft also provides a free debugger, the Microsoft Script Debugger. It is available for download at http://www.microsoft.com/script/debugger. Script Debugger supports many of the key debugger features, such as the ability to view and step through code, set breakpoints, and view and change variable values.

No matter which browser you use, you are bound to find the ability to step through complex JavaScript programs very useful. For small scripts, adding debugging code may be all you need to find problems. But when your program contains a lot of functions and you need some of the advanced debugging features such as breakpoints, a good JavaScript debugger can be the programmer's best friend.

The next chapter deals with some of the important concepts around using **try-catch** statements to intercept system errors before the browser does. You will also see how to use exceptions in your own programs.

What a Breakpoint Is

In debugging, a *breakpoint* is a line of code designated by the programmer as the point where the debugger will pause (or *break*) the program. The programmer can perform a number of tasks inside the debugger before letting the program continue executing.

The benefit of having a debugger that supports breakpoints is that instead of having to step through every single line of code in a script manually, you can let the debugger execute all lines automatically until it reaches its first breakpoint. Once you have checked the contents of some data variables, you can either step through the program manually or let it run automatically until it reaches the next breakpoint.

13

Chapter 14

Make Your Program Errorproof

How to...

- Understand exceptions and how they are caused
- Catch exceptions using the **try** and **catch** statements
- Create exceptions using the **throw** statement
- Design programs that are easy to debug from the start

Designing and developing programs that are immune to errors is a difficult task when using programming languages such as Visual Basic and Java. But it is in some ways even more difficult when working with JavaScript.

One of the reasons this is true is that, as a scripting language, JavaScript is generally distributed as source code. In normal circumstances, there is no compiler to catch syntax errors before users see the final program in action. With other languages, the compilation step provides a layer of protection against certain types of errors.

Another reason for the difficulty is that JavaScript is often developed using nothing more than a basic text editor. Languages such as Visual Basic are created using integrated development environments (IDEs) that help developers create better code and include built-in debuggers.

And yet another reason is that the number of target environments (browsers and operating systems) is so diverse—literally dozens of combinations—that it becomes practically impossible to test the program in all the possible environments.

But there are some techniques developers can use to make sure the JavaScript programs they create will work properly in as many environments as possible. In this chapter, we will examine some of the most practical ways to ensure programming success.

Learn the Basics of Exceptions

In the early days of web programming, when JavaScript encountered a error while executing a program the result was always fatal: the browser would stop executing the code and report the error to the user. In effect, errors were always reported directly to the browser—the application had no opportunity to try and handle the error itself. You can imagine how impossible it was to create an errorproof program when you couldn't even detect when an error occurred.

In addition, JavaScript developers had to invent their own ways of returning errors back to the program. Take the following example:

```
function simple_addition(a, b) {
    // This function will add two numbers,
    //    but only if they both are between 0 and 9
    if (a < 0 || a > 9) {
        return "First number is not between 0 and 9.";

    } else if (b < 0 || b > 9) {
```

```
       return "Second number is not between 0 and 9.";

  } else {
     return a + b;

  }
}
```

Every place inside the program that made a call to this function had to have several extra lines of code (more **if** statements) to check the return value to see whether an error occurred before using the number. Other programmers might solve the same problem differently, with special return codes (like using the value –1) to return an error.

JavaScript uses *exceptions* to pass system errors back to the program for handling. In addition, JavaScript programmers can use the same system of exceptions inside their code to return application-specific errors back from functions. For example, we can rewrite the source code from the previous example to use exceptions instead, by using the **throw** statement.

```
function simple_addition(a, b) {
    // This function will add two numbers, but only if they are less than 10
    if (a < 0 || a > 9) {
       throw "First number is not between 0 and 9.";

    } else if (b < 0 || b > 9) {
       throw "Second number is not between 0 and 9.";

    } else {
       return a + b;

    }
}
```

You will learn more about the statements that deal with creating and capturing exceptions in the next two sections.

Catch Exceptions Using the try and catch Statements

The **try-catch** statement was introduced in JavaScript 1.4; it is modeled on similar statements in Java and C++. When JavaScript encounters a **try-catch** statement in code, it will begin to execute the block of code contained inside the **try** clause. If any of the statements inside that block cause an exception to occur, JavaScript will not execute any of the remaining statements inside that block and will jump immediately to the code contained inside the **catch** clause. Of course, if no exceptions occur inside the **try** clause, the code inside the **catch** clause will never be executed.

14

The following code shows how the **try-catch** statement can be used to protect the code from exceptions.

```
var isIE = (navigator.userAgent.indexOf("MSIE")) > -1;

try {
    var a = 1;
    var c = a / b;
    alert("The result of a / b is " + c);
}
catch (e) {
    var msg = "JavaScript encountered the following error:\n\n";
    // IE and Netscape pass errors differently to the catch clause
    if (isIE) {
        msg += e.description;
    } else {
        msg += e;
    }
    alert (msg);
}
```

NOTE   *IE and Netscape each has its own way of passing errors to the **catch** clause. IE passes the error as an Error object—in order to get the actual error message you have to access one of the properties of that object. Netscape passes the error as a string, which can be used like any other string.*

The preceding code attempts to use an undefined variable, b, inside the **try** block. As soon as our code attempts to use that variable in an expression, an exception occurs, and the rest of the code inside the block does not execute. The error message generated by the **catch** clause for IE looks like this.

Netscape encounters the same error when executing the code inside the **try** block. Its error message is worded slightly differently, however:

Understand Exception Bubbling

The **try-catch** statement can also capture errors generated inside function calls within the **try** clause. For instance, say we were to move some of the code from the previous example into a function of its own.

```
var isIE = (navigator.userAgent.indexOf("MSIE")) > -1;

function calculate() {
    var a = 1;
    return a / b;
}

try {
    var c = calculate();
    alert("The result of a / b is " + c);
}
catch (e) {
    var msg = "JavaScript encountered the following error:\n\n";
    // IE and Netscape pass errors differently to the catch clause
    if (isIE) {
        msg += e.description;
    } else {
        msg += e;
    }
    alert (msg);
}
```

14

The **try-catch** statement will still receive notification of the error, even though it occurs inside the calculate() function. This is because exceptions, like events, bubble. *Exception bubbling* is the term that is used to describe the process of how an exception will seek out the first **try-catch** statement eligible to handle it. If there is no **try-catch** statement immediately surrounding the line of code with the error, control will jump back to the code that called the function containing the error. If there is no **try-catch** there, control will jump back to the code that called it, and so on, until either a **try-catch** is found or the browser handles the exception by displaying it to the user.

For example, the following code generates an error after several levels of function calls have been made. The exception still manages to make its way back to the **try-catch** statement surrounding the first function call.

```
var isIE = (navigator.userAgent.indexOf("MSIE")) > -1;

function fn1 () {
    // The first function (fn1) calls the second (fn2)
    fn2();
}

function fn2 () {
    // The second function (fn2) calls the third (fn3)
    fn3();
}

function fn3 () {
    // The third function (fn3) calls the fourth (fn4)
    fn4();
}

function fn4 () {
    // The fourth function (fn4) calls the fifth (fn5)
    fn5();
}

function fn5 () {
    // The fifth function (fn5) contains an error
    return some_undefined_variable;
}

// MAIN program
try {
    fn1();
} catch (e) {
    var msg = "JavaScript encountered the following error:\n\n";
    // IE and Netscape pass errors differently to the catch clause
    if (isIE) {
        msg += e.description;
    } else {
        msg += e;
    }
    alert (msg);
}
```

As you can see from the following screenshot, both Netscape and IE are able to pass the exception properly to our **catch** clause.

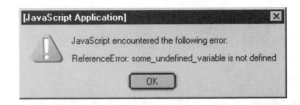

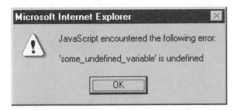 NOTE *You do not always have to respond to an exception by displaying a message to the user. You could always ignore the error and continue.*

Use the IE Error Object

As we observed in the previous section, Internet Explorer passes an Error object to the parameter of the **catch** clause. The Error object contains two properties:

- **number** A numeric value related to the error
- **description** A string describing the error

NOTE *The code in this section will work only in Internet Explorer.*

IE automatically creates an Error object whenever an exception occurs, but you are also free to create your own error using the following **new** statement syntax:

```
var myerr = new Error (1000,
          "Value falls outside acceptable range of 0-81.");
```

Using this object allows your program to easily distinguish between different types of errors while also retaining the plain-English description to display to the user.

```
// Error 1000: Ignore, set return code to 0
if (e.number == 1000) {
    var returncode = 0;

// Error 1001: Exit loop, set return code to 9999
} else if (e.number == 1001) {
    var returncode = 9999;

// Other error code: Can't handle this, report to user
} else {
    alert(e.description);
}
```

14

The only real problem with this method is that Netscape uses a different approach, which means you have to have browser-sniffing code in order to create cross-platform-compatible code.

Use Netscape-Only catch Clauses

Netscape has a special syntax for **catch** clauses that allows for more than one of them to exist in a **try-catch** statement. Netscape calls them *conditional catch blocks*.

 IE does not support this syntax, and it is not part of the official ECMA standard.

Basically, Netscape allows developers to insert an **if** keyword to determine which **catch** block is called after an exception is thrown:

```
try {
    var input = get_user_input();
    edit_check (input);
}
catch (e if e == "Value too high") {
    // What do we do when the user enters a value that is too high?
    // ...
}
catch (e if e == "Value too low") {
    // What do we do when the user enters a value that is too low?
    // ...
}
catch (e if e == "No value entered") {
    // What do we do when the user does not enter a value?
    // ...
}
catch (e) {
    // Some other error occurred
    // ...
}
```

I recommend that this proprietary method be avoided if at all possible. Since adding an **if-else** statement into a single **catch** clause can generate the same effect, there is no benefit to coding it like this.

Use Nonstandard finally Clauses

Java and C++ programmers will recognize the optional **finally** clause in the **try-catch** statement, although those familiar with the official ECMAScript specification will not. Both Netscape and

IE web browsers support this clause, even though it does not exist in the official standard and therefore is not supported by all JavaScript environments.

Basically, the **finally** clause contains code that will always be executed, regardless of whether an exception occurs in the **try** block or not. Even if there are **return** statements inside the **try** or **catch** clauses (which triggers an exit from the function), the **finally** clause is guaranteed to run.

NOTE *The only time the **finally** clause will not be executed is if an unhandled exception occurs inside the **catch** clause. An unhandled exception is an exception that has to be handled by the browser, since there are no remaining **try-catch** statements to handle it.*

For example, the following code triggers an exception inside the **try** clause, and both the code inside the **catch** clause and the code inside the **finally** clause are executed before the control is passed back outside the function.

```
function function_that_will_fail() {
    var a = 1;
    var b = 2;
    this_function_does_not_exist(a, b);
}

function capture_error() {

    try {
        document.write("<b>try</b>: ");
        document.write("Calling the function.<br><br>");
        function_that_will_fail();
    }
    catch (err) {
        document.write("<b>catch</b>: ");
        document.write("An error has occurred.<br><br>");
        return;
    }
    finally {
        document.write("<b>finally</b>: ");
        document.write("This code is guaranteed to execute.<br>");
    }
}

capture_error();
```

As you can see from Figure 14-1, even though there is a **return** statement inside the **catch** clause, the **finally** clause does indeed execute.

14

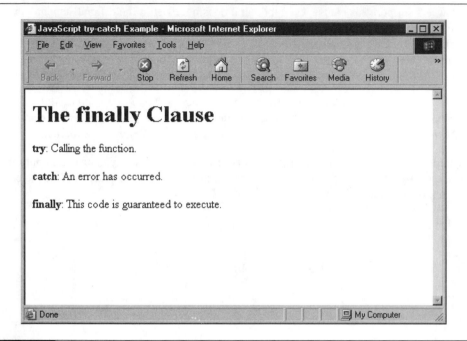

FIGURE 14-1 The **finally** clause gets the last say: exception or no exception.

Create Exceptions Using the throw Statement

One thing that makes the **try-catch** statement more useful is the **throw** statement. The **throw** statement allows developers to create their own exceptions. This means that you can have a single set of **try-catch** statements to capture all system and application errors, which certainly saves a lot of coding effort.

It also allows you to leverage the exception bubbling mechanism in order to pass an error message from deep inside a function up to the **try-catch** statement waiting several function calls back. Without this exception bubbling, we would have to write a lot of extra code in order to capture errors inside each function and then remember to diligently pass them back up to the next level.

For example, the following code causes an exception to occur. By definition, processing inside the function stops immediately, and the exception is passed to the waiting **try-catch** statement one level back.

```
function throw_an_error() {
    throw "Ouch! I stubbed my toe!";
```

```
}

try {
    throw_an_error();
    document.write("This line will never be executed.");
} catch (myerr1) {
    document.write("The following error occurred: <br>");
    document.write(myerr1);
}
```

Notice that I was able to use the myerr1 variable as a string and did not have to include browser-sniffing code to determine whether or not we need to use the IE Error object. The reason is that since we used the **throw** statement to pass a string literal, the **catch** clause receives only the string. IE does not automatically create an Error object for you if you choose to throw a string.

You can, however, create your own Error object and throw it.

Did you know?

How to Re-throw an Exception

When the **try-catch** statement encounters an exception that it does not want to handle, it can use the **throw** statement to send the exception back to another **try-catch** defined elsewhere in the program. This is called *re-throwing* it.

For example, the following code re-throws an error that it is not prepared to handle:

```
function calculate_total() {
    try {
        var subtotal = get_item_amount();
    } catch (e) {
        if (e = "No items remaining") {
            return 0;
        } else {
            // must have been a system error,
            // let JavaScript handle it
            throw e;
        }
    }
}
```

14

```
function throw_an_error() {
    var eobj = new Error ( 0, "Ouch! I stubbed my toe!" );
    throw eobj;
}
```

However, this code works only in Internet Explorer, since there is no Error object in Netscape. So with this approach we would need to introduce browser-sniffing code as well.

The best approach is to throw a string, as you would expect. In the **catch** clause, test to see whether the parameter passed is a string or an object.

```
catch (myerr1) {
    if (myerr1 instanceof Error) {
        var errstring = myerr1.description;
    } else {
        var errstring = myerr1;
    }
    document.write("The following error occurred: <br>");
    document.write(errstring);
}
```

The preceding **catch** clause works in both IE and Netscape and will properly detect whether the parameter passed is an Error object or just a string.

Design Programs That Are Easy to Debug from the Start

Certain programming styles lead to less bugs (and less debugging hassles), while others have the opposite effect. Whenever your JavaScript program looks like it is going to be long and complicated, you may save yourself some time and headaches later if you take the right design approach from the start.

We discussed the four programming styles in some detail in Chapter 3:

- **Unstructured**   Sequence of statements acting on global data
- **Procedural**   Main program that calls functions to perform certain tasks
- **Modular**   Main program that uses modules to group related functionality
- **Object-oriented**   Main program that uses objects to group related data and functionality

Each of these methodologies has its pros and cons when it comes to writing errorproof programs. The unstructured technique is good for small scripts but terrible for large ones. Object-oriented is the opposite—good for large programs and poor for short scripts. Having a rough idea of the complexity of your program beforehand will help you decide on the best approach.

Avoid Unstructured Programming

Unstructured methodology is usually best for short, simple scripts. Essentially, this program consists of a set of JavaScript statements that do not define or use any functions, modules, or objects.

In some ways the unstructured technique is the simplest of them all, but when your program exceeds more than a page or two of code, you should think about breaking it up into more manageable pieces.

The biggest problem you'll encounter with a large program of this type is the complexity and number of interdependencies in the code. Statements later on in the program will rely on variables set several hundred lines earlier. Making a change to one part of the program might break the code in another area.

Building a program in such a fashion is similar to building a house out of one large piece of wood. One small adjustment, such as relocating a window, becomes next to impossible without starting over completely. That is OK only if your house is very small.

Break Code into Manageable Chunks

There's a reason houses aren't made in one big piece, but one wall, roof, floor, and staircase at a time. That way, relocating a window does not affect other walls or other structural elements, and the worst thing that such an adjustment can do is cause you to have to rebuild a single wall. Houses are built of separate components, and computer programs generally should be as well.

The easiest way to "componentize" a program is to organize it into several functions. It is best if these functions fall into separate areas of responsibility, if at all possible, so that two or more functions are not working at cross-purposes or doing the same task. For example, the following code snippet shows how using functions improve program organization and readability:

```
function groceries () {
    var grocerylist = get_grocery_list();
    drive_to_store();
    for (var item in grocerylist) {
        get_item(item):
    }
    pay_cashier();
    drive_home();
    put_food_away();

    return;
}
```

We could have alternatively used an unstructured program that attempted to do all those tasks in order. But that program would have been harder to read, test, and make changes to.

14

To test a function, we only need to make sure that it performs the tasks and returns the value that is expected of it. Most functions rely on the way the rest of the program is structured, so you can never be 100 percent sure that nothing will go wrong. Because functions are easier to test, you will find that procedural programming offers a higher sense of reliability than unstructured programming does.

Reuse Code Using Classes and Objects

The other way to componentize your code would be to break it into a number of classes and objects. Classes allow you to separate all related functions and variables into a single module. This allows you to create classes that can be easily reused in other applications.

For instance, you can create a class that represents an item in the user's online shopping cart. Since this item code is generic, the exact same code can be reused in other applications that need access to an item, say, an inventory program.

```
class Item {
    var SKU : String;
    var productName : String;
    var size : String;
    var color : String;
    var retailPrice : Number;
    var wholesalePrice : Number;

    function Item(inSKU : String, inName : String,
                  inSize : String, inColor : String,
                  inPrice1 : Number, inPrice2 : Number) {
        this.SKU = inSKU;
        this.productName = inName;
        this.size = inSize;
        this.color = inColor;
        this.retailPrice = inPrice1;
        this.wholesalePrice = inPrice2;
    }

    // More methods would follow...
}
```

Classes and objects are much easier to test as well. You would only need to check once to make sure the object behaves the way it is expected to. As long as there are no code changes in the class, the object can be considered completely tested.

Test Your JavaScript Code Thoroughly

The final key to ensuring that your program is immune from errors is to perform thorough testing on it. Testing involves running the program many different times under many different scenarios to make sure it operates as expected.

For short scripts, testing does not have to be complicated. For instance, testing mouse rollover effects may just entail rolling the mouse across an image several times to make sure that it toggles as expected. For more complicated scripts, such as those involving DHTML or interframe communication, more rigorous testing may be required.

Create a Testing Harness

A *testing harness* is a program whose job it is to help test other programs. In JavaScript programming, a testing harness generally takes the form of a custom web page that exposes buttons and form fields used for testing the behind-the-scenes scripts.

Figure 14-2 shows an example of a good testing harness. The web page allows a developer or tester to manually trigger certain events or to force-feed certain values to functions embedded on the page.

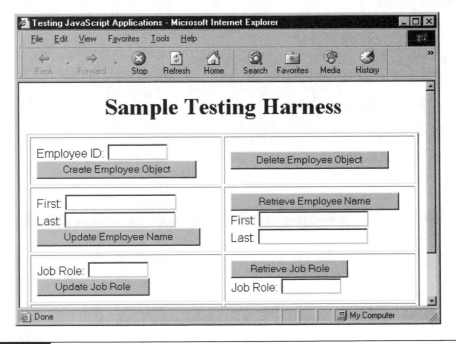

FIGURE 14-2   Use a testing harness to help test JavaScript programs.

310 How to Do Everything with JavaScript

To see a testing harness in action, let's start with a small JavaScript script that we wish to test.

```
// This script will validate an e-mail address
function validate_email (inputstr) {
    // The following complex regular expression pattern checks
    // for a valid e-mail address:  user.name@domain-name.com
    var pattern =
        /^[a-zA-Z0-9_\-.]+@([a-zA-Z0-9\-]+\.)+[a-zA-Z]{2,3}$/;

    if (inputstr.search(pattern) > -1) {
        return true;
    } else {
        return false;
    }
}
```

Now we could just choose to use this straight in our program, but it would be a good idea to verify that it is completely working before doing so. By creating the following HTML testing harness that includes our script, we can test dozens of different e-mail addresses in an easy and straightforward fashion.

```
<html>
  <head>
    <title>HTML Testing Harness</title>
    <script language="JavaScript" type="text/javascript">

// This script will validate an e-mail address
function validate_email (inputstr) {
    // The following complex regular expression pattern checks
    // for a valid e-mail address:  user.name@domain-name.com
    var pattern =
        /^[a-zA-Z0-9_\-.]+@([a-zA-Z0-9\-]+\.)+[a-zA-Z]{2,3}$/;

    if (inputstr.search(pattern) > -1) {
        return true;
    } else {
        return false;
    }
}
    </script>
  </head>
  <body>
  <center>
  <h1>HTML Testing Harness</h1>
```

```
<h2>for E-mail Checker</h2>
</center>

<form action="#" method="get">
  E-mail address: <br>
  <input type="text" name="email">
  <input type="button" value="Test"
      onclick="alert(validate_email(document.forms[0].email.value))">
</form>
</body>
</html>
```

The preceding HTML code exists only to test the JavaScript function validate_email(). It consists of a simple HTML form that contains a text box and a push button. Using this form, testers and developers can type in dozens of different test e-mail addresses to verify that our script is working as expected.

If this process is repeated with each complex function in a program, you will reduce the likelihood of users discovering strange behavior when using your web page.

Force Errors to Test Error-Handling Code

One thing that occurs when developers test their own programs is what I call "Sunny Day Syndrome." We tend to use only valid dates when functions are expecting a date in a parameter field or use only numbers when functions expect numeric values.

But it's important to see what happens when you send an invalid date (such as "02/29/2005" or "12/33/2005") to such a field—or even to try sending something that's not a date (such as the string "Boo"). How does your function respond to invalid inputs? How is your error-handling code?

You might even have to modify the code to force such errors. For example, in the following code, I have hard-coded an array to be empty in order to see how the code handles empty arrays. This is only to test the error-handling capabilities of the code that called this function.

```
function print_listing() {

    var itemarray = get_product_list();

    // BEGIN TESTING:: Empty array added just for testing
    //      Forcing an error
    itemarray = new Array();
    // END TESTING

    for (var item in itemarray) {
        // Rest of code ...
    }
}
```

14

We only modify the code to see what would happen were something to go wrong. This is a very easy way to test for things that rarely happen in real life.

Try Your Program in Many Different Environments

After you have used the **try-catch** statement to capture and handle errors and have designed your program in a modular, easy-to-test manner, there is only one thing left to do: system testing. *System testing* is the process of trying a program on all the different software environments it could possibly run on.

JavaScript programs embedded in web pages still need to be checked in several different browsers and operating systems in order to be considered errorproof. You might not have that many operating systems at your disposal, but it isn't difficult to download and install two or more web browsers so you can at least test your program in those environments.

It is fairly difficult to get multiple versions of IE running on the same machine, but it can be done. It has always been much easier to get several versions of Netscape— all you have to do is install them in different directories.

The web site http://browsers.evolt.org contains a copy of almost every browser ever produced. It's a pretty impressive site. If you ever want to see what the Internet of today looks like in Netscape 0.9 , you can download and install it to find out.

You probably don't have to test every browser ever produced, but at a minimum you should check your scripts using IE 5, Netscape 4 and 7, and Mozilla 1.

The next chapter is the final chapter of the book. It explores how JavaScript can be used to interact with multimedia objects on the page. JavaScript was originally developed to interact with Java, but it can also deal with movies and music embedded in web pages.

Chapter 15

Use JavaScript to Manage Browser Plug-Ins

How to...

- Insert scriptable objects into HTML web pages
- Include Sun Java applets
- Embed movies and music in web pages
- Use the Microsoft Calendar Control in web pages

Since its initial release in December 1995, JavaScript has been primarily used for web site automation. Tens of thousands of useful scripts have been created for everything from handling web site navigation to running online shopping carts. The widespread adoption of JavaScript has meant that web pages now display information in a more interesting and dynamic manner.

Over the years, many companies have created their own technologies to enhance the web experience for users even further. These companies have developed and distributed their own applications, called *browser plug-ins*, so that users of the various web browsers can view these enhancements.

There are two standards for creating these browser enhancements: the Netscape Plug-In API and Microsoft ActiveX. These two standards are not compatible, so developers must create versions of their plug-ins for both. Throughout this chapter, I will refer to components developed under either architecture as "plug-ins," for the sake of convenience.

As you may have guessed from the way the two standards are named, browsers based on the Mozilla engine (including Netscape browsers) only support the Netscape Plug-In API standard, and Microsoft Internet Explorer only supports the ActiveX standard. Plug-in developers often need to support both types of plug-ins, since the browser companies do not appear to be settling on any one standard.

 You can download many ActiveX controls for IE from http://activex.microsoft.com. At http://home.netscape.com/ plugins Netscape also provides a place to download plug-ins.

There are literally dozens of plug-ins available for download, and some browsers ship with several of the popular ones already loaded. The following list contains some of the most popular plug-ins and the URLs where they can be downloaded:

- Macromedia Flash, http://www.macromedia.com/software/flash
- Macromedia Shockwave, http://www.macromedia.com/software/shockwaveplayer
- Sun Java, http://sun.java.com
- RealNetworks RealOne Player, http://www.real.com
- Apple QuickTime, http://www.apple.com/quicktime
- Microsoft Windows Media Player, http://www.microsoft.com/windows/windowsmedia

Users are required to install plug-ins in order to view some content because browsers only know how to display two types of content without help: text and images. For web pages that include other types of content, such as movies, music, and 3-D virtual reality models, browsers must rely on external plug-ins to handle the content.

In this chapter, we will examine how to add these different types of content to a web page and how to use JavaScript to control them. From Java applets to ActiveX controls, we'll see how JavaScript can call the methods and functions that those objects provide.

Insert Scriptable Objects into HTML Web Pages

Web browsers treat content managed by plug-ins as they would any other content on the web page—like an object. The movies, music, and Java applets embedded on a page become one more node in the Document Object Model hierarchy. Since they often also provide properties and methods that can be manipulated by JavaScript, we call them *scriptable objects*.

There are three HTML tags that are able to add these scriptable objects to a web page:

- <applet>
- <embed>
- <object>

Of the three, only <object> is part of the official HTML standard. Both <applet> and <embed> have been available in web browsers since Netscape 2, but the Internet standards body had decided that those tags were ill conceived, and instead encourages web developers to use the alternative <object> element.

Include Sun Java Applets

Java is an easy-to-use programming language that is used by many different types of developers— from serious corporate types to the home user. The Java Virtual Machine (JVM) was one of the first plug-ins ever released, and it was actually included with the Netscape Navigator 2 web browser. A version of the JVM is available for dozens of platforms, including:

- Cell phones
- Personal digital assistants (PDAs)
- Web browsers
- Personal computers that run Microsoft Windows XP, Apple Mac OS, Linux
- Business computers that run Sun Solaris, Microsoft Windows 2000, Unix

Applets are small Java programs that are designed to run inside a web browser. On the Internet today, applets are frequently used to provide stock tickers, interactive charts and graphs, crossword puzzles, and chat rooms.

15

To see how easy it is to include Java applets in a web page, let's look at a simple example of some Java code. The following code needs to be saved in a text file named HelloWorld.java:

```java
/* My first Java program */

import java.applet.Applet;
import java.awt.Graphics;

public class HelloWorld extends Applet {
  public void paint(Graphics g) {
    g.drawString("Hello world!", 75, 75);
  }
}
```

Since Java programs are compiled, we first need to run this code through a compiler before it can be used inside a web browser. The process of compiling turns a plain-text .java code file into a binary .class file. This .class file can be executed on any computer with a JVM, since binary Java files are platform-independent code that does not rely on a specific operating system.

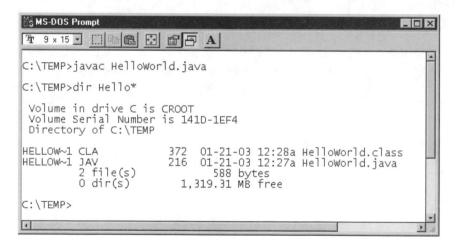

In HTML, Java programs are added to a web page using the <applet> tag. Although <applet> is not part of the official HTML 4.01 specification, both Netscape and IE support it. For example, the following HTML embeds a Java applet into a web page:

```html
<applet code="HelloWorld.class"
        width="250"
        height="150"
        id="myapplet">
</applet>
```

How to ... Download the Java SDK

Sun Microsystems provides several pieces of its Java platform free to anyone who wants to download them, including the JVM (which is part of the Java Runtime Environment, or JRE) and the Java compiler (which is part of the Java Software Development Kit, or SDK).

In order to ensure you have the latest JVM, head over to the Sun Java web site at http:// java.sun.com/getjava/index.html. That page will make sure your web browser has the latest version of Java installed and ready to go.

If you would like to download a compiler so that you can try your hand at creating Java applets, you can download your own SDK for free from http://java.sun.com/j2se/ downloads.html. There are several good tutorials available on the Sun Java web site to help you create your first Java program.

Using this HTML code, the web browser will attempt to load the Java applet called HelloWorld.class and will reserve an area on the screen for it that is 250 pixels wide by 150 pixels tall.

You can see how this Java applet will look in the web browser in Figure 15-1.

The HTML <applet> tag has a number of optional attributes that can be used to further define the applet's properties inside the browser. Table 15-1 lists these attributes.

Attribute	Purpose
code	The class file name
codebase	The class file subdirectory
archive	The name of the .zip file containing the class file
alt	Text that should be displayed by browsers that don't support the <applet> tag
align	How the applet should be aligned with text and images placed beside it
height	The height of the applet in pixels or as a percentage
width	The width of the applet in pixels or as a percentage
hspace	The amount of horizontal space to reserve around the applet in pixels
vspace	The amount of vertical space to reserve around the applet in pixels
mayscript	Permits the applet to access JavaScript
name	The name of the applet to be used in the DOM

TABLE 15-1   Attributes of the HTML <applet> Tag

15

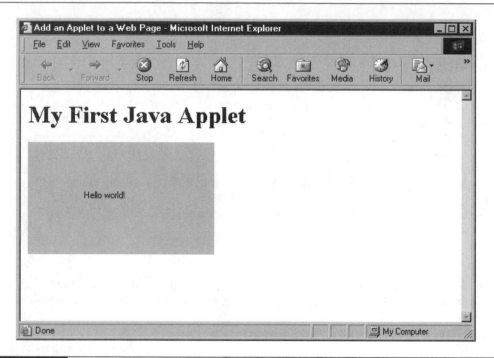

FIGURE 15-1   A simple Java applet inserted into a web page

Web page developers also have the option of passing in several parameters to the Java applet to help customize it using the HTML <param> tag. For instance, we can modify our Hello World Java applet to accept one parameter:

```
/* My first Java program */

import java.applet.Applet;
import java.awt.Graphics;

public class HelloWorld extends Applet {
  String displayString;

  public void init() {
    // We are expecting a <param> named "display"
    displayString = getParameter("display");
```

```
    }

    public void paint(Graphics g) {
      g.drawString(displayString, 75, 75);
    }
}
```

We can then use the HTML <param> tag inside the <applet> tag to pass a customized string to display to the applet, like so:

```
<applet code="HelloWorld.class"
        width="250"
        height="150"
        id="myapplet">
    <param name="display" value="This is my applet!">
</applet>
```

Using this new parameter, we can change the string our Java applet displays without having to recompile the code. An applet can accept multiple parameters, so your Java applet can be designed to be completely configurable from outside the compiled code.

Connect to Java Applets Using JavaScript

As you would expect, JavaScript is able to call the public methods and set the public properties of any Java applet. The Java applet we created in the last section already has a number of public properties and methods, some of which are automatically provided by HelloWorld's parent class—Applet.

We can create a small JavaScript function that will modify the string being displayed and force the applet to refresh by calling the appropriate public properties and methods, as follows:

```
<script language="JavaScript" type="text/javascript">
function displayString() {
    var applet = document.getElementById("myapplet");
    applet.displayString = "String is set here";
    applet.repaint();
}
</script>
```

This JavaScript function starts by creating a variable that will point to the Java applet on our HTML web page using the familiar document.getElementById() function.

We then modify the displayString property, which was defined inside the HelloWorld Java applet. In order to get Java to display our new string to the screen, we have to call the applet's repaint() method.

15

Of course, it would also be helpful to display a small button or other user control in order to trigger this JavaScript function with an onclick event.

```
<applet code="HelloWorld.class"
        width="250"
        height="150"
        id="myapplet">
    <param name="display" value="This is my applet!">
</applet><br><br>

<form action="#">
<input type="button" value="Modify Applet"
    onclick="displayString()">
</form>
```

This HTML code will add a small push-button control underneath the applet window. Clicking the button will cause the string displayed by our applet to be altered, as you can see in Figure 15-2.

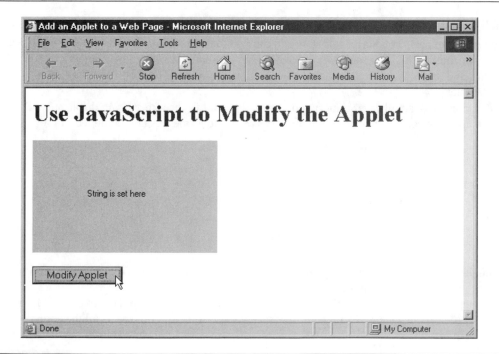

FIGURE 15-2   The applet has been modified as a result of our JavaScript function.

Embed Movies and Music in Web Pages

Embedding movies and music in web pages is handled quite differently from embedding Java applets. First, the <applet> tag cannot be used to embed these types of files into a web page (unless you use a Java applet to display them, of course).

The first way to insert a multimedia file into a web page is by using the <embed> tag. Using the <embed> tag is certainly easier than using the <object> tag, but when using it, remember that <embed> is not part of the official standard.

```
<embed src="myMovie.avi" autostart="true" loop="true"
    width="160" height="120"></embed>
```

With the <embed> tag, you pass all the parameters to the plug-in using attributes inside the tag itself. There is no <param> tag for <embed>. The <embed> tag supports three parameters for itself—src, width, and height. The source URL for the embedded content is passed using the **src** attribute. The amount of space reserved inside the browser is passed using the **width** and **height** attributes.

NOTE   *Your computer would need a browser plug-in that could handle Windows AVI files in order to see the movie in our example. Most of the popular video players can, however, including Windows Media Player, Apple Quicktime, and RealNetworks RealOne Player.*

In the preceding example, the plug-in that is responsible for playing the movie is being passed the autostart parameter, as well as the loop parameter. It is up to the plug-in software, of course, to interpret what they mean and what to do with them.

NOTE   *IE is currently the only browser that supports ActiveX controls such as Windows Media Player.*

We can also use the official <object> tag to embed the movie in our web page. The <object> tag is slightly more complex, particularly since plug-ins are referred to using an extremely long hexadecimal number.

```
<object id="ActiveMovie1"
 classid="CLSID:05589FA1-C356-11CE-BF01-00AA0055595A"
 width="320" height="240">
    <param name="ShowDisplay" value="1">
    <param name="ShowControls" value="1">
    <param name="AutoStart" value="1">
    <param name="PlayCount" value="10">
    <param name="FileName" value="myMovie.avi">
</object>
```

The preceding HTML code inserts an object using the Microsoft ActiveMovie control, which is identified using that long **classid** attribute. ActiveMovie is the ActiveX control installed with

15

Embed a Windows Media Player 9 Object in a Web Page

With the release of Windows Media Player 9, Microsoft has further enhanced the capabilities of its video and music playback application. Windows Media Player 9 also includes an ActiveX control that allows developers to embed music and movies in web pages.

However, since not everyone has had an opportunity to upgrade to this new player yet, it might be better not to force your visitors to download it in order to see your content. But if you can be reasonably sure that your audience already has this software installed, you can easily include this new <object> tag in your web pages.

Notice in the following HTML code that the **classid** value is different, as is the name of the parameter used to specify the name of the media file.

```
<object id="Player" height="0" width="0"
 classid="CLSID:6BF52A52-394A-11d3-B153-00C04F79FAA6"
 width="160" height="120">
    <param name="URL" value="myMovie.avi">
</object>
```

Microsoft Windows Media Player 6.4 that manages the details of the display and playback of movies. Developers can pass the ActiveMovie control several properties to control the size, volume, balance, and position. You can see an example of the ActiveMovie control in Figure 15-3.

If we do not want to rely on Windows Media Player to play our movie, we can use the **classid** attribute belonging to the Apple Quicktime Player, as follows:

```
<object id="QuicktimeMovie1"
    classid="clsid:02BF25D5-8C17-4B23-BC80-D3488ABDDC6B"
    width="320" height="240"
    codebase="http://www.apple.com/qtactivex/qtplugin.cab">
    <param name="src" value="myMovie.avi">
    <param name="autoplay" value="true">
    <param name="controller" value="false">
</object>
```

The preceding code will use the Apple Quicktime Player plug-in instead to display our movie. Again, this will only work in web browsers that support ActiveX controls.

Connect to Music and Media Objects Using JavaScript

Just as we could use JavaScript to reset the properties and call the method of Java applets, we can also use that same principle when handling other embedded objects. For instance, the following

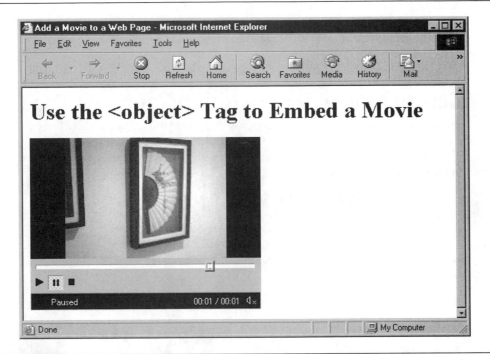

FIGURE 15-3   Embedding a movie in an HTML page

JavaScript functions can be used to stop and start the movie displayed in our ActiveMovie control.

```
<script language="JavaScript" type="text/javascript">
var movie = document.getElementById("ActiveMovie1");
function startMovie() {
    movie.Run();
}
function stopMovie() {
    movie.Stop();
}
</script>
```

The preceding JavaScript code gets a variable reference to the element named ActiveMovie1, which happens to be our embedded movie control. We can then call the Run() and Stop() methods of that control to start and stop the movie.

We can take advantage of these functions by adding two HTML push-button controls to the web page, allowing users to stop and start the movie themselves.

```
<form action="#">
    <input type="button" value="Start Movie" onclick="startMovie()">
    <input type="button" value="Stop Movie" onclick="stopMovie()">
</form>
```

Use the Microsoft Calendar Control in Your Web Pages

Microsoft provides some interesting ActiveX controls that you can use in your HTML web pages. One such control is the Microsoft Calendar Control, which can be used to display a calendar and allows your users to choose a date. For choosing dates in the near past or future, this tool can be a valuable time-saver.

NOTE *IE is currently the only browser that supports ActiveX controls such as the Calendar Control.*

Figure 15-4 gives an idea of how the calendar control looks in a web browser. Of course, knowing the class ID of the calendar control makes adding it to a web page fairly easy, using the <object> tag.

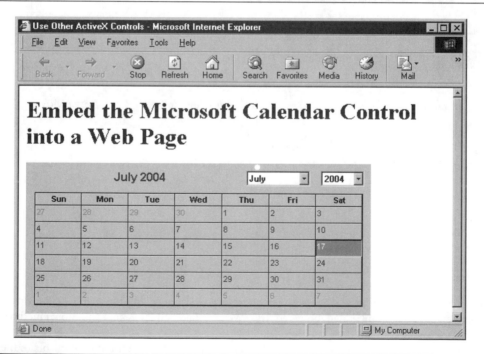

FIGURE 15-4   The predefined calendar control can be used to select a date.

```
<object id="myCalendar" width="480" height="190"
 classid="CLSID:8E27C92B-1264-101C-8A2F-040224009C02">
    <param name="Year" value="2004">
    <param name="Month" value="7">
    <param name="Day" value="17">
</object>
```

We can pass the current year, month, and date to be displayed using the familiar <param> syntax.

Of course, the calendar control is scriptable, like most other objects embedded in the web page. So all we need is a variable that contains a reference to the object and then we are free to modify its properties and settings using JavaScript.

The basic principles introduced in this chapter can be extended to almost any type of content you can imagine. Macromedia Flash animations, virtual reality 3-D models, and Adobe Acrobat PDF documents can all be handled inside the browser window using plug-ins. And most of those objects can be scripted using JavaScript.

JavaScript has firmly implanted itself as a core technology in web site development. As the Internet moves into the age of XML and XHTML, and away from the age of HTML, we can trust that JavaScript will remain a popular standard, since there is no better technology to bring automation and interactivity to web pages.

Appendix A HTML 4.01 Tags

The following table lists each of the HTML 4.01 tags and gives a brief description of its use. But note that Microsoft and Netscape have in some cases added their own tags, so their lists might not match this.

Tag Name	Purpose
\<a>	Creates a hyperlink, or defines a bookmark inside a page
\<abbr>	Denotes an abbreviated form
\<acronym>	Denotes an acronym
\<address>	Denotes a mailing address
\<applet>	Officially deprecated; embeds a Java applet
\<area>	Part of the client-side image map syntax
\<b>	Defines the enclosed text as bold print
\<base>	Defines the base URI for the document
\<basefont>	Officially deprecated; defines the base font size for the document
\<bdo>	Internationalization (i18n BiDi override)
\<big>	Defines the enclosed text as extra large print
\<blockquote>	Defines the enclosed text as a block quotation
\<body>	Indicates the body of the web page
\ 	Inserts a new line
\<button>	Adds a command button to a form
\<caption>	Adds a caption to a table
\<center>	Officially deprecated; centers text horizontally
\<cite>	Citation
\<code>	Defines the enclosed text as code
\<col>	Defines a table column's properties
\<colgroup>	Groups columns in a table
\<dd>	Definition description for a definition list
\<del>	Defines the enclosed text as deleted text
\<dfn>	Instance definition
\<dir>	Officially deprecated; creates a directory list
\<div>	Defines a block of text as an entity
\<dl>	Creates a definition list
\<dt>	Definition term for a definition list
\<em>	Defines the enclosed text as emphasis print
\<fieldset>	Form control group
\<font>	Officially deprecated; sets the font type for the enclosed text

Tag Name	Purpose
<form>	Defines an HTML web form
<frame>	Defines framed content
<frameset>	Defines a group of frames
<h1>	Defines heading text, level 1 (largest)
<h2>	Defines heading text, level 2
<h3>	Defines heading text, level 3
<h4>	Defines heading text, level 4
<h5>	Defines heading text, level 5
<h6>	Defines heading text, level 6 (smallest)
<head>	Indicates the head section of the web page
<hr>	Inserts a horizontal rule
<html>	The parent tag of every other element
<i>	Defines the enclosed text as italic print
<iframe>	Defines a floating frame
<img>	Inserts an image
<input>	Adds a form control to a form
<ins>	Defines the enclosed text as inserted text
<isindex>	Officially deprecated; single line prompt
<kbd>	Defines the enclosed text as text to be entered by the user
<label>	Inserts a label into a form
<legend>	The legend for a fieldset
<li>	A list item for a list
<link>	A media independent link
<map>	Defines a client-side image map
<menu>	Officially deprecated; defines a menu list
<meta>	Inserts data related to the HTML document (called meta data)
<noframes>	Alternate content for browsers that do not support frames
<noscript>	Alternate content for browsers that do not support scripting
<object>	Inserts an object into the document
<ol>	Defines an ordered list
<optgroup>	Defines a group of options
<option>	Defines an option for a select list
<p>	Indicates a paragraph
<param>	Provides a property to be passed to embedded content

A

Tag Name	Purpose
\<pre\>	Defines the enclosed text as preformatted
\<q\>	Defines the enclosed text as a short inline quotation
\<s\>	Officially deprecated; defines the enclosed text as strikethrough
\<samp\>	Defines the enclosed text as sample program output
\<script\>	Defines an embedded script
\<select\>	Inserts a list box control into a web form
\<small\>	Defines the enclosed text as small text
\<span\>	Defines inline text as an entity
\<strike\>	Officially deprecated; defines the enclosed text as strikethrough
\<strong\>	Defines the enclosed text as strong text
\<style\>	Defines an embedded style sheet (CSS)
\<sub\>	Defines the enclosed text as subscript
\<sup\>	Defines the enclosed text as superscript
\<table\>	Creates a table
\<tbody\>	Defines the table body
\<td\>	Inserts a new cell into a table
\<textarea\>	Inserts a multiline text form control into a web form
\<tfoot\>	Defines the table foot
\<th\>	Inserts a new header cell into a table
\<thead\>	Defines the table head
\<title\>	Gives the document a title
\<tr\>	Inserts a new row into a table
\<tt\>	Defines the enclosed text as monospace (fixed-width) text
\<u\>	Officially deprecated; defines the enclosed text as underlined
\<ul\>	Creates an unordered list (bullet points)
\<var\>	Defines the enclosed text as a program variable

Appendix B

JavaScript Quick Reference

This appendix lists the statements and system objects available for use in JavaScript. Table B-1 shows all the statements available for use in JavaScript 1.5. No new statements have been added to the list for JavaScript 2.0. Tables B-2 and B-3 list the system objects for JavaScript 1.5 and 2.0, respectively.

Statement	Description
//	Creates a single line of comments
/* ... */	Creates a block of comments
break	Jumps out of a loop or **switch** statement
continue	Starts a loop over at the next iteration
do-while	Creates a loop that executes one or more statements as long as the specified condition is true, but always executes it at least once
for	Creates a loop that executes one or more statements until a counter reaches a set value
for-in	Creates a loop that iterates over the properties of an object or the contents of an array
if-else	Only executes code if the specified condition is true
label	Allows **break** or **continue** statements to jump out of nested loops
return	Causes a function to exit, optionally returning a value
switch	Chooses to execute only one of several cases based on the value of the specified expression
throw	Causes an exception to be raised
try-catch	Intercepts an exception and handles it
while	Creates a loop that executes one or more statements as long as the specified condition is true
with	Allows access to the properties and methods of an object without having to use that object

TABLE B-1   Statements Available in JavaScript 1.5 and 2.0

Class Name	Description
Array	Allows lists of data to be stored in a single variable
Boolean	A wrapper for Boolean values
Date	Lets you work with dates and times
Function	Allows you to define a function programmatically
Math	Contains convenient mathematical constants and functions
Number	A wrapper for primitive numeric values
Object	All objects derive from this data type
RegExp	Provides support for regular expressions in JavaScript
String	A wrapper for string values

TABLE B-2   Built-in System Objects Available in JavaScript 1.5

Class Name	Description
Array	Allows lists of data of type Object to be stored in a single variable; equivalent to the Array[Object] data type
Array[*type*]	Allows lists of data of type *type* to be stored in a single variable
Boolean	Supports variables that can store only the values true and false
char	Supports variables that can store only a single character
ConstArray	Allows lists of data of type Object to be stored in a single constant; is equivalent to the ConstArray[Object] data type
ConstArray[*type*]	Allows lists of data of type *type* to be stored in a single constant
DynamicArray[*type*]	Allows resizable lists of data of type *type* to be stored in a single variable
Function	The "data type" of functions
Integer	Supports variables that can only store integers
Never	Supports variables that cannot contain any value
Null	Supports variables that can only store the value null
Number	Supports variables that can only store numbers
Object	Supports variables that can contain any value
Prototype	Supports variables that contain prototype-based objects (JavaScript 1.5's way of handling objects)
StaticArray[*type*]	Allows writable lists of data of type *type* to be stored in a single variable
String	Supports variables that can only store strings
Type	The "data type" of data types
Void	Supports variables that can only store the value undefined

TABLE B-3   Built-in System Objects Available in JavaScript 2.0

B

Index

INTERNATIONAL CONTACT INFORMATION

AUSTRALIA
McGraw-Hill Book Company Australia Pty. Ltd.
TEL +61-2-9900-1800
FAX +61-2-9878-8881
http://www.mcgraw-hill.com.au
books-it_sydney@mcgraw-hill.com

CANADA
McGraw-Hill Ryerson Ltd.
TEL +905-430-5000
FAX +905-430-5020
http://www.mcgraw-hill.ca

GREECE, MIDDLE EAST, & AFRICA
(Excluding South Africa)
McGraw-Hill Hellas
TEL +30-210-6560-990
TEL +30-210-6560-993
TEL +30-210-6560-994
FAX +30-210-6545-525

MEXICO (Also serving Latin America)
McGraw-Hill Interamericana Editores S.A. de C.V.
TEL +525-117-1583
FAX +525-117-1589
http://www.mcgraw-hill.com.mx
fernando_castellanos@mcgraw-hill.com

SINGAPORE (Serving Asia)
McGraw-Hill Book Company
TEL +65-863-1580
FAX +65-862-3354
http://www.mcgraw-hill.com.sg
mghasia@mcgraw-hill.com

SOUTH AFRICA
McGraw-Hill South Africa
TEL +27-11-622-7512
FAX +27-11-622-9045
robyn_swanepoel@mcgraw-hill.com

SPAIN
McGraw-Hill/Interamericana de España, S.A.U.
TEL +34-91-180-3000
FAX +34-91-372-8513
http://www.mcgraw-hill.es
professional@mcgraw-hill.es

UNITED KINGDOM, NORTHERN, EASTERN, & CENTRAL EUROPE
McGraw-Hill Education Europe
TEL +44-1-628-502500
FAX +44-1-628-770224
http://www.mcgraw-hill.co.uk
computing_neurope@mcgraw-hill.com

ALL OTHER INQUIRIES Contact:
Osborne/McGraw-Hill
TEL +1-510-549-6600
FAX +1-510-883-7600
http://www.osborne.com
omg_international@mcgraw-hill.com